Police Report Writing

The essential guide to crafting effective police reports

Police Report Writing

The essential guide to crafting effective police reports

Benjamin J. Smith

Police Report Writing: The essential guide to crafting effective police reports

Special editions of this book, including customized covers and content, are available for law enforcement agencies wishing to adopt this guide as a resource for their agency. Contact info@policewriting.com for more information.

10 9 8 7 6 5 4

R A L C C, w/l

9798392329663 (paperback)
9798874344023 (hardcover)

www.policewriting.com

The body text of this book is set in Adobe Garamond Pro, designed by Robert Slimbach. Headings and example text are set in Poppins, designed by Jonny Pinhorn and Ninad Kale. Images used in the "Two Groups of Readers" diagram are from Flaticon.com.

To those whose daily acts of service
are the stuff police reports are made of.

Brief Contents

Page

Preface   xv

Introduction   xix

PART I   **Getting to Know Your Readers**

Chapter 1   Why Police Reports?   3

Chapter 2   Who Reads Your Reports?   17

Chapter 3   You As a Primary Reader   31

PART II   **Gathering and Organizing Information**

Chapter 4   Identifying Relevant Facts   45

Chapter 5   Guiding Your Readers   61

Chapter 6   Structuring Your Report   71

Part III   **Adopting an Appropriate Style**

Chapter 7   Ten Style Guidelines   85

Chapter 8   Describing Your Actions & Observations.   99

Chapter 9   Describing People, Places, and Things   121

Chapter 10   Describing Uses of Force   159

PART IV   **Grammar, Punctuation, and Usage**

Chapter 11   Basic Sentence Composition 185

Chapter 12   Sentence Errors 215

Chapter 13   Punctuation 221

Chapter 14   Usage and Formatting 247

Chapter 15   Commonly Confused Words. 273

PART V   **Writing Aids and Resources**

Chapter 16   The Writing Process 317

Chapter 17   Report Writing Walkthrough 325

Chapter 18   Relevant Facts Checklists 345

Chapter 19   Model Phrases. 361

Chapter 20   Sample Reports 367

Appendix

Appendix A   Tables 383

Appendix B   Figures 384

Appendix C   Example Police Incidents 385

Appendix D   Referenced U.S. Supreme Court Cases 387

Appendix E   Suggested Readings 389

Index   391

Detailed Contents

Page

Preface   xv

Introduction   xix

PART I   **Getting to Know Your Readers**

Chapter 1   Why Police Reports?   3

          1.1   The Six Purposes of Police Reports   4

Chapter 2   Who Reads Your Reports? 17

          2.1   Two Groups of Readers   18

          2.2   Questions Your Readers May Ask   22

Chapter 3   You As a Primary Reader 31

          3.1   Reports as Memory Aids   32

          3.2   Influence on Future Investigations   33

          3.3   Tools to Help You Learn from Your Reports   36

          3.4   How to Handle Mistakes   38

PART II   **Gathering and Organizing Information**

Chapter 4   Identifying Relevant Facts 45

          4.1   What is a Fact?   46

          4.2   What Makes a Fact Relevant?   49

Chapter 5	Guiding Your Readers	61
	5.1 Officer-Chronological Order	61
	5.2 Additional Techniques to Guide Your Readers	68
Chapter 6	Structuring Your Report	71
	6.1 Paragraphs, Headings, and Subheadings	72
	6.2 Five Parts of a Police Report Narrative	73
	6.3 Additional Parts	79

Part III   Adopting an Appropriate Style

Chapter 7	Ten Style Guidelines.	85
	7.1 Write From the First-Person Point of View	86
	7.2 Favor the Past Tense	88
	7.3 Don't Predict the Future	89
	7.4 Tell What Happened	90
	7.5 Use the Active Voice	91
	7.6 Use Concrete Language	93
	7.7 Use Simple Sentence Constructions	94
	7.8 Support Conclusions with Facts	95
	7.9 Choose Clarity Over Brevity	96
	7.10 Remain Consistent	96
Chapter 8	Describing Your Observations and Actions . . .	99
	8.1 Describing Observations	100
	8.2 Describing Actions	108
	8.3 Supporting Information	117
Chapter 9	Describing People, Places, and Things	121
	9.1 Referring to People By Name	123
	9.2 Describing People's Physical Characteristics	129
	9.3 Describing Injuries	136
	9.4 Documenting Verbal Statements	139
	9.5 Describing Places	146
	9.6 Describing Things	152

Chapter 10   Describing Uses of Force 159

    10.1   Identifying Relevant Facts   160
    10.2   The Three-Part Use of Force Model   172
    10.3   Guidelines for Documenting Uses of Force   175
    10.4   Sample Use of Force Report   177

PART IV   **Grammar, Punctuation, and Usage**

Chapter 11   Basic Sentence Composition 185

    11.1   What Makes a Sentence?   187
    11.2   Nouns   191
    11.3   Verbs   193
    11.4   Adjectives   204
    11.5   Adverbs   205
    11.6   Pronouns   206
    11.7   Prepositions   211
    11.8   Articles   212
    11.9   Conjunctions   213
    11.10 Interjections   214

Chapter 12   Sentence Errors 215

    12.1   Run-on Sentences   215
    12.2   Tense Shifts   216
    12.3   Subject-Verb Number Agreement   217
    12.4   Pronoun-Antecedent Agreement   218
    12.5   Pronoun-Antecedent Confusion   219
    12.6   Misplaced and Dangling Modifiers   220

Chapter 13   Punctuation 221

    13.1   Period (.)   224
    13.2   Comma (,)   227
    13.3   Semicolon (;)   232
    13.4   Colon (:)   233
    13.5   Question Mark (?)   234
    13.6   Exclamation Point (!)   235
    13.7   Quotation Marks (" ")   235

13.8	Apostrophe (')	237
13.9	Hyphens and Dashes (- – —)	239
13.10	Parentheses (( ))	242
13.11	Brackets ([ ])	243
13.12	Slash (/)	243
13.13	Spaces	245

Chapter 14   **Usage and Formatting** **247**

14.1	Bias-Free Language	249
14.2	Jargon	252
14.3	Abbreviations	255
14.4	Contractions	259
14.5	Lists	259
14.6	Numbers	261
14.7	Capitalization	269
14.8	Text Formatting	271

Chapter 15   **Commonly Confused Words** **273**

PART V   **Writing Aids and Resources**

Chapter 16   **The Writing Process** **317**

16.1	The Six-Step Writing Process	318
16.2	The COPS Method	321

Chapter 17   **Report Writing Walkthrough** **325**

17.1	Description of Police Incident	326
17.2	Preparing to Write	327
17.3	Organizing Your Information	331
17.4	Writing Your Report	333
17.5	Sample Report with Annotations	337

Chapter 18   **Relevant Facts Checklists** **345**

18.1	Basic Legal Principles	346
18.2	Police Procedure	352
18.3	Incidents Involving People	355
18.4	Incidents Involving Property	357
18.5	Custom Lists	359

Chapter 19	Model Phrases.		361
	19.1	Initial Response	362
	19.2	Describing Actions	363
	19.3	Describing Observations	364
	19.4	Case Disposition	365
Chapter 20	Sample Reports		367
	20.1	Basic Report	368
	20.2	Basic Report with Headings and Subheadings	369
	20.3	Detailed Follow-Up Report	372

Appendix

Appendix A	Tables	383
Appendix B	Figures	384
Appendix C	Example Police Incidents	385
Appendix D	Referenced U.S. Supreme Court Cases	387
Appendix E	Suggested Readings	389

Index 391

Preface

I took my first police ride-along when I was sixteen years old. The day must have seemed uneventful to the officer I rode with—we handled a minor accident, wrote a few tickets, and "drove code" to a fight in progress that ended before we arrived—but to me, the experience confirmed the exciting and meaningful job that police officers do each day.

At the conclusion of the shift, the officer showed me around police headquarters: here was the prisoner holding area, the evidence processing room, the supervisor's office, and the report writing area. In this last room, enormous metal paper organizers lined one of the walls. These organizers held dozens of forms. "We have to document nearly everything we do," the officer told me, sweeping his hand in front of him. "We kill a lot of trees in police work."

If you have been a police officer for even a short time, you already know that 90% of what happens on television police dramas accounts for only about 10% of what real police officers do on a daily basis. The excitement of a hot call is quickly balanced by the hours of follow-up investigation, evidence processing, crime scene security, court appearances, and, yes, report writing. One author observed that police work is "three hours of boredom, followed by two minutes of terror, concluding with six hours of report writing."[1]

If report writing takes up such a significant amount of an officer's time each shift—and consequently, such a large portion of an officer's career—why is so little time spent teaching this important topic? Part of the reason may be that many police officers see report writing as a necessary evil, something to get done so they can get back to doing "real" police work. This mentality is reflected in an anonymous message that was posted on an NYPD bulletin board: "We're not report takers," the note read, "we're the police."[2] While some police officers believe report writing is distinct from actual police work, other officers take a different view. When I was in field training, a veteran officer who greatly influenced my early career told me that, in his opinion, modern police officers were little more than report takers. I believe the truth lies somewhere between these two extreme viewpoints.

Effective police reports are inseparable from effective policing. Even if you didn't use police reports to communicate information, you still wouldn't be the most effective police officer you could be without the ability to write effective police reports. That's because, simply put, part of being an effective police officer is being able to articulate why you did what you did in a manner that will stand up to the scrutiny of the courts, your agency, and the public. Police reports form the foundation for that articulation.

Poorly articulated police reports can lead to mishandled criminal investigations, unwarranted acquittals, or unneces-

---

[1] Kirschman, Ellen. 2018. *I Love a Cop: What Police Families Need to Know.* New York: The Guilford Press.

[2] Wexler, Chuck, Mary Ann Wycoff, and Craig Fischer. 2007. *"Good to Great" Policing: Application of Business Management Principles in the Public Sector.* Washington, D.C.: Police Executive Research Forum. https://cops.usdoj.gov/ric/Publications/cops-w0767-pub.pdf.

sary internal affairs investigations. This isn't because your police work is based solely on your reports, but because unclear writing is often a symptom of unclear thinking.

Although this is a book about writing, it is also, at its heart, a book about articulation. By adhering to the rules, guidelines, and techniques described in this book, you will be better equipped to articulate the actions and split-second decisions your job as a police officer requires. Doing this will also help you better understand *why* you took the actions you did and *how* your split-second decisions were justified. As you repeat this process, report after report, day after day, year after year, you will become a more knowledgeable, articulate, and effective police officer.

If all this sounds like too ambitious a goal, rest assured. This book also serves as a practical companion while you navigate what can sometimes be the mundane, tedious, repetitive, and even frustrating process of writing police reports. And if I can't convince you that police report writing is anything more than something to get done so you can get back to doing "real" police work, then I hope this book will help you do so a little less painfully and a lot more effectively.

Benjamin J. Smith
Virginia
2023

Introduction

Policing is complex work.

During any shift, you may be required to break up a fight, hold a suspect at gunpoint, search for a missing child, perform CPR, interview an assault victim, secure a crime scene, assist someone having a mental health crisis, make an arrest, or engage in dozens of other activities. Each incident requires you to combine your training, experience, legal knowledge, and tactical abilities to safely and lawfully resolve (or stabilize) the situation. This is no simple task.

It is precisely these challenging circumstances that make police work appealing and exciting to many officers.[1] But you may also find these circumstances frustrating when you attempt to document your actions in a police report. At first, writing a police report may seem as complex as the incidents you respond to; however, like those incidents, even the most complex reports can be broken down into smaller, more manageable components. Once you learn these components and how to apply them

---

[1] The terms used throughout this book—*officer, agency,* etc.—are meant to be understood in their broadest context. *Officers* includes sheriff's deputies, constables, detectives, special agents, and the many other positions within the law enforcement profession. *Agency* includes police departments, police bureaus, sheriff's offices, federal agencies, tribal agencies, and any other law enforcement organizations.

consistently, you will find that writing effective police reports becomes a simple, quick, and intuitive process. This book will teach you how.

What Is An Effective Police Report?

Police reports are not just documentation tools; they are communication tools. Your police reports communicate information about an incident to people who need that information to do their jobs. To be an effective communication tool, your police reports must tell the *right people* the *right information* in the *clearest way possible*. This definition includes three components.

1. *The right people.* Since police reports are communication tools, you must first determine who you are communicating with. Writing a well-written report for the wrong readers is the same as writing a poorly-written report for the right readers: they both fail to communicate effectively. Chapters 1–3 will introduce you to your readers, help you understand their purposes for reading your reports, and explore some of the questions they will expect your reports to answer.

2. *The right information.* Your readers expect your reports to provide specific information in a particular format. Since each incident presents you with hundreds—if not thousands—of discrete pieces of information, this may seem like an impossible task. Fortunately, most information falls into just a few categories, and that information can be organized and presented in a logical way. Chapters 4–6 will teach you methods for determining what information is relevant to your reports and how best to organize that information.

3. *The clearest way possible.* Since police reports are written documents, readers expect them to adhere to standards

of English grammar, punctuation, and usage. Additionally, readers expect you to adopt a style of language and composition common to police reports. Chapters 7–15 cover matters of style, grammar, punctuation, and usage. Chapters 16–20 give you techniques and examples to make your reports as clear as possible.

To help you achieve each of the three objectives described above, this book presents a reader-centric approach to police report writing. Before, during, and after you decide what to write and how to write it, you must ask yourself, "Who are my readers? What do they care about most?"

Ultimately, it doesn't matter how clear your police reports are if they clearly communicate the wrong information. And it is impossible to know the right information until you know who your readers are and what information they care about.

What this Book Does Not Cover

This is a book about how to write an effective police report narrative. Police reports are divided into two sections: the incident details, which are captured through a series of form fields (e.g., last name, address, date of birth), and the report narrative, which is a long-form description of what happened at an incident. This book addresses the latter section and purposefully ignores the former. The reason for this is simple: the requirements for what information to include in the incident details section of your reports are usually dictated by the report writing software you are using. Since these requirements are agency-specific, any advice given in this area would have to be so generic—*be sure to spell someone's name correctly*—that it would be essentially useless.

How to Use This Book

This book is both an instructional guide and a reference manual. It progresses from the more conceptual to the more practical. In the first seven chapters, you will learn what makes a report effective, how to think about the report writing process, and how to determine what information should be included in your reports. In the remaining chapters, you will learn practical rules and guidelines for putting pen to paper (or fingers to keyboard). Because of this, there are three ways to use this book.

First, you can read the entire book from front to back. This may be helpful if you are new to writing police reports. By reading each chapter in the order it is presented, you will better understand why police reports exist and why this book instructs you to do things in certain ways.

Second, you can use this book as a reference guide by seeking out specific answers to specific questions. If your questions are more conceptual—*why are police reports necessary?*—then you'll find your answer toward the beginning of the book (see Chapters 1–3 for this question specifically). If they are more practical—*how do I properly use a comma?*—then you'll find these answers closer to the end of the book (see section 13.2 for this question). The index, located at the end of the book, can also help you find whatever you're looking for.

Third, you can combine the first two methods, reading some chapters completely and referring to others as the need arises. If you choose this method, you may find it beneficial to read Chapters 1–7 and 16–17 entirely and save the rest of the book as a reference when specific questions arise.

However you decide to use this book, it will be most helpful if you use it as a companion during your report-writing process. Keep it stored in a desk drawer or tucked in a patrol bag. Dog-ear the pages and underline, high-light, or mark up the contents to make it easy to refer back to later.

Also, for ease of reference, this book divides content into numbered sections and subsections, which you will find in the left margins. The detailed table of contents lists every chapter and section in the book, while the first page of each chapter lists that chapter's sections and subsections.

Throughout the book, examples demonstrate how the rules, guidelines, and techniques described in that section translate into actual police reports. Examples are indented and set in a sans-serif font, like this:

> After arriving at the burglary scene, I taped off the crime scene and started a crime scene log.

Some examples include words shaded in gray. These words prompt you to include specific information in your sentences. Shaded words in *italics* prompt you to choose between the word choices presented; shaded words in SMALL CAPS prompt you to include information of a particular category:

> I interviewed *Mr./Ms.* LAST NAME on DATE.

The challenge with any writing guide, including this one, is to strike the correct balance between *prescribing* (directing you on what to do without offering much explanation) and *informing* (offering a lot of explanation without much direction). A middle ground could be called *advising*—giving you enough information to make an informed decision, suggesting the best option, and then leaving the decision up to you. This is the approach taken in this book. Although this book always tries to offer you the best advice, you are the author of each police report you write. With that responsibility comes the right to adapt or ignore any rules, guidelines, or techniques presented in this book, including well-established ones. As you do so, keep two pieces of advice in mind: first, your police reports are work products you are required to produce for your employer; therefore, your employer's direction—barring anything illegal or unethical—must trump any personal preferences about writing you have. Second, every decision you make should be based on how well it helps you communicate the right information to your readers in the clearest way possible, for that is the ultimate test against which all your police reports will be measured.

Part I
Getting to Know Your Readers

When you sit down to write a police report, you may be tempted to ask, "What do I need to write about?" Although this question is essential, it is not the first question you should answer. Before you can know what to write about, you need to know who you are writing for. In other words, you need to know who your readers are and what information they hope to gain. Once you figure this out, determining what to write about is easy: you simply answer your readers' questions.

People do not typically read police reports for fun or pleasure. (Arguably, you don't write them for fun or pleasure either.) Just as part of your job is to document your actions and observations in a police report, someone else's job is to use this information to fulfill their own responsibilities. Like each step in an assembly line affects the steps that come after it, the effectiveness of your police report has the potential to affect how well others perform their jobs. When readers can easily use the information you have written to perform their duties, you will know you have crafted an effective police report.

Trying to answer all your readers' questions may seem impossible. Fortunately, most of your readers want your reports to achieve a few common purposes. These purposes are explained in Chapter 1. Once you understand these purposes, you can better identify specific questions your readers expect your reports to answer. Chapter 2 will help you do this. Finally, Chapter 3 will discuss how viewing yourself as the primary reader of your reports can help you become a more effective police officer.

1. Why Police Reports?

1.1 The Six Purposes of Police Reports

    1.1.1   Purpose #1: Document constitutional policing

    1.1.2   Purpose #2: Document compliance with agency policy

    1.1.3   Purpose #3: Document the reasonableness of your actions

    1.1.4   Purpose #4: Build a criminal case

    1.1.5   Purpose #5: Share information

    1.1.6   Purpose #6: Create a permanent record

Most police officers will go an entire career without firing their weapon at another person, but almost none will go a single shift without documenting some of their actions in an official report. Even in our era of body cameras, dash cameras, cell phones, digital recorders, and electronic reporting systems, the long-form police report narrative remains the standard method for documenting your actions and observations.

One reason for this is that the United States criminal justice system depends not only on understanding *what* happened during a police incident but also on understanding *why* it happened. Cameras and other recording devices capture a relatively accurate account of what happened, but they can't capture the underlying thought processes and reasoning that led you to make certain decisions and take specific actions. Only you can provide that information. Your police report narrative is your opportunity to do so.

When officers first learn how to capture the chaos of a police incident in their reports, many begin writing immediately, hoping the report will work itself out as it goes. This rarely happens. Often, the report turns out more chaotic than the incident itself. Even officers who are otherwise talented writers struggle when they first begin writing police reports. This isn't due to their grasp of the English language but rather to their lack of understanding of the larger purposes police reports have.

The six purposes of police reports described in this chapter will help you situate your reports in the larger context of your profession. Understanding these purposes will make it easier to understand why the many rules, guidelines, and techniques described in this book are helpful. Ultimately, achieving these purposes in your reports will allow you to take the chaos of a police incident and present it clearly and methodically to your readers.

1.1   The Six Purposes of Police Reports

The six purposes of police reports described in this chapter give you a simple way to think about what your reports are trying to achieve. The first three purposes apply to every report you write. If your report fails to meet any of these purposes, it will not be fully effective. Because these three purposes are so essential, you can think of them as primary purposes:

- Purpose #1: Document constitutional policing.
- Purpose #2: Document compliance with agency policy.

- Purpose #3: Document the reasonableness of your actions.

The final three purposes are also important, but their importance changes with the type and severity of the incident you are writing about. Additionally, as you focus on documenting the *constitutionality, compliance,* and *reasonableness,* of your actions, many of the final three purposes will be achieved naturally. Because of this, you can think of these as secondary purposes:

- Purpose #4: Build a criminal case.

- Purpose #5: Share information.

- Purpose #6: Create a permanent record.

1.1.1   **Purpose #1. Document constitutional policing.** Properly documenting constitutional policing is fundamental because the United States Constitution affects nearly every interaction you have with citizens. As a police officer, you are an official representative of the government. Whenever the government interacts with its citizens, those citizens have certain rights guaranteed by the United States Constitution. Some common rights include the right against unreasonable searches and seizures, the right against questioning without an attorney present, the right to freedom of speech, and the right to bear arms.

Your job as a police officer is a constant balancing act between people's rights to individual liberty and the government's right to intrude into their private lives to maintain order and enforce laws. Readers of your police reports will look for how well you maintain this balance while performing your duties.

Suppose you develop a strong criminal case against a suspect but do so using unconstitutional means. In that case, you are almost guaranteed to lose your case and jeopardize your job or your freedom. Now, suppose you develop a strong criminal case using constitutional means, but the way you write your report makes it *sound* as if your actions were unconstitutional. This is a huge problem.

Consider the two police report excerpts presented below. This officer has responded to a larceny at a convenience store. Upon arriving, the officer detains two individuals at the scene. Which example best demonstrates that the officer's actions were in harmony with the Constitution?

Example 1:

Upon arriving at the scene, I immediately detained two subjects who were standing outside the front door of the convenience store.

Example 2:

As I arrived on scene, I saw two male subjects standing outside the front door of the convenience store. One was wearing a red shirt and blue shorts. The other was wearing a green shirt and blue shorts. These subjects matched the lookout description given by dispatch; consequently, I told both subjects they were being detained.

The constitutional issue in both examples is the officer's right to temporarily detain the two subjects based on reasonable suspicion that they are involved in criminal activity. This is commonly called an investigative detention or "Terry stop."

Which of these examples convinces you that the officer lawfully seized the two individuals outside the convenience store? Notice how the second example clearly meets the legal threshold for an investigative detention. The first example provides no such justification. If the first officer had arrived on scene and found six people standing outside the convenience store, including a father and his three young children, would the officer have detained them also? It is impossible to tell by the way this officer writes their report. Since the first example contains no justification for the officer's actions, it is impossible to tell if these actions were constitutionally reasonable.

You don't have to mention the Constitution or case law specifically to document constitutional policing. You only need to explain your actions in such a way that readers understand you both know the law and follow it.

1.1.2   **Purpose #2. Document compliance with agency policy.** Agency policies and procedures exist to ensure officers uphold the Constitution and state laws and to ensure the efficient operations of your agency. In many cases, your agency's policies place tighter restrictions on your actions than the Constitution or state laws. For this reason, many readers will want your reports to show you have complied with agency policy.

Imagine you respond to an incident where an individual is using a baseball bat to smash out car windows in a parking lot. As you arrive on the scene, the subject sees you, immediately drops the bat, and surrenders. You see twelve broken windows. Numerous witnesses tell you the subject with the bat did, in fact, break each of the windows. It's an open-and-shut case, so you take the suspect into custody. But after you place the suspect in your cruiser, he begins banging his head against the cruiser window. Before you can stop him, he has smashed out the entire window, and his forehead is now bleeding. It looks like there are now thirteen broken windows.

Nothing in the United States Constitution says what you should do for this prisoner. Do you take him straight to jail? Do you summon medics? Do you notify a supervisor? Do you place a padded helmet on him to prevent him from further hurting himself or damaging property? Your agency's policies provide this sort of guidance. Your readers will be interested to know if you have followed your policies since making the wrong decision in this situation can open you and your agency up to civil liability. Which of these examples best demonstrates the officer's compliance with agency policy in this situation?

Example 1:

Upon seeing the blood on the suspect's forehead, I immediately opened the door to prevent him from hurting himself further. I summoned medics and my supervisor to the scene. Medics arrived and treated the suspect's wounds. He declined to go to the hospital. After my supervisor documented the incident, I transported the suspect to the jail.

Example 2:

Upon seeing the suspect's bloody forehead, I asked him if he wanted medics to evaluate him. He remained silent and stared straight ahead. I asked him again. He again ignored me. I saw that he was still breathing and alert, so I transported him to the jail.

The first example clearly shows that the officer followed a pre-established procedure to deal with the injured suspect. In the second example, the officer appeared to interpret the suspect's lack of acknowledgment as a denial of medical treatment. The readers of the second report will undoubtedly have follow-up questions, especially if the suspect later files a complaint or if his medical condition deteriorates while at the jail.

1.1.3   **Purpose #3. Document the reasonableness of your actions.** If police work were as simple as following a predefined number of policies and procedures, someone could build a robot to do your job for you. Program in enough directives, and the robot would have sufficient information to make the correct decision in every situation. Sadly, some agency policy manuals appear as if they are attempting to do just this. Of course, the officer on the street knows policing is more complex. No two situations are identical, and officers must make difficult—often life-or-death—decisions in a split second, without all the facts, and certainly without referencing the policy manual. There's a reason the courts have long upheld the concept that officers' actions are not to be evaluated by whether they made the best, or even the correct, decision during an incident, but only if that decision was *reasonable* given the totality of the circumstances.[1]

Even while abiding by constitutional law and agency policy, you are still given wide latitude to determine how you will handle each situation. Depending on the incident, you may need to decide whether to make an arrest, give someone a warning, mediate a dispute, call someone a ride home, or make one of many other available decisions. By the end of your police report, your readers don't have to agree that they would have made the same decision you did (indeed, defense attorneys are paid to disagree), but they should agree that your decision was reasonable given the circumstances of your incident.

---

[1] See *Graham v. Connor*, 490 U.S. 386 (1989)

Consider this example: an officer has just finished investigating a suspect believed to be driving under the influence. It is three o'clock in the morning, and the suspect has driven their car onto a curb and crashed into a lamp post, causing it to fall onto an unoccupied vehicle parked on the side of the road. This excerpt describes the officer's summary of the incident:

> Based on the circumstances of this incident, including the property damage caused by the crash, the strong odor of an alcoholic beverage emanating from the driver, the six empty beer cans in the passenger seat, and the driver's slurred speech, inability to focus, and admission to drinking "a whole six-pack," I decided to...

How do you expect the officer to finish this sentence? Do you expect the officer to arrest the driver? Put them in a taxi? Drive them home in the back of their cruiser? Allow them to walk or drive away from the scene? Some of these options sound much more reasonable than others. Your readers will think so too.

Your readers should not be surprised when they finish reading your reports; you are not writing a mystery novel, after all. If your readers end your report with questions about your actions, there are two explanations: either you have failed to adequately articulate the *constitutional, compliant,* and *reasonable* nature of your actions, or your actions were not constitutional, compliant, or reasonable to begin with. The latter issue is addressed in Chapter 3. Fixing the former issue is the purpose behind this book.

1.1.4   **Purpose #4. Build a criminal case.** Not all police incidents rise to the level of illegal activity, which is why not all your reports need to build a criminal case. For example, a found wallet turned in to the police station probably isn't evidence of a crime, but a police report will still be required. Your agency needs a way to document how it came to possess the wallet, the efforts taken to find the owner, and where the wallet will be stored for safekeeping in case the owner comes looking for it. The primary purpose of such a report is to document compliance with agency policy (see 1.1.2).

But what about the many incidents you respond to that are criminal in nature? By ensuring that your report is *constitutional, compliant,* and *reasonable,* won't you also ensure that you effectively document everything needed for a criminal case? Mostly. But a few things are required for a criminal case that are worth mentioning specifically.

Criminal cases are built on a foundation of probable cause. The simplest definition of this legal standard is "a reasonable ground to suspect that a person has committed or is committing a crime."[2] For your police reports to fulfill their purpose of building a criminal case, you must document the facts and circumstances uncovered during your investigation that satisfy both parts of this definition:

1. that a crime has occurred or is occurring, and

2. that the person to be arrested has committed the crime

All crimes have specific elements that must be met before a person can be convicted. Broadly speaking, every crime has three elements:

1. the act (*actus reus*)

2. the intent (*mens rea*)

3. causation between the intent and the act

---

[2] Bryan A. Garner, ed., *Black's Law Dictionary: Sixth Pocket Edition* (St. Paul: Thomson Reuters, 2021), 632.

Readers will look for all three elements when determining if you have sufficiently documented your criminal case. One of your readers, the prosecutor, will use the information in your report, along with your testimony (which will also be based on your report), to review the facts of the case and determine its likely outcome. Your report, therefore, becomes a tool that helps determine if a suspect goes free, pleads to a lesser charge, gets probation, pays a fine, or gets sent to jail.

In addition, you may not be the only officer or the last officer to investigate the crime you are writing about. Even if your report documents only one or two elements of the crime, other officers may be able to use this information to fill holes in their own investigations.

1.1.5   **Purpose #5. Share information.** No law enforcement agency exists in isolation. While police officers do not typically investigate crimes outside their jurisdictions, criminals don't respect jurisdictional boundaries. A crime you document today may be related to crimes in neighboring jurisdictions tomorrow, making it even more essential that your reports be written so they are understandable to a broad law enforcement audience. Here are a few example situations where your reports may be shared outside your agency:

- You make an arrest, and a prosecutor reviews your case to determine how to proceed with the prosecution.
- You work a larceny where a large retail store has surveillance video of a suspect stealing pairs of shoes. Although you don't recognize the suspect, you include a thorough physical description and photograph of the suspect from the surveillance video in your report. A crime analyst reads your report and links your suspect to multiple other thefts in the region.

- You document an investigation into massage parlors you suspect of offering illicit massages. Your reports are entered into a nationwide database. An FBI task force uses information from your reports to build a human trafficking case.

In addition to interagency sharing, your reports may be shared within your agency. Here are a few examples:

- You take an initial report for an auto theft. Your report is forwarded to a detective to continue working the case.

- You take a report of social media messages that threaten violence at a local high school. Your report is shared with school resource officers, who then brief the school principal and security staff about the situation.

- You respond to a bar fight that ends in a non-fatal stabbing. A curious elected official who drove by the scene calls your chief of police the next day to find out what happened. Your chief consults your report to get the details.

- A narcotics case you've been working on for over a year finally ends with a search warrant and multiple arrests. Your agency wants to share the results with the public, so your Public Affairs Bureau drafts a press release based on what you've written.

- One night, you find a subject sleeping in a vehicle behind a shopping center. Something doesn't seem right, so you document your interaction in a short report. A few weeks later, there's a burglary at one of the businesses in the shopping center. Your report provides an investigative lead for detectives.

- You are involved in a use of force incident where your Taser fails to deploy properly. Your training division reviews your report to identify training opportunities and determine if there is justification for upgrading to a newer Taser model.

There are many more examples, but these should demonstrate that your police reports and the information in them have the potential to reach a broad audience. Chapter 2 will help you identify some of these potential readers and questions they hope your reports will answer.

1.1.6   **Purpose #6. Create a permanent record.** Most police careers last between 20 and 30 years. During this time, you are likely to write hundreds or even thousands of police reports. Because of the importance of such records, state laws dictate how long your agency must retain your reports. Often, these retention periods are measured in decades. This means the first report you write as a police officer may sit in an archive or digital repository long after you retire.

There are many benefits to having your reports stored for the long term in a centralized records system:

- Your reports will be kept safe if your personal files are ever lost or corrupted.

- Your reports will be centrally located and accessible to other officers or employees.

- The information in your reports can be aggregated with other data to help your agency plan for future equipment, training, and staffing needs.

- Your agency can compile crime statistics to publish in annual reports, grant proposals, or requests for additional funding from your local or state government.

- Your agency can more easily comply with Freedom of Information Act (FOIA) requests.

- Your agency can systematically provide other people access to your reports without requiring you to be directly involved.

The six purposes discussed in this chapter provided a high-level overview of why police reports are essential to policing. Every report you write should achieve the three primary purposes by demonstrating that your actions were *constitutional, compliant,* and *reasonable.* The importance of fulfilling the three secondary purposes will vary based on the type of incident you are reporting. Now you know these purposes, you are ready to begin identifying specific questions your reports must answer to achieve them.

2. Who Reads Your Reports?

2.1   **Two Groups of Readers**

     2.1.1   Primary readers

     2.1.2   Secondary readers

2.2   **Questions Your Readers May Ask**

     2.2.1   The life of a report

     2.2.2   Primary readers' questions

     2.2.3   Secondary readers' questions

     2.2.4   List of sample questions

Police reports aren't just documents written *by* police officers; they are also documents written *about* the interactions police officers have with the public. And whenever police officers interact with the public, questions naturally arise from a number of different sources. A prosecutor wants to know what witnesses to call to try the case. A supervisor wants to know who should be notified about an incident. A detective wants to know what follow-up actions are required. To adequately document your interactions as a police officer, you must first learn who will read your reports and what questions they expect your reports to answer.

2.1   Two Groups of Readers

The number of people who read your reports may vary from a few to a few dozen. Depending on the type of incident you are writing about, hundreds or even thousands of people may become aware of the information you have included in your reports via the news media or public court records. It would be impractical to consider all these individuals while writing your reports.

To make it more manageable, you can divide your readers into two groups: primary readers and secondary readers. Your primary readers are those people you are writing your reports *for*. They're the people who will hold your reports in their hands and read the words you've written on the page. Your secondary readers are those people who may become *aware* of the information in your reports but who won't necessarily read them directly. By understanding both groups of readers, you can begin to anticipate what information your readers need and what questions they will ask. You can then craft your reports in response to these questions.

2.1.1   **Primary readers.** When you sit down to write, you may have someone's voice in the back of your head. Maybe it's your field training officer warning you not to leave out essential details. Maybe it's your supervisor questioning why you made certain decisions. Or perhaps it's that detective whose high report writing standards you can never seem to meet. Whatever the case, these are examples of people you anticipate reading your reports. They are your primary readers because they will read the actual words you have written. Primary readers need the information you have written to make decisions related to their jobs. These decisions may be as simple as, "Do I need to follow up with this incident?" or "Who do I need to share this

Example Primary and Secondary Readers

Primary Readers

Crime Analyst

Defense Attorney

Detective

Prosecutor

Public Information Officer

Records Personnel

Supervisor

Secondary Readers

Accreditation Manager

Chief of Police or Sheriff

Child/Adult Protective Services

Command Staff

Court Clerks

Elected Officials

Federal Law Enforcement Agencies

General Public

Insurance Companies

Internal Affairs

Judge

Jurors

News Media

Other Law Enforcement Agencies

Probation Officers

Suspect

Task Force Officers

Training Staff

Victim

Victim's Family

Witnesses

information with?" Typical primary readers include your supervisor, attorneys, detectives, analysts, records personnel, and public information officers.

The list of primary readers is usually small, but it may grow or shrink based on the incident you are investigating. For example, if you are the first officer to arrive at a homicide, you can expect the detective who takes the case to read your report. If you take a report for potential terrorism-related activities, the FBI will likely make the list of primary readers.

2.1.2 **Secondary readers.** Secondary readers aren't technically readers because they won't read your reports directly, but they may become aware of the information contained in your reports. How do they become aware of information in your reports if they don't read them? Usually through one of your primary readers (see diagram on the facing page).

For example, crime victims are unlikely to read your reports, but they may become aware of certain details after the prosecutor reads your report and then interviews them about the case. The public is not likely to read the full text of your reports, either. Still, they may become aware of certain details through the media, who receive the information in press releases generated by your public information officer. Other ways that secondary readers may become aware of information in your reports include courtroom testimony, wanted posters, crime bulletins, and briefings to elected officials.

Since secondary readers don't see the actual text of your reports, they don't care about punctuation, spelling, and grammar, but they do care about substance. For this reason, always assume that what you write may become available to the general public in one form or another.

Two Groups of Readers

Primary Readers
will read your report

Secondary Readers
*may become aware of
information in your report*

2.2   Questions Your Readers May Ask

Now that you've identified your primary and secondary readers, you can begin to think about what questions each type of reader expects your reports to answer. Since your readers can change depending on the incident, let's use an example incident to make it easier to identify some of your readers and their questions.

2.2.1   **The life of a report.** The following example demonstrates the role that primary and secondary readers play throughout the life of a police report. In this example, imagine you are the first officer on the scene of a gas station robbery with a deadly weapon. You have just finished writing your report[1] and are about to submit it to your supervisor for review.

Each step listed below describes how one or more primary or secondary readers will interact with your report over its lifetime. Primary readers appear in boldface type, and secondary readers are italicized. Underneath each step, you'll find a few questions those readers may ask. See if you can identify other relevant readers or questions for this incident.

1. Your **supervisor** reviews your report before forwarding it to a detective for follow-up.

    •   Did you follow agency policies?

    •   Who needs to be notified about the incident?

    •   Who will be responsible for follow-up activities?

    •   Is the report free of grammatical and factual errors?

---

[1] For simplicity, this example refers to a *report*, singular. In reality, many incidents involve *reports*, plural, written by numerous officers. Readers would use a combination of these reports to answer their questions.

2. The **assigned detective** from the robbery division reviews your case and decides that significant follow-up activity is needed, including collecting surveillance footage from nearby businesses.

   - What follow-up investigation do I need to do?
   - Is anything in this case urgent or time-sensitive?
   - What are the gaps in the investigation?
   - What evidence still needs to be collected?

3. *Uniformed officers* are enlisted to help canvass local businesses for surveillance video.

   - What are the basic facts of the incident?
   - What timeframe should the video cover?

4. While all this is happening, **records department personnel** are reviewing your report.

   - What type of crime was committed?
   - Is the case actively being investigated?

5. Meanwhile, a **crime analyst** reads your report so they can draft a "Request for Information" flyer.

   - What is the suspect's physical description and M.O. (*modus operandi*)?
   - Is there any information that should be kept private?
   - To whom should the flyer be disseminated?

6. Since armed robbery is a major crime, the **public information officer** has written a press release and disseminated it to the *news media*. A summary of the incident is also posted on social media, where *a few thousand members of the public* view the post.

- What information can I share with the public?
- Are there leads that citizens should know about?
- Are community members safe?

7. The Request for Information flyer is now showing up in email inboxes of *officers in 17 other law enforcement agencies*. Unfortunately, no leads are generated from this flyer.

- Do I recognize this suspect?
- Could this be related to crimes in my jurisdiction?

8. A few months pass. You have had dozens more cases and have all but forgotten about this robbery until you receive a subpoena for court; it looks like the detective has identified a *suspect* and made an arrest.

- Do they have enough evidence to convict me?
- How did they link me to the crime?

9. On the court date, you speak briefly with the **prosecutor**, who tells you the **defense attorney** is unwilling to agree to a plea. The case will go to trial.

- Is there proof beyond a reasonable doubt?
- Are there constitutional issues with the way the case was investigated?
- What evidence needs to be examined more closely?

10. Before the trial date, **you** take some time to review your report and refresh your recollection of events.

- What was my role in the case?
- What facts did I learn, and how did I learn them?
- Are there significant holes in my documentation, and can my memory fill the gaps?

11. You give your testimony from the witness stand. The *victim* and the *owner of the gas station* are in the courtroom.

    - Did the police do a thorough investigation?
    - Will we recoup monetary losses?
    - Will this suspect be taken off the streets?

12. After a two-day trial, the *jury* spends 90 minutes deliberating before returning a guilty verdict.

    - Is there proof beyond a reasonable doubt?
    - Were there holes in the prosecution's case?

The above example is a realistic depiction of how police reports (and the information they contain) are regularly used, especially for significant crimes. If this incident occurred in your jurisdiction, would there be other readers? As you followed this report over its lifetime, did you think of any additional questions your readers may have asked?

2.2.2 **Primary readers' questions.** In the gas station robbery example, your readers had many questions. You may have noticed that some questions were specific to your incident while some were more general: they would have been asked about any report you wrote. The best way to identify your primary readers' specific questions is to learn what information each reader needs to do their job. You will learn this gradually throughout your career. Some of the general questions will come up again and again: *Is there probable cause? Who should be notified about this incident? Is the community safe?* You will also become better at answering these questions as you progress through your career, but the sample questions in 2.2.4 and the checklists in Chapter 18 can also help you identify this information.

2.2.3   **Secondary readers' questions.** Although your reports are written for your primary readers, sometimes your secondary readers will ask identical questions. This was the case in step #6 of the gas station robbery example (see 2.2.1). The public information officer (primary reader), the news media (secondary readers), and the members of the public (secondary readers) were all curious if there were any leads and if the public was safe.

     Sometimes, the relationship between your primary and secondary readers is not as clear. In step #11 of the gas station robbery example, the victim (secondary reader) and business owner (secondary reader) wanted to know if they would recoup their monetary losses. The judge or jury (both secondary readers) would ultimately answer this question. You had no way of knowing this information when you wrote your report, so how could you possibly address the question directly? You couldn't. Instead, you include the information the judge or jury would need to ultimately make this determination. Think about where the judge or jury gets their information about the total monetary loss. From the prosecutor's case. Where does the prosecutor get this information? From your report, since the prosecutor is a primary reader. By including a simple but precise sentence about the total monetary loss—*the suspect stole $2005.11 from the safe*—you help your primary reader transfer information to secondary readers.

2.2.4   **List of sample questions.** The following pages contain typical questions asked by some of your readers. Sample questions are also listed throughout section 2.2.1. As you write more reports, you may want to consider creating your own lists of readers and their questions.

Sample Questions Your Readers May Ask

Reader	Sample Questions
Accreditation Manager	Is the agency in compliance with accreditation standards?
Chief/Sheriff	Will I be required to provide answers to elected officials?
	Are there agency-wide issues?
Child/Adult Protective Services	Is there immediate danger?
	Do we have the authority to intervene?
Command Staff	Have we correctly allocated resources?
	Do our policies need to be updated?
Defense Attorney	Are there facts that may lead to reasonable doubt?
	What will I find during discovery?
Detective	Do I need to investigate further?
	Is there additional evidence that needs to be collected?

Sample Questions, cont.

Reader	Sample Questions
Elected Officials	Will there be public outcry? What is the implication for public policy?
Insurance Company	Is there potential fraud? Who was at fault?
Internal Affairs	Were agency policies followed?
Journalist/ Media	Is the public safe? Is there a story here?
Judge/Jury	Is there proof beyond a reasonable doubt? Was the rule of law upheld?
Other Officers	Does this affect me/my agency? Are there officer safety concerns?
Prosecutor	Should I try or plead the case? Were all the elements of the crime satisfied?

Sample Questions, cont.

Reader	Sample Questions
Supervisor	Do I need to provide additional supervision/guidance?
	Should I notify anyone about the incident?
Suspect	Is there enough evidence to convict me?
Task Force Officer	Are additional resources or personnel needed?
	Is there a nexus to other crimes?
Training Staff	Do we need to provide additional training?
Victim	Did the police do everything they should have?
Witnesses	Was my account of events accurately documented?
You	Do I have enough information to answer my readers' questions?

3. You As a Primary Reader

3.1   **Reports as Memory Aids**

3.2   **Influence on Future Investigations**

    3.2.1   Documentation vs. evaluation

    3.2.2   The investigation-report cycle

3.3   **Tools to Help You Learn from Your Reports**

    3.3.1   Mini-debrief

    3.3.2   Cross-examination

    3.3.3   Lessons learned

    3.3.4   Unanswered questions

    3.3.5   Swipe file

3.4   **How to Handle Mistakes**

    3.4.1   Choices between good and better

    3.4.2   Genuine mistakes made in good faith

    3.4.3   Intentional errors

The previous chapter only briefly mentioned the most important reader of your reports: *you*. Other primary readers (see 2.1.1) may also read the words you've written; however, *you* are the one who experienced everything you have written about. Your report won't be giving testimony in a courtroom, briefing out a search warrant execution, or answering questions in an internal affairs investigation. *You* will. This chapter will explore reasons you should consider yourself *the* primary reader of your reports and offer you tools to help you use your reports to become a more effective police officer.

3.1   Reports as Memory Aids

Many criminal cases take weeks, months, or even years before they find their resolution in a courtroom. In that time, you may have worked dozens or hundreds of other incidents, transferred to a new assignment, or received a promotion. You may not have thought about the incident since you first responded to it. This can pose a problem when it comes time to testify in court. If you have only a vague recollection of the incident, you had better hope your report fills in all the necessary details. Many reports seem clear and complete immediately after you finish writing them, but that's only because your mind fills in the gaps left in your writing. Once time passes and your memory fades, those gaps become apparent.

Police reports help you recall the facts of an incident, but when properly written, they also help you better explain your actions out loud. When you spend the time necessary to properly capture your actions in writing, you force yourself to think through the rationale behind your decisions. Since no police report can contain all the information needed to answer every possible question asked by your readers, this process of careful consideration prepares you to articulate the answers to any questions that may be derived from information in your reports, even if the facts aren't described explicitly.

The benefits of your police reports extend far beyond being memory aids, however. After all, many of your reports will never see the inside of a courtroom or even be looked at once they are stored in your agency's records management system. Is it worth spending the time and effort to make these reports as effective as they can be? Yes, because effective report writing can lead to more effective policing.

3.2   Influence on Future Investigations

Many officers view report writing as the last step in their response to an incident. Chronologically, this is accurate. You respond to a call, conduct your investigation, take necessary actions, and then document what happened in a police report. Your report is the last thing you must do before you can "cross the incident off your list" and move on to the next call. Thinking about reports in this way may look something like this:

Investigation   Report

But viewing police reports in this way overlooks a crucial element that can help you become not only a more effective police report writer but also a more effective police officer.

3.2.1   **Documentation vs. evaluation.** Writing a police report is not just an exercise in documentation; it is also an opportunity for evaluation. Writing forces you to think about what you did and why you did it. By articulating your decisions, you may expose errors in your thinking or gaps in your knowledge. *Why* did *I detain that person in handcuffs instead of telling them to sit on the curb? Were they making furtive movements? Which furtive movements specifically? Which case law supports detention based on furtive movements? What even* is *a furtive movement?*

This type of internal questioning is the difference between an officer who uses their reports as evaluation and improvement tools and an officer who uses them simply for documentation. One officer sees report writing as the culmination of their incident. The other sees it as the culmination of their incident *and* the foundation for future interactions with the public. Yes, the report may still read, "I placed him in handcuffs," but the officer who takes the few minutes to reflect on the legal justification for this action comes away from the incident with more knowledge that will help them in the future. The process of using your reports as tools to evaluate your actions is called the Investigation-Report Cycle.

3.2.2 **The investigation-report cycle.** Rather than having a linear view of police report writing, consider your reports as one part of an ongoing cycle of investigating and reporting. Effective investigations lead to effective police reports. In return, effective police reports lead to effective future investigations. Thinking about reports in this way may look something like the diagram on the facing page.

Let's revisit an example from section 1.1.1 to see this cycle in action:

> Upon arriving at the scene, I immediately detained two subjects who were standing outside the front door of the convenience store.

As established in Chapter 1, this is a poor example of articulating the legal grounds for a Terry stop.[1] If you have just finished writing the report that contains this sentence, you have two choices:

---

[1] We'll assume for purposes of this discussion that additional legal justification insn't provided anywhere else in the report.

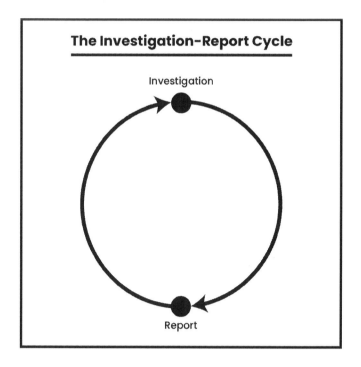

The Investigation-Report Cycle

Investigation

Report

1. Breathe a sigh of relief that your report is finished, submit it, and move on to the next call.

2. Take a few extra minutes to reflect on why you detained these subjects, refresh your memory on the factors contributing to reasonable suspicion for an investigative detention (see 18.1.2), and then add a sentence or two to clarify your actions.

If you make the second choice, you end up with a clearer description of your actions (see the revised example in 1.1.1), refreshed legal knowledge, and the ability to better articulate your actions in the future. Most importantly, you better understand why you did what you did, making you more competent and confident when you must detain people in the future. Conversely, if you make the first choice, you end up with nothing more than a poorly articulated sentence and a questionable Terry stop.

3.3 Tools to Help You Learn from Your Reports

Nothing in this chapter is meant to suggest that you need to scrutinize every word in your reports to death—you don't have time for that, anyway—but only that you shouldn't waste obvious opportunities to improve both your writing and your policing abilities. The tools discussed in this section will help you move through the investigation-report cycle more quickly.

3.3.1 **Mini-debrief.** Debriefs are meetings where multiple stakeholders discuss lessons learned during a police incident. Such meetings usually occur after major incidents because of the increased risk and liability those incidents entail. On the other hand, mini-debriefs can be conducted by yourself or with another officer. They are a powerful tool to help you articulate your actions, identify areas for improvement, see the incident from others' perspectives, and document lessons learned.

To conduct a mini-debrief, review your report and identify key decisions you made during the incident. Try to come up with reasonable alternatives to those decisions. Practice articulating the pros and cons of your decision versus the alternative choices.

3.3.2 **Cross-examination.** In court, a cross-examination allows opposing counsel to discredit a witness. If you have ever been cross-examined, you know it is an uncomfortable but beneficial experience because it forces you to clarify details and explain the rationale behind your actions

To conduct a cross-examination on your reports, find another officer you trust. Have them read your report and attempt to find holes in your investigation or areas of poor articulation. Let them ask you questions as if you were the one on the witness stand. Try to answer their questions using only the information you have written in your report. If this isn't possible, work through the articulation aloud and then revise what you've written.

3.3.3 **Lessons learned.** When you learn something that will help you with a future report or investigation, write it down on paper or in your phone. Routinely glance at the list to remind yourself what you've learned. Plus, just the act of writing down what you've learned will make you much more likely to remember it.

3.3.4 **Unanswered questions.** Similar to keeping a list of lessons learned, when you come across something you don't know and don't have the time to figure out at the moment, add it to a running list of things you want to learn later. Each time you have a few spare minutes, look up the answer to one of the questions and write it on your list of lessons learned.

3.3.5 **Swipe file.** A swipe file is a collection of writing samples you can use as a pattern for your reports. These samples may come from other officers' reports, books about report writing, or reports you've written in the past.

One of the most effective ways to learn how to write police reports is to read other officers' reports. If you review a random report or two every shift, you'll read a few hundred reports in a year. When someone's writing style or articulation resonates with you, collect a snippet of their writing in your swipe file. Next time you have to write a report, adapt an example from your swipe file to your specific incident.

You can do the same thing with your reports. The first time you deal with a drunk person, it may take you significant time and effort to articulate their signs of intoxication in your report. But if you take the time to properly document what happened, you will have a pattern to use the next time you have a similar incident (the specific facts will be different, of course). Putting this time and thought into the reports you write early in your career, will allow them to serve as helpful templates long into the future.

3.4   How to Handle Mistakes

As you consistently evaluate your reports and actions, you will inevitably encounter things you wish you had done better during your investigation. You may also discover genuine mistakes you made while acting in good faith. Making mistakes is part of growing as a police officer and a writer so long as you handle them appropriately.

3.4.1   **Choices between good and better.** Sometimes, you will reflect on an incident and realize that you didn't do anything wrong, but you could have made better decisions. In other words, your actions were *good*, but they could have been *better*. If you've identified choices like these, congratulations: that's the purpose behind everything discussed in this chapter. Use one of the tools discussed in section 3.3 to capture what you learned, and then make adjustments to do better next time.

3.4.2   **Genuine mistakes made in good faith.** No one, including your agency and the courts, expects you to make perfect decisions 100% of the time. But after you've had the time to think about what happened and write it down, no one will tolerate you covering up or spinning the truth. If you make a genuine mistake while acting in good faith, follow this simple rule: *fix promptly, document honestly.*

Let's say your agency has adopted the common practice of collecting names and birthdates from people you interact with during an incident. You sit down to write your report and realize you forgot to collect a birthdate from one of the witnesses, but you did get their phone number. What should you do? *Fix promptly, document honestly.*

Give the witness a call, get their birthdate, and then include it in your report as usual. Unless this delay in obtaining their birthdate significantly impacts your investigation, there's no need to articulate that you obtained it later. It's not a relevant fact (see Chapter 4).

What about more significant mistakes? *Fix promptly, document honestly.* Say you respond to a call of a man in a park trying to attack another man with a machete. You and your backup arrive on scene and, due to the nature of the call, immediately prone out both subjects at gunpoint and place them in handcuffs. You separate the subjects by placing the suspect into the back of your cruiser before questioning him. When you ask him what happened, he tells you everything, including how he came to the park under the pretense of buying drugs from the other subject, but with the true intent of robbing him. When the victim drug dealer refused to give up the money, the suspect removed the machete from his jacket and began hacking.

Congratulations, you've just gotten a confession, but you've also got a problem: you forgot to Mirandize the suspect before questioning. Upon realizing this, you quickly Mirandize him and start questioning again, but now he stays silent. What should you do? *Fix promptly, document honestly.*

You did everything you could to fix the problem while on the scene. This is commendable. Since you can't go back in time and change what happened, the best you can do is clearly, objectively, and accurately document what happened:

> After securing the suspect, Mr. Escobar, in the back of my cruiser, I asked him what happened. He told me he came to the park intending to rob the victim, Mr. Hays. After approaching Mr. Hays, Mr. Escobar demanded all his money. Mr. Hays refused and began to walk away, which is when Mr. Escobar removed a machete from his jacket and struck Mr. Hays on his right arm.
>
> After hearing this information, I Mirandized Mr. Escobar using my department-issued Miranda warning wallet card. I asked Mr. Escobar to tell me what happened again. He refused to speak to me.

Your police reports shouldn't become confessionals for every mistake you make, but you also don't want the reputation of spinning or obscuring the truth. As demonstrated above, the best way to achieve this balance is to state what happened without additional commentary. It also might not hurt to give a heads-up to your supervisor if your investigation contained significant mistakes.

3.4.3   **Intentional errors.** The term "intentional errors" is just a kinder way of saying *misconduct* or *abuse of authority*. It should go without saying that the intentional violation of people's rights or disregarding of policy has no place in policing, much less in police reports. Good police reports cannot cover up bad policing, and nothing in this book should be construed as intending to help you achieve this end.

Some officers run into problems when their poor articulation makes it appear that they intentionally disregarded the law or policy when this is not the case. This often happens when officers fail to include sufficient relevant facts to support their actions. Take, for example, an officer who describes patting down a suspect without first articulating their reasonable suspicion that they were armed. Or an officer who describes entering someone's residence without first articulating the exigent circumstances that allowed this entry in the first place. In each case, these officers may have complied with policy and law, but these reports will read as if they blatantly disregarded both. If you implement the rules, guidelines, and techniques discussed in this book, you will avoid this trap.

Part II
Gathering and Organizing Information

Police incidents provide an almost endless stream of information. Imagine a domestic violence call. As soon as you are dispatched, you become flooded with choices. Which route will you take to get to the incident? Is this an in-progress call or a delayed report? Will you respond with lights and sirens? How will you approach the residence safely once you arrive? Is backup on the way? Do you know the people who are involved? Are there weapons present? Is the suspect still on the scene? Could this be an ambush? Each question forces you to gather and evaluate information before making an informed decision.

Once you arrive on the scene, you receive more information. The victim tells you what happened. The suspect tells you something else. Dispatchers update you over the radio. Your backup officers tell you what they saw or heard. You make observations about the victim's injuries. You discover evidence. The list goes on and on.

When arriving at an unknown, chaotic situation, you don't know what information will be relevant to conducting your investigation and keeping you safe, so you must keep an open mind; however, when it comes time to document the incident, much of the information you were overwhelmed with at the scene is no longer relevant.

Newer officers often struggle to distinguish between information *they knew* at the scene and information *their readers need to know* to understand what happened. *Does it matter that I parked my cruiser two houses away from the incident location? Is it important that the victim was wearing no shoes?* The answer to these and millions of other questions is usually unsatisfactory: *it depends on your incident.*

To provide more guidance, Chapter 4 gives tools to help you evaluate what information is relevant to your incidents and what should be left out. Chapter 5 provides a few techniques to guide your readers through your relevant facts sequentially. Finally, Chapter 6 describes how to organize your relevant information into a clear, logical structure.

4. Identifying Relevant Facts

4.1   What is a Fact?

4.1.1   Definition of a fact

4.1.2   Two categories of facts

4.1.3   How incident facts and general facts work together

4.2   What Makes a Fact Relevant?

4.2.1   Definition of a relevant fact

4.2.2   Facts relevant to every incident

4.2.3   Grouping incident facts with general facts

4.2.4   Example of identifying relevant facts

4.2.5   Using a T-Chart diagram to document relevant facts

You've probably been told police reports contain "just the facts." While this statement is fundamentally true, it fails to provide practical direction when you are struggling to understand what information to include in your reports. Which facts are important? And to whom? If you include irrelevant facts in your reports, you waste your time and risk confusing your readers. If you leave out relevant facts, you risk leaving your readers' questions unanswered. This chapter will help you identify which facts are relevant and which aren't.

4.1   What is a Fact?

4.1.1   **Definition of a fact.** A fact is a piece of information that accurately portrays reality.[1] At every police incident, you are presented with an overwhelming number of facts. The date and time of your incident are facts. The names of your suspects, victims, and witnesses are facts. The statements given to you by those suspects, victims, and witnesses are also facts.[2] Facts include the radio transmissions you hear, the speed you drive to get to the incident, the names of other officers who were on the scene, the time, the weather, and the list goes on. But just because these facts exist does not mean they are all relevant to your report. To begin determining which facts are relevant, it helps to divide them into two categories.

4.1.2   **Two categories of facts.** The facts that exist during any police incident may be separated into one of two categories:

1. *Incident facts.* Incident facts apply specifically to the incident you are handling. They include the observations you make, the actions you take, and the information you learn during your investigation. Incident facts are important because they help readers understand what happened during your incident. Here are just a few examples of incident facts:

---

[1] Black's Law Dictionary gives this definition of *fact*: "Something that actually exists; an aspect of reality. Facts include not just tangible things, actual occurrences, and relationships, but also states of mind such as intentions and the holding of opinions."

[2] A person's statement does not have to be true to be considered a fact. Someone who tells you they are the reincarnation of Abraham Lincoln sent to take over the government has not accurately portrayed reality; however, it *is* a fact that they hold this opinion and that they made this statement to you.

- The incident date, time, and location
- Names and addresses of witnesses
- A license plate number
- A description of someone's injuries
- The dollar value of damaged property

2. *General facts.* General facts exist even outside the context of the incident you are handling. They include information related to case law, criminal statutes, agency policies, and your training and experience. General facts are important because they help you determine which incident facts are relevant to your report. Here are just a few examples of general facts:

- Your agency's policy on handcuffing
- Your legal knowledge of reasonable suspicion and the requirements for an investigative detention
- Your prior dealings with a suspect

At every incident, incident facts and general facts work together to help you make decisions, further your investigation, and ultimately make arrests or otherwise conclude the incident.

4.1.3   **How incident facts and general facts work together.** Incident facts and general facts depend on each other to make them relevant to your investigation. To understand the relationship between incident facts and general facts, imagine the following scenario:

> You are called to a shoplifting in progress at a local convenience store. While you are en route, dispatch tells you that a suspect came in and stole a beer. Dispatch describes the suspect as a white male with brown hair wearing a black tee shirt, jeans, and a

baseball cap. As you arrive on the scene, you see a person matching that description standing in front of the convenience store. He is holding a beer in his hand. You speak to the suspect and tell him he is being detained while you conduct your investigation.

Can you identify the incident facts and general facts in this example? The incident facts are straightforward:

- The alleged crime is shoplifting of a beer at a convenience store.

- The suspect is a white male with brown hair wearing a black tee shirt, jeans, and a baseball cap.

- When you arrived, a suspect matching this description was standing in front of the store.

- The suspect had a beer in his hand.

- You detained the suspect.

What are the general facts in this example? Remember, general facts are those pieces of information that exist outside the context of your incident. Here are the general facts:

- Shoplifting is a crime.

- One of the elements of shoplifting is taking merchandise past the point of sale without first making a purchase.

- The United States Supreme Court allows you to detain a suspect on less than probable cause when you reasonably suspect they are involved in criminal activity.

- Reasonable suspicion must be based upon more than a hunch, such as the description of a suspect that matches a lookout and the suspect's proximity to the crime location.

You can begin to see how general facts and incident facts work together. The description of the suspect (an incident fact) supports your legal justification for a detention (a general fact). Likewise, your knowledge of the elements of the crime of shoplifting (a general fact) supports your ability to determine that someone taking a beer without paying (an incident fact) has shoplifted.

Understanding the relationship between general facts and incident facts is key to understanding which facts are relevant to your report. The next section will provide you with a few tools to determine which facts are relevant and which are not.

4.2   What Makes a Fact Relevant?

4.2.1   **Definition of a relevant fact.** A fact becomes relevant when it helps your police report accomplish its purpose or answer your readers' questions. The elements of this definition have already been covered extensively in Chapters 1 and 2, so we won't address them more here except to say this: it is impossible to overstate the importance of keeping your readers in mind while you write your reports. Understanding your readers and their questions is the gold standard for determining what information to include and what to leave out. In short, whatever facts your readers require are, by definition, relevant.

4.2.2   **Facts relevant to every incident.** Certain facts are relevant to every report you write, regardless of whether that report documents a complex robbery or a simple lost property case. By including these facts, you help your readers answer a few basic questions. These questions and the facts necessary to answer them are presented below in checklist format because your goal should be to locate the facts in every report you write and check them off the list.

1. *When did the incident take place?* This question helps your readers understand the date and time that the incident occurred. Relevant facts include:
   - ☐ The date and time the incident was reported to police
   - ☐ The date and time, or date and time range, the incident occurred

2. *Where did the incident take place?* This question helps your readers understand the geographic location where your incident occurred. Relevant facts include:
   - ☐ The location where the incident was reported to police, including:
       - ☐ the full street address
       - ☐ when applicable, the business name
   - ☐ The location(s) where the incident occurred, including:
       - ☐ the full street address
       - ☐ when applicable, the business name

3. *Who was involved?* This question helps readers understand each person you interacted with and their role in your investigation. Relevant facts include:
   - ☐ The identification of each person involved in the incident, including their:
       - ☐ first and last name
       - ☐ salutation (e.g., Mr., Ms., Dr., Officer)
       - ☐ role in the incident (e.g., witness, victim, suspect)

4. *What brought police to the scene?* This question helps readers understand why police were involved in the

incident, including any crimes being investigated. Relevant facts include:

- ☐ The incident type (e.g., arson, lost property)
- ☐ How you became involved (e.g., dispatched, self-initiated)
- ☐ When applicable, the law(s) that was allegedly violated, including:
  - ☐ the statute number
  - ☐ a brief description of the statute (e.g., driving without a license, brandishing a firearm)

5. *What should happen now?* This question helps readers understand what follow-up actions, if any, are required. Relevant facts include:

- ☐ The status of the case (e.g., closed, open for further investigation)
- ☐ When applicable, who is responsible for the follow-up investigation

These questions may seem obvious, but their answers form the foundation for every report you write. If you forget to include any associated facts, your readers will have difficulty understanding the remainder of your report.

You probably noticed that these questions are based on the familiar *who–what–where–when–why* pattern. You probably also noticed that there are no *why* questions on the list. That's because answering the most important *why* question—*why did you make the decisions you did?*—requires you to think critically about your decisions and which facts led to those decisions. Fortunately, this becomes much easier as you group your incident facts with general facts.

4.2.3   **Grouping incident facts with general facts.** As discussed previously, you can separate facts into two categories: incident facts and general facts. An incident fact becomes relevant when it is needed to support a general fact. Because of this, the easiest way to determine which incident facts are relevant is first to determine which general facts are relevant. You can then group your incident facts with each of your general facts.

Imagine an incident where you searched someone's vehicle without a warrant (i.e., a "Carroll doctrine" search). For a vehicle search to qualify under the Carroll doctrine, you must have probable cause to believe:

1. A vehicle
2. contains contraband or evidence of a crime

These two requirements of the Carroll doctrine are *general facts*. Once you have identified these, you need to match the *incident facts* that prove each of these requirements was satisfied. Assuming each of the following facts is true within our imaginary vehicle search, your list may look something like this:

1. A vehicle
   - The suspect car was a blue Audi A6.
   - The car pulled over in the 1600 block of Gilmer Street.

2. contains contraband or evidence of a crime
   - The car matched the getaway vehicle description from a bank robbery that happened ten minutes prior.
   - A gun and ski mask were visible in the back window.

If this were a real-life incident, you'd likely have a more comprehensive list. But this brief example demonstrates the usefulness of evaluating each of your incident facts based on whether or not they satisfy one of the general facts required by your incident. The next sections will present a more complete example and introduce a tool that helps capture your incident's relevant facts.

4.2.4   **Example of identifying relevant facts.** To provide a more robust example of identifying the relevant facts of your incident, let's expand on the example from section 4.1.3. As you read this incident, try to identify any general facts first, followed by the incident facts that support them.

> You are running radar in your cruiser one day when a call comes out for a shoplifting in progress at a local convenience store (1127 Farland Avenue). It's not in your beat, but you are nearby and decide to respond.
>
> While you are en route, dispatch tells you that a suspect came in and stole a beer. Dispatch describes the suspect as a white male with brown hair wearing a black tee shirt, jeans, and a baseball cap. As you drive to the scene, you notice at least three people who partially match that description: a woman wearing a black tee shirt and jeans, a male teenager wearing a baseball cap and riding a skateboard, and an Asian male wearing all the indicated clothing. *Witnesses get descriptions wrong all the time*, you think, but you don't believe any of these people are suspects, so you continue to the scene.
>
> As you arrive on the scene, you see a person matching the suspect's description standing in front of the convenience store. He is holding a can of Steel Reserve. The convenience store parking lot is busy, so you must park on the street, about fifty feet from the

store. As you walk up, you notice a couple of empty beer cans in the gutter. In fact, there seems to be a lot of trash in the gutter—cigarette butts, food wrappers, even a shoe!

When you step foot in the parking lot, you announce yourself to the suspect in a friendly manner—you don't want him to take off running. You have him place the beer on the ground and wait with your backup officer, who has just arrived on scene, while you continue your investigation.

You first speak with the clerk. He confirms that the person standing outside the door is the suspect, and the can of beer he is holding is priced at $3.50. He also tells you he's been working at this location for five years, and he is sick of people stealing all the time. He'll do whatever it takes to make it stop. You ask if he has any video of the theft, and he lets you into the back room so you can review the surveillance footage. In the video, you witness the suspect take a can of Steel Reserve from the drink cooler and place it into his jacket pocket. The video then shows the suspect exiting the store without paying.

You return outside and speak with the suspect. As you explain what your investigation has revealed, you notice that he is swaying back and forth on his feet, his eyes are glassy, and he has trouble concentrating on your conversation. You recognize these as signs of intoxication.

When you ask the suspect if he is intoxicated, he laughs and says, "Not enough! That's why I needed one more!" He points to the can of Steel Reserve at his feet.

About this time, you notice a group of people—including the teenager on the skateboard you saw earlier—gathered at the corner of the store. They are watching you intently. You aren't sure what they're up to, but you want to wrap up your investigation and get out of this parking lot.

You place your suspect under arrest for public intoxication and larceny. You handcuff him, double-lock the cuffs, and search him incident to arrest while your backup officer checks the prisoner compartment of your cruiser. You then place the prisoner in the back seat and head to jail.

This description has much more information than you need to report. But this is how actual police incidents are. As a police officer walking into an uncertain situation, you don't yet know which facts will be relevant and which won't. Good officers keep their minds open to all the facts and possible outcomes of an incident.

When it comes time to write your report, however, you don't want to occupy your readers' time with anything but the relevant details of your incident. As you read the scenario above, did you identify facts that you immediately knew weren't relevant? Were there some facts that even now you question whether or not to include in your report?

Let's first break down this incident by summarizing what it was *really* about. It wasn't about you getting interrupted while running radar or considering the possibility that the witness got the suspect's description wrong. It wasn't about the amount of trash in the gutter or any officer safety concerns you had with the group at the corner. You can summarize what this incident was about in a few short sentences:

> I responded to a shoplifting of a can of beer. I detained the suspect, investigated the crime, and ultimately arrested the suspect for public intoxication and shoplifting.

Once you've simplified this incident to its most basic parts, you can more easily identify its general facts:

1. One crime was shoplifting.
2. Another crime was public intoxication.
3. You detained the suspect in an investigative detention.
4. You arrested the suspect.

Now that you know these general facts, it is much easier to go back through the incident and determine which incident facts are relevant and which aren't. The following section will use a simple diagram to demonstrate how to group your incident facts and general facts.

4.2.5   **Using a T-Chart diagram to document relevant facts.** You can determine which facts are relevant by drawing a simple diagram called a "T-Chart," so named because the vertical and horizontal lines of the chart form the capital letter *T*. To create this diagram, take out a piece of paper and draw a horizontal line a few inches from the top of the page. Now, draw a vertical line under that horizontal line, dividing the paper into left and right sections. Your paper should look something like the diagram on the facing page.

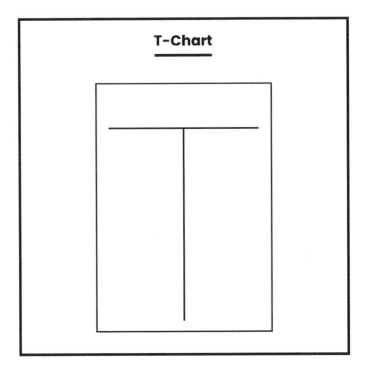

Above the horizontal line, write a brief synopsis of your incident. Then, in the left-hand column, write down each general fact you identified. In the right-hand column, write each incident fact that supports the general fact across from it. Once your chart is complete, you will have a convenient list of all the relevant facts that must be addressed in your report. The following pages contain a T-Chart[3] for the example incident in 4.2.4.

---

[3] The elements of the crime of public intoxication and shoplifting used in the example T-Chart are taken from Bryan A. Garner, ed., *Black's Law Dictionary: Sixth Pocket Edition* (St. Paul: Thomson Reuters, 2021), 432, 727.

Incident Synopsis

I responded to a shoplifting of a can of beer. I detained the suspect, investigated the crime, and ultimately arrested the suspect for public intoxication and shoplifting.

General Facts	Incident Facts
Elements of the crime of shoplifting:	
willfully taking	A witness and surveillance cameras saw the suspect take beer and put it into his pocket.
merchandise	The beer was housed in the store's refrigerator case and sells for $3.50.
from a store	The store is Corner Convenience, located at 1127 Farland Avenue.
without paying	A witness and surveillance cameras saw the suspect exit the store without first paying for the item.
with the intent of converting the goods to one's personal use	I saw the suspect drinking the beer outside the store.

Elements of the crime of public intoxication:	
diminished ability to act with full mental and physical capabilities	Suspect was swaying back and forth; glassy eyes; couldn't concentrate on the conversation.
	Admitted to being "not [drunk] enough."
because of alcohol consumption	I witnessed him drinking beer while standing outside the store.
	Stated he needed "one more," implying he had already consumed alcohol.
In a place open to the general public	Suspect was standing in front of Corner Convenience.
Initial detention of suspect based on reasonable suspicion	The suspect matched the lookout description (white male, brown hair, black tee shirt, jeans, baseball cap).
	The suspect was standing in front of the crime location.
	The suspect was holding the allegedly-stolen merchandise.

Agency policy on arrests:	
handcuffs double-locked	I applied handcuffs and double-locked them.
prisoner searched	I conducted a prisoner search. No contraband was located.
prisoner compartment of cruiser searched before and after transport	Backup Officer Vaughan checked the prisoner compartment.

Much like you used a checklist to identify the *facts relevant to every incident* (see 4.2.2), your T-Chart now becomes your custom checklist for ensuring you include all the relevant incident facts in your report.

You will notice that the facts presented in the above T-Chart are in no particular order; the purpose of a T-Chart is only to determine their *relevance*. In the next chapter, you will learn how to take this list of facts and present it in a logical way that guides your readers through your incident.

5. Guiding Your Readers

5.1   **Officer-Chronological Order**

    5.1.1   Chronological vs. officer-chronological order

    5.1.2   Examples of officer-chronological order

    5.1.3   When to avoid officer-chronological order

5.2   **Additional Techniques to Guide Your Readers**

    5.2.1   Position events in time and place

    5.2.2   Use transitional phrases

Once you have identified the relevant facts of your incident, you must present them in a way that leads your readers step by step along a clear fact pattern toward a logical conclusion. As stated in Chapter 1, whether or not your readers agree with the decisions you made, they should always end your report with an understanding that your actions were *constitutional*, *compliant*, and *reasonable*. This chapter gives you techniques to do just that.

5.1   Officer-Chronological Order

5.1.1   **Chronological vs. officer-chronological order.** If you were to write your reports in true chronological order, you would take all the facts of your incident and present them from the first occurring fact to the last. You would first describe the events leading up to the criminal act you are investigating. You would then describe the commission of the criminal act itself. Finally, you would describe the aftermath of the criminal act. Reports written in chronological order would be arranged something like this:

The problem with trying to document your incidents in true chronological order is that *this is not the order in which you experience them.* Usually, you become involved in an incident during or immediately after the commission of a crime. (Rarely will you come across a crime before it happens.) When you arrive on the scene, you first ensure the safety of the people involved. You then work backward, trying to understand what happened and why. After you conclude your initial investigation, you or other officers may revisit the case over the following days, weeks, months, or years with a series of follow-up activities. Although the events of the incident still occur in order, your involvement with the events follows a different sequence, known as *officer-chronological order.*

Documenting an incident in officer-chronological order presents events in the order you experienced them. When compared with true chronological order, officer-chronological order looks something like the diagram depicted on the facing page.

Although this distinction may be subtle, it is extremely important. When you become involved in an incident, you make decisions and take actions based on the facts you have *at the time.* Your knowledge about what happened may change significantly as you continue to investigate. It may even change to the point where, had

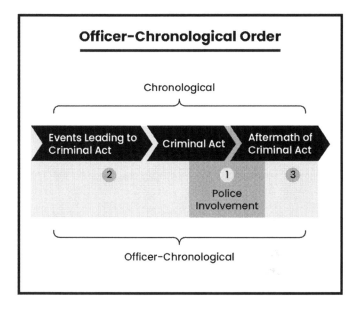

you known that information earlier, you may not have acted as you did. This concept is known as *hindsight*, and the United States Supreme Court has been clear about the role of hindsight in evaluating police actions, particularly in the context of uses of force:

> The "reasonableness" of a particular use of force must be judged from the perspective of a reasonable officer on the scene, rather than with the 20/20 vision of hindsight.[1]

When you write your reports in officer-chronological order, you present the facts of your incident to your readers in the order you experienced them. This means that, at any given point in your report, your readers have no more and no less information than you did at the time.

---

[1] *Graham v. Connor*, 490 U.S. 386 (1989)

5.1.2   **Examples of officer-chronological order.** To understand the importance of writing in officer-chronological order, imagine you respond to a call of someone walking down the street with a gun. When you arrive on the scene, the subject yells, "I'll kill you," and points the gun at you, forcing you to discharge your weapon. Only hours later do investigators determine that the gun was a non-working replica; there was no way it could have harmed you or anyone else. Based on the limited facts presented here, are readers likely to find that your actions were *constitutional, compliant,* and *reasonable?* Anyone familiar with the law and police procedure will say that they were; however, if you were to present this incident in true chronological order in your report, your readers may question why you made the decisions you did:

> I responded to a subject walking down the street with a non-working replica firearm. When I arrived on the scene, the subject yelled, "I'll kill you," and pointed the replica at me. I discharged my service pistol.

This description is highly problematic, not because the facts are wrong (they aren't) but because it presents them out of order. In this scenario, you had no way of knowing that the gun was a replica; that fact wasn't discovered until hours later. But this report makes it seem as if you knew this information upon arriving at the scene. By presenting the facts out of officer-chronological order, you provide your readers with information that even you didn't have at the time. In other words, you allow your readers the luxury of hindsight to evaluate your decisions when you didn't have the same luxury while making them!

Consider how a few minor edits can present these same facts in officer-chronological order and provide your readers with the information you had when you had it:

> I responded to a report of a subject walking down the street with a gun. When I arrived on the scene, the subject yelled, "I'll kill you," and pointed the gun at me. I discharged my service pistol.

Now, readers have the same information you had while you were making split-second decisions at the scene. They know the facts in the order that you experienced them. Although the gun later turned out to be a replica, you didn't know this information at this point in your report; therefore, your readers shouldn't either.

Remember, the point of presenting facts in officer-chronological order is to give readers no more and *no less* information than you had when you had it. If you had arrived on the scene suspecting that the gun was a replica because, for example, dispatch had informed you of this information, then this fact becomes relevant. To leave out this fact with the intention of misleading your readers would be nothing short of unethical.

As one final example, look back at the example police incident presented in section 4.2.4. The table on the following page compares how you would present these facts in chronological order versus officer-chronological order.

Chronological Order	Officer-Chronological Order
1. Suspect walked into the store	1. Police received a call about a shoplifter
2. Suspect removed a beer can from the cooler	2. Dispatch broadcast a description of the suspect
3. Suspect placed the beer can into his jacket pocket	3. Police arrived on scene
4. Suspect exited the store	4. Police identified a suspect matching the lookout description who was drinking a beer outside the store
5. Suspect stood outside drinking the beer	5. Police spoke to the clerk
6. Store clerk called the police	6. Police reviewed the surveillance video
7. Police arrived	7. Police determined that the suspect took the beer from the cooler and put it into his pocket

Once you have placed your relevant facts into officer-chronological order, you have taken the most important step to guiding your readers through your incident.

5.1.3   **When to avoid officer-chronological order.** Although presenting facts in officer-chronological order is usually the best way to present information clearly, there are two circumstances when using officer-chronological order may make your reports *less* clear.

The first circumstance occurs when two events happen simultaneously and the sequence of the events isn't relevant to your incident. Imagine an incident where you are trying to interview two eyewitnesses to a robbery. Both eyewitnesses are still feeling the effects of adrenaline and they keep interrupting each other as you try to interview them. Trying to document their statements in officer-chronological order would be confusing:

> I spoke to one of the witnesses, Ms. Andrea Tolley. She told me the suspect was wearing green pants and a black shirt. Another witness, Mr. Alex Juhl, interrupted her and said he thought both the pants and shirt were black. Ms. Tolley said the suspect ran south on Hill View Street. Mr. Juhl added that he saw the suspect turn east onto Canal Way. Ms. Tolley disagreed and said the suspect ran past Canal Way.

These facts are presented in officer-chronological order, but it's hard to keep straight which witness said what. Since the sequence of these statements doesn't have any real bearing on your actions, you can solve this problem by grouping similar information:

> I first interviewed one of the witnesses, Ms. Andrea Tolley. She told me the suspect was wearing green pants and a black shirt. She saw the suspect run south on Hill View Street past the intersection with Canal Way.
>
> I then interviewed the second witness, Mr. Alex Juhl. He told me the suspect was wearing black pants and a black shirt. He also remembered the suspect running south on Hill View Street but believed the suspect turned east onto Canal Way.

A second circumstance where it makes sense to avoid officer-chronological order occurs when you document administrative actions. Usually, these are actions required by your agency's policies, such as documenting that your body camera was activated, that you checked the rear seat of your cruiser before prisoner transport, or that you turned in a particular form at the end of your shift. Since it only matters that you document these facts—not that you document them in order—it makes sense to group them at the end of your report. This will be discussed more in section 6.2.5.

5.2   Additional Techniques to Guide Your Readers

5.2.1   Position events in time and place. Police incidents happen in the real world and are always describable by time and place. When describing events in your reports, readers should understand precisely when and where the events took place.

One way to accomplish this is to begin a paragraph with a phrase or sentence that describes when and where the events in that paragraph took place. Here are a few examples of how those phrases and sentences may look:

> On 09 July 2023, at 1755 hours, I responded to 2581 Maplewood Lane.

> On August 5, 2023, at 1200 hours, I spoke to the complainant by phone.

> At 1530 hours, I returned to the crime scene.

> I then took cover behind a nearby dumpster.

Notice from these examples that there are a variety of ways that time and place can be described. The first example explicitly names the date, time, and location of the described event. The second example explains that the "place" was "by phone" but doesn't mention where exactly the phone call took place, presumably because this isn't a relevant fact. The third example gives a time and a generic label for the location (i.e., "the crime scene"); this technique works only if the date and specific location of the crime scene were described earlier in the report. Finally, the last example works only if readers understand where you were before taking cover behind the dumpster.

5.2.2   **Use transitional phrases.** Transitional phrases help readers know when you change from describing one event to the next. Since your reports present events in officer-chronological order, many transitional phrases indicate the passage of time and can be used to string together sequences of events:

> Upon my arrival...
>
> I then...
>
> After speaking with the victim, I...
>
> First, I.... Next, I.... Last, I...
>
> I first interviewed.... I then interviewed...
>
> As a result of..., I...
>
> She then told me...
>
> I then ordered him to...

When using transitional phrases, be careful not to accidentally choose phrases that describe events out of officer-chronological order. Instead, rephrase them to be in the proper sequence:

Not this:

Prior to placing him in my cruiser, I double-locked the handcuffs and checked them for proper fit.

But this:

I double-locked the handcuffs and checked them for proper fit. I then placed him in my cruiser.

6. Structuring Your Report

6.1 Paragraphs, Headings, and Subheadings

    6.1.1   Paragraphs

    6.1.2   Headings and subheadings

6.2 Five Parts of a Police Report Narrative

    6.2.1   Overview of the model

    6.2.2   Pre-Arrival

    6.2.3   Initial Investigation

    6.2.4   Follow-Up Investigation

    6.2.5   Administrative Actions

    6.2.6   Case Disposition

6.3 Additional Parts

    6.3.1   Header

    6.3.2   Synopsis

    6.3.3   Attachments

    6.3.4   Dissemination

Structure describes both the order in which relevant facts are presented to your readers and the physical layout of your reports. A consistent structure makes your reports easier to write, read, and refer back to. By organizing information consistently each time, you will find that writing your reports becomes a much quicker endeavor, and your readers will learn that answers to their questions appear in a predictable manner each time they read your reports. The *Five Parts of a Police Report Narrative* described in section 6.2 provides a clear, intuitive way to structure your reports.

This chapter goes hand-in-hand with the techniques described in Chapter 5. You can't guide your readers through your incident without adopting an appropriate structure, and you can't adopt an appropriate structure if you are using ineffective techniques to guide your readers.

6.1 Paragraphs, Headings, and Subheadings

6.1.1   **Paragraphs.** The basic structural unit of your report is the paragraph. A paragraph is one or more sentences grouped together because they share a similar theme. One paragraph may contain statements made by a witness, another may describe a suspect, and another may describe techniques you used to dust for fingerprints. There is no exact science to creating paragraphs, but shorter, focused paragraphs are usually the easiest for your readers to navigate.

6.1.2   **Headings and subheadings.** Headings and subheadings label sections of your reports. They are comprised of text that is boldface, underlined, or set in all caps. The boldface text that begins section 6.1 (*Paragraphs, Headings, and Subheadings*) is a heading. The boldface text at the beginning of this paragraph (*Headings and subheadings*) is a subheading.

Headings and subheadings provide a quick way for readers to find the information they need. The first time someone reads a report, they are likely to read it straight through, from beginning to end, like a novel. If they need to refer to your report after their initial reading, however, they will probably do so because they need to find specific information; therefore, the more likely your readers will be to refer to your report at a later date, the more beneficial it will be to include headings and subheadings.

Headings and subheadings also add visual structure by separating multiple paragraphs into sections and subsections. It is a matter of practicality that it is easier to read a document that is broken into smaller sections. For this reason, if your reports extend past one typewritten page, consider using headings and subheadings to break your document into more manageable chunks. See the last page of this chapter for examples of headings and subheadings.

6.2 Five Parts of a Police Report Narrative

6.2.1 **Overview of the model.** The *Five Parts of a Police Report Narrative* uses headings and subheadings to divide your report into five major sections, each corresponding to the order in which you handle a police incident (i.e., officer-chronological order). Organizing your reports this way guides readers through your incident (see Chapter 5). The five parts are:

1. *Pre-Arrival.* Information you learned before arriving at the incident location (1–2 sentences)

2. *Initial Investigation.* Actions taken and observations made while at the incident scene (multiple paragraphs)

3. *Follow-Up Investigation.* Investigative actions you took in the hours, days, months, or years after concluding your initial investigation (multiple paragraphs)

4. *Administrative Actions.* Paperwork, notifications, evidence logging, and other administrative matters that aren't essential to document in officer-chronological order (multiple paragraphs)

5. *Case Disposition.* The status of your case as of the date of the report (1–2 sentences)

These five parts describe a general way to organize your reports. Depending on your incident, you may want to use the five parts as headings within your report, or you may need to develop headings more specific to your incident. Begin with the structure outlined above, but don't be afraid to adapt it to best suit the needs of your readers. We'll now look at each of the five parts and the possible subheadings contained under each one.

6.2.2   **Pre-Arrival.** Every report begins with pre-arrival information, which tells readers how you came to be involved in your incident. Information typically included in the *pre-arrival* section includes:

- The incident date and time
- The incident location
- The type of incident (e.g., robbery, assault, burglary)
- Whether the call was dispatched or self-initiated
- Relevant information you learned before you arrived on the scene

Notice how most of the *facts relevant to every incident* (see 4.2.2) are included in this first section of your report.

Pre-arrival information is comprised of one or two sentences and follows a basic pattern (see 19.1 for more examples of formatting pre-arrival information):

On DATE at TIME, I was dispatched to LOCATION for *a/an* INCIDENT TYPE *in progress/report*.

Pre-arrival information should be concise, so no subheadings appear in this section.

Five Parts of a Police Report Narrative

Part	Description (Length)
Pre-Arrival	Information you learned before arriving at the incident location (*1–2 sentences*)
Initial Investigation	Actions taken and observations made while at the incident scene (*multiple paragraphs*)
Follow-Up Investigation	Investigative actions you took in the hours, days, months, or years after concluding your on-scene investigation (*multiple paragraphs*)
Administrative Actions	Paperwork, notifications, and other administrative matters that aren't essential to document in officer-chronological order (*multiple paragraphs*)
Case Disposition	The status of your case as of the date of the report (*1–2 sentences*)

6.2.3 **Initial Investigation.** Once you arrive on the scene, your initial investigation begins. This part of your report includes all the actions and observations you made while at the scene of your incident. Information typically included in the *initial investigation* section includes:

- Observations you made
- Actions you took
- Interviews you conducted
- Descriptions of suspects, evidence, crime scenes, injuries, etc.

The *initial investigation* section usually comprises many paragraphs and may extend to multiple pages. Because your initial investigation has the potential to be quite lengthy, it is often helpful to divide this section into smaller sections by using subheadings. Some subheadings that may go in this section include:

Interview with PERSON'S NAME

Description of Use of Force

Description of Crime Scene

Review of Surveillance Footage

Description of OBJECT NAME

Chapters 8–10 and 19 provide more guidance about documenting things that appear in the *initial investigation* section.

6.2.4 **Follow-Up Investigation.** After you wrap up your initial investigation, you may still have work left to do. For example, you may need to obtain a warrant, conduct follow-up interviews, or research persons of interest in a police database. The *follow-up investigation* section includes all the investigative steps you took in the hours, days, months, or years after the initial investigation took place. These steps may be documented in your original report or in report supplements. Information typically included in the *follow-up investigation* section includes:

- Interviews you conducted
- Phone calls you made
- Records you checked
- Evidence you processed

Some subheadings that may go in this section include:

Interview with PERSON'S NAME

NCIC checks

Open Source Searches

Evidence Chain of Custody

6.2.5   **Administrative Actions.** This section includes information you are required to document (perhaps by policy) but that doesn't need to appear in officer-chronological order. Information typically included in the *administrative actions* section includes:

- Whether your body camera was recording
- Whether you checked the back seat of your cruiser before and after prisoner transport
- Agency forms you completed
- NCIC entries
- Notifications made to supervisors

Some subheadings that may go in this section include:

Evidence Chain of Custody

Warrant Entry

Supervisor Notification

Completion of FORM NAME

Because many of these items may simply be acknowledgments that you have performed an action, you may include each administrative action as its own short paragraph and eliminate the subheadings altogether. For example:

My body camera was activated.

I notified Sergeant Gilbert of this incident.

6.2.6   **Case Disposition.** The final part of each report you write should be the disposition of your case as of the date of your report. Information typically included in the *case disposition* section includes:

- Whether or not the case is actively being investigated
- Who is responsible for any follow-up investigation

Notice how this section covers the last *fact relevant to every police incident* (see 4.2.2). Case disposition information is comprised of one or two sentences:

This case is closed by arrest.

This case is CASE STATUS. It is turned over to *detectives/crash reconstruction/school resource officers/*ETC. for further investigation.

Case disposition information should be concise, so this section contains no subheadings.

6.3 Additional Parts

The *Five Parts of a Police Report Narrative* makes it easy to organize the information in your police reports, but, in special circumstances, you may find it helpful to add one or more of the additional parts listed in this section.

6.3.1 **Header.** A header is a block of text that appears before your police report narrative begins. The purpose of a header is to quickly give your readers key information. Here are some possible subheadings that may be included in your header:

Case Number

Incident Date

Incident Time

Incident Type

Incident Location

Victim/Suspect/Witness Information

Primary Officer

Investigator

Case Disposition

6.3.2 **Synopsis.** A synopsis is a 3–5 sentence summary of your report. The synopsis gives your readers the most important information upfront, allowing them to determine if they need to read your entire report. A synopsis can be especially helpful when numerous reports are written about a single incident. For example, in a complex homicide investigation where multiple officers and detectives wrote reports, having a synopsis makes it easy for readers to determine which report contains the information they are looking for.

6.3.3   **Attachments.** The attachments section points readers to information that supplements what you have written in your report. Attachments may be physically attached to a hardcopy report, uploaded to a records management system, or stored separately in a case file. Either way, your readers should be able to gain access to these documents if they need to. Some common attachments include:

- Photographs
- Copies of agency forms
- Sketches and diagrams
- Financial records
- Witness, victim, or suspect statements
- Interview transcripts and recordings

Notate attachments at the end of your report in a comma-separated list preceded by the word *Attachments*.

6.3.4   **Dissemination.** The dissemination section is usually unnecessary because modern reporting systems allow you to control who will receive a copy of your report; however, if you want to specifically notate people who were given a copy, then indicate these people as the very last line of your report, next to the abbreviation *cc*, which stands for *carbon copy*.

Sample Report with Sections, Headings and Subheadings

Case Number: 202300238
Incident Date: January 14, 2023
Incident Time: 2354 hours
Incident Type: Robbery — Home Invasion
Incident Location: 4111 Laurel Rd. #136-A
Victim: Luis Nagy (DOB: 08/14/2001)
Suspect #1:   Alisha Beltran (DOB: Unknown)
Suspect #2:   Unknown B/M
Investigator: Detective T. Luther (#1346)
Disposition: ACTIVE

Synopsis

The victim, Mr. Luis Nagy, alleged that on 14 January 2023, he invited Ms. Alisha Beltran over to his apartment. Shortly after her arrival, an unidentified male entered the apartment, pointed a gun at Mr. Nagy, and robbed him of $750 in cash. This report documents crime scene processing and an interview with the victim.

INITIAL SCENE SURVEY

I responded to the scene of this incident on 14 January 2023 at approximately 2245 hours.

Incident Location Description

This incident occurred at a residential condominium located at 4111 Laurel Road, #136-A (hereafter "the Apartment"), which belonged to the victim, Mr. Luis Nagy. The Apartment was located on the second level of the apartment building in the northeast corner. I accessed the Apartment by ascending fifteen concrete steps to the building entrance and then two...

~ ~ ~

Attachments: Crime Scene Log, Interview recording

cc: Evidence Section

Part III
Adopting an Appropriate Style

S tyle describes how words, sentences, and paragraphs combine to convey meaning. Just as no two police officers share the same style of policing, no two officers use the same style when they write their reports. Even so, some style decisions are more acceptable than others.

Your agency may dictate certain style choices, or you may adopt some as a matter of personal preference. For example, your agency may require you to set a person's name in ALL CAPS the first time it appears in a report. Or, you may decide to begin each paragraph by stating the date and time that the incidents in that paragraph took place. Some style decisions are arguably more effective than others, but so long as you do not violate your agency's policies or well-established rules of grammar, spelling, and punctuation, such choices are generally left to your discretion as the author.

The following chapters contain style guidance. Chapter 7 presents ten commonly accepted style guidelines. Chapter 8 describes effective styles for documenting your actions and observations. Chapter 9 gives specific guidance for describing people, places, and things. Finally, Chapter 10 addresses the documentation of use of force incidents.

7. Ten Style Guidelines

7.1   Write From the First-Person Point of View

7.2   Favor the Past Tense

7.3   Don't Predict the Future

7.4   Tell What Happened

7.5   Use the Active Voice

7.6   Use Concrete Language

7.7   Use Simple Sentence Constructions

7.8   Support Conclusions with Facts

7.9   Choose Clarity Over Brevity

7.10   Remain Consistent

Your writing style is like a fingerprint you leave on your reports. For better or worse, your readers will be able to look at what you've written and say, "Oh, I know who wrote this!" Although there is no single accepted style for police reports, this chapter contains ten of the most common style guidelines for effective report writing. Many of these guidelines are explained in more detail elsewhere in this book, but they are presented here as a set so you have a place to turn when you want ten simple ways to dramatically improve your writing.

As with any guidelines, deciding which to adopt (or ignore) is up to you. Determining your unique style is part of both the fun and frustration of writing. Finding your style usually only happens through a long process of trial and error, by adhering to the guidelines most of the time, deviating from them occasionally, and ultimately figuring out what works best for you.

7.1   Write From the First-Person Point of View

When you respond to a police incident, everything is experienced by *you*. Even when someone tells you what happened to them, *you* are still the one hearing their account. If your partner places handcuffs on the suspect while you hold the suspect's arm, your partner may be the one handcuffing, but *you* are the one witnessing what has happened. Everything you do at the scene is filtered through your point of view. Since this is how you experience a police incident, it makes sense this is how you would report one.

Writing has three basic points of view: first-person, second-person, and third-person. The first-person point of view describes an incident from your perspective. The second-person point of view describes an incident from the perspective of your reader. The third-person point of view describes an incident from the perspective of someone else mentioned in your report.

When writing from the first-person point of view, you only report on what you personally did or witnessed. Readers must always be clear about how you came to know each piece of information. Look at the following example, which switches between the first- and third-person points of view.

> I yelled at the suspect to freeze, but he immediately began running east on Mason Street. He then turned north into an alley and disappeared from my sight.

> While he was in the alley, he dropped the gun from his waistband onto the ground. I turned the corner and saw him attempting to climb onto a dumpster so he could jump over a brick wall. He knew I would lose sight of him if he got over the brick wall.

This example begins from the officer's perspective. The officer yells at the suspect, who runs off and then turns down an alley. Readers understand that the officer had first-hand access to all this information: they see these events from the officer's perspective.

The point of view shifts suddenly, however, when the writer describes the suspect dropping the gun in the alleyway. According to the writer's own words, this action happened after the suspect disappeared from sight and before the officer turned the corner into the alley. How could the officer possibly know what the suspect was doing with the gun while he was all alone in the alley? This action was written from the third-person point of view.

The point of view then shifts again. Suddenly, readers are back with the officer in the foot pursuit. The officer turns the corner and witnesses the suspect attempting to jump onto a dumpster. But then readers are thrust into the suspect's mind (third-person point of view) as the officer declares what the suspect knew. How could the officer know the suspect's thoughts? Or was the officer projecting their conclusions onto the suspect? Both options are problematic.

If you are the officer writing this report, you may think, "But the fact that the suspect dropped the gun and could have hidden from me are both relevant facts. I can't leave them out of my report." Nor should you. What you should do is recast all the events from your perspective. In the following example, notice how the italicized changes describe the same events from the officer's point of view.

I yelled at the suspect to freeze, but he immediately began running east on Mason Street. He then turned north into an alley and disappeared from my sight. *I turned the corner into the alley and saw a black gun lying on the pavement. This looked like the same gun the suspect had in his waistband when I first approached him.* I then saw the suspect attempting to climb onto a dumpster *near* a brick wall. *I knew* I would lose sight of him if he crossed the brick wall.

This is now an acceptable description of events because it is clear to readers that all events are filtered through the officer's perspective.

7.2   Favor the Past Tense

In English, every sentence exists somewhere in time, either in the past, the present, or the future (see 11.3.4). The past tense describes things that have happened, the present tense describes things that are happening currently, and the future tense describes things that will happen. Since police reports tell readers what happened in the past, it makes sense to write them in the past tense. Here is the same event described in the past, present, and future tenses respectively:

I knocked on the apartment door.

I knock on the apartment door.

I will knock on the apartment door.

The first sentence tells readers that you knocked on the apartment door at some point in the past. The second sentence makes it seem like you are writing your report while knocking on the door. The third sentence makes it clear you have not knocked on the door yet but plan to do so in the future.

Writing in the past tense makes it clear to readers that the events they are reading about have already occurred. But what if you are trying to describe an event that was happening in the past when it was interrupted by something else, as in the below example? To accomplish this, use a special variation of the past tense known as the past progressive tense (see 11.3.9):

> I was knocking on the apartment door when I heard a gunshot.

Although the past tense should be your default choice, there are situations where writing in the present tense is acceptable, such as when explaining habits or information that is generally true:

> The security guard patrols this lot at 10 p.m. every weekday.

> This neighborhood is known for drug activity.

Using the present tense in these cases tells readers that the statement is likely still true when they read your report.

Is there any situation where writing in the future tense is acceptable? Probably not, as explained in the next section.

7.3   Don't Predict the Future

As explained in the previous section, you should favor the past tense when writing your reports. Sentences written in the future tense pose practical problems:

> I will follow up with the victim on Tuesday.

> I will obtain video footage during my next shift.

These statements commit you to taking future action. Despite your best intentions, a critical incident, sick day, temporary assignment, or other unforeseen circumstance may prevent you from doing what you have just committed to do in an official document.

Instead of committing to something in the future, document only those things that have happened in the past. If you still have work to do, simply do it and document it in a supplemental report.

There is an important distinction between predicting the future (which you should not do) and reporting someone's past statements about something that is expected to happen in the future (which you should do). Consider these sentences:

> Ms. Sawyer said she would send me the video footage on Saturday.

> The unknown suspect threatened to blow up the school on April 19.

While these two sentences mention future events, the sentences themselves occur in the past. The first sentence describes what Ms. Sawyer said in the past; the second sentence describes threats made in the past by the suspect. Since both sentences describe past events, they are acceptable to include in a report.

7.4   Tell What Happened

Your reports should not force readers to deduce what happened during an incident by describing everything that *did not* happen:

> I did not find any fingerprints at the scene.

> He did not say he wanted to prosecute.

In these examples, readers will wonder if you looked for fingerprints or if you bothered asking the victim if he wanted to prosecute. These statements are written ambiguously. You may not have found fingerprints because you never looked, and the victim may have never said he wanted to prosecute because you never asked.

If you find yourself beginning your sentences with negative constructions—*did not*, *had not*, etc.—ask yourself what *did* happen. Then, rephrase your sentence to explain what actually occurred:

> I dusted for fingerprints and found no viable results.

> He said he did not want to prosecute.

Are there cases where omissions are important? Yes, as in the case of a suspect who leaves out a key piece of information in a statement. In these cases, describe what happened and then mention the omission explicitly:

> The suspect told me he went to the grocery store and the gym before coming home. He failed to mention that he stopped by the bowling alley.

7.5   Use the Active Voice[1]

When you write in the active voice, the subject of the sentence performs the action:

> I arrested the suspect.

> Detectives canvassed the neighborhood.

> The victim saw him walking east.

---

[1] A more technical description of the active voice is found in section 11.3.13.

The opposite of the active voice is the passive voice, in which the subject of the sentence receives the action:

The suspect was arrested by me.

The neighborhood was canvassed by detectives.

He was seen walking east by the victim.

You can see that the examples written in the active voice are shorter, snappier, and more specific. The examples written in the passive voice slow down the action by making readers wait until the end of the sentence to figure out who the sentence is about. If that were the only problem with writing in the passive voice, then it may not be an issue, but there is a larger problem: sentences written in the passive voice make it easy to omit the subject altogether:

The suspect was arrested.

The neighborhood was canvassed.

He was seen walking east.

These examples raise questions: *Who* arrested the suspect? *Who* canvassed the neighborhood? *Who* saw the suspect walking east? From the way these sentences are written, it is impossible to tell.

If you have trouble distinguishing the active voice from the passive, look for *was…by* constructions in your sentences. Because the passive voice tends to drop the subject altogether, keep in mind that the "by" part of that equation may also be missing:

She <u>was</u> fingerprinted <u>by</u> me.

He <u>was</u> punched <u>by</u> the suspect.

My cruiser <u>was</u> struck [<u>by</u> a citizen's vehicle].

To fix each of these sentences, identify the true subject of the sentence and place it at the beginning:

I fingerprinted her.

The suspect punched him.

A citizen's vehicle struck my cruiser.

7.6 Use Concrete Language

Concrete language uses nouns that readers can picture in their minds:

She wore a red shirt.

He had both hands in his pockets.

I saw him walk around the corner.

The opposite of concrete language is abstract language, which expresses ideas or concepts. Abstract language leaves plenty of room for interpretation:

Her clothing was disheveled.

She posed an officer safety risk.

He was evasive.

As will be covered extensively in Chapter 8, writing from your senses is the most effective technique for using concrete language; however, don't get tricked by sentences that appear to originate from your senses but that actually use abstract language:

I saw that she was frightened.

The car had been rummaged through.

What led you to believe she was frightened? How did you know the car had been rummaged through? Imagine yourself as a movie director trying to recreate the incident you experienced. What would you expect viewers to *see* on the screen when they watched the movie?

She couldn't stop shaking, and she kept looking over her shoulder.

The glove compartment was open, and its contents were lying on the passenger floorboard.

7.7   Use Simple Sentence Constructions

Each word in a sentence takes your readers on a small journey from the sentence's beginning to its end. Likewise, each sentence and paragraph leads your readers from one thought to the next. Although complex sentences may be grammatically correct, simpler sentences are usually more effective at conveying meaning.

Not this:

While I was reviewing surveillance video footage, I saw the suspect smash the store's front window with a brick, after which the suspect entered the store and proceeded to the cash register, where he removed the money, placed it into his duffel bag, exited the store, and then rode away on a bicycle.

But this:

I reviewed surveillance video footage. In the video, I saw the suspect smash the store's front window with a brick. The suspect entered the store through the window and walked to the cash register. He placed the money from the cash register into his duffel bag. He then exited the store through the smashed window and rode away on a bicycle.

The first example presents the incident as one long sentence, forcing your readers to maintain a single train of thought. The second example separates each thought into a new sentence. This gives your readers places to rest. It also helps them easily understand the sequence of events. Chapter 11 will discuss sentence structure in more detail.

7.8   Support Conclusions with Facts

A conclusion is a determination you make based on your investigation. Contrary to popular belief, conclusions *do* have a place in your police reports. But readers need more than your word as the writer before they can agree the conclusion was reasonable. Writing that someone was drunk is a conclusion. While the person may have been drunk, the only way for readers to agree with your conclusion is for you to support it with concrete, verifiable facts:

Based on his slurred speech, the strong odor of alcohol, and his admission to drinking a fifth of vodka, I concluded that he was drunk.

The goal of your police reports is not to eliminate your conclusions. Indeed, you were called to the scene precisely to draw conclusions based on your investigation. The goal of your reports is to present enough information so that your readers understand how you came to your conclusions. You do this by supporting your conclusions with facts. A conclusion not supported by facts is called a *baseless conclusion*.

Supporting your conclusions with facts is what it means for your report to be *objective*. It's not that you have eliminated every mention of yourself and the decisions you made, but that your readers understand your decisions were made without any distortion by your personal feelings or opinions.

7.9 Choose Clarity Over Brevity

Short reports are good; clear reports are better. Short and clear reports are the best of all. Unfortunately, you won't often have the time to make your reports strike this perfect balance. When you are forced to choose between clarity and brevity, always choose clarity.

Not this:

The car left the roadway.

But this:

The blue Toyota 4Runner skidded on a patch of black ice, jumped the curb, and crashed into a concrete planter.

7.10 Remain Consistent

Policing and writing both offer you considerable discretion. Just as there are many ways to handle a police incident successfully, there are many ways to describe that incident in your report. The choice of which style to adopt is ultimately up to you. Whichever choices you make, however, remain consistent. Readers will get confused if you adopt one writing style in the first paragraph and a different style in the next.

Be especially careful to maintain consistency when:

- Referring to people by name
- Giving physical descriptions of people and places
- Formatting dates and times
- Structuring your reports
- Adopting a conversational yet professional tone

Suggestions for maintaining consistency in these and other areas are presented in the remaining chapters.

8. Describing Your Observations and Actions

8.1 Describing Observations

8.1.1   Write from your senses

8.1.2   Begin each observation with a sensory verb

8.1.3   Replace abstract language with concrete nouns

8.1.4   Eliminate obvious verbiage

8.1.5   Documenting observations captured on body camera

8.2 Describing Actions

8.2.1   Write in action-reaction sequences

8.2.2   Start with the actions of others

8.2.3   Link your reactions

8.2.4   Eliminate irrelevant actions

8.2.5   Special considerations when describing actions

8.3 Supporting Information

8.3.1   Background information

8.3.2   Conclusions

Nearly everything that happens during a police incident can be categorized as an observation or an action (a third category—*supporting information*—will be discussed at the end of this chapter). Observations are things you learn through your five senses.[1] Actions are things you do, such as driving, arresting, interviewing, or collecting evidence. This chapter will teach you how to combine sensory descriptions of your observations with action-reaction sequences to create powerful descriptions of what happened during an incident.

8.1 Describing Observations

8.1.1 **Write from your senses.** Policing is a sensory profession. You *see* a traffic violation, you *hear* someone crying, you *feel* a gun in the suspect's waistband, you *smell* drugs, or you *taste* blood on your lip. Since the information you collect at an incident is filtered through your senses, the easiest way to document that information is by using sensory language:

> I heard two people arguing.

> I felt resistance when I pushed against the door.

> I saw a knife on the passenger seat.

Notice how each of these examples tells your readers not just *what* you learned but also *how*—or through which senses—you learned it. Compare how changing a few words in the same sentences makes them less clear:

> I noticed two people arguing.

> I could tell something was blocking the door.

> I believed there was a knife on the passenger seat.

---

[1] Throughout this book, the word *observation* is used to describe any information you gather through your senses, not just what you see with your eyes.

These sentences raise more questions than they answer. *What made you notice two people arguing? How could you tell something was blocking the door? What led you to believe there was a knife on the passenger seat?* If these questions are left unanswered in your reports, they will undoubtedly be asked by prosecutors, defense attorneys, supervisors, and other readers. The answers to these questions lie somewhere in the senses you used to obtain this information.

To effectively describe your observations using sensory language, follow all three of these rules in the order they are presented:

1. Begin each observation with a sensory verb.

2. Replace abstract language with concrete nouns.

3. Eliminate obvious verbiage.

8.1.2   **Begin each observation with a sensory verb.** In every sentence where you describe your observations, make it clear to readers which sense you used to gather the information. The simplest way to achieve this is to begin each sentence with a sensory verb:

I saw   I felt   I heard

I tasted   I smelled

For example, imagine you are dispatched to a possible disorderly subject. The only information you receive from dispatch is that a man is walking in and out of traffic on a major roadway during rush hour. An excerpt from your police report about this incident may read like this:

As I arrived on the scene, the man was still walking in the middle of the roadway. He was yelling at passing vehicles and preventing them from passing.

These two sentences will raise questions with observant readers. *How did you learn this information? Did you witness it yourself, or did a citizen tell you? What made you believe the man was yelling at passing vehicles? How exactly was he preventing cars from getting around him?*

Remember, *you* were at the incident, so *you* know how you learned this information, but your readers don't. Your reports need to stand on their own. Let's begin answering your readers' questions by identifying each observation:

Observation 1: The man was walking on the roadway.

Observation 2: The man was yelling at passing vehicles.

Observation 3: The man was preventing vehicles from passing.

After identifying the three observations you made, rephrase each observation so it begins with a sensory verb. Here's what the resulting excerpt from your police report may look like now:

As I arrived on the scene, I saw the man walking in the middle of the roadway. I heard him yelling at passing vehicles. I saw him preventing vehicles from passing.

You can see that the first rule—*begin each observation with a sensory verb*—makes it clear to your readers that you *saw* the man walking, and you *heard* the man yelling. Your readers can imagine what they would have observed had they been sitting in the passenger seat of your cruiser.

But what about the last sentence? Even though it begins with a sensory verb, it doesn't clarify *how* the man was preventing vehicles from getting around him. To solve this problem, let's turn to the second rule.

8.1.3   **Replace abstract language with concrete nouns.** Abstract language describes concepts or ideas. Concrete nouns are people, places, or things that can be perceived through the senses. Your readers could point to a concrete noun if it were in front of them. For example, they could point to the Washington Monument (a concrete noun) but not to "gratitude," which is an abstract concept the Washington Monument embodies.

With this in mind, let's look again at the last sentence of the police report excerpt:

> I saw him preventing vehicles from passing.

"Preventing" is a concept. It is not something you learn through your senses. The second rule is to replace such language with concrete nouns. To do this, ask yourself what observations led to your conclusion that he was preventing cars from getting by (as opposed to attempting to flag them down for help or to direct them around a road hazard). Here's how this revised sentence may read:

> I saw the man wave his hands above his head and jump up and down. I saw him step in front of cars. I saw cars' brake lights as they stopped suddenly. I saw other cars swerve around him to avoid striking him. One vehicle had to stop so suddenly that I heard its tires screeching.

When using concrete nouns, your readers have a much more vivid description of what led you to believe that the man was preventing vehicles from passing.

Although this paragraph paints a vivid picture, it is repetitive. Do you really need to state what sense you used for *every* observation, especially the obvious ones? No, which leads to the third rule.

8.1.4   **Eliminate obvious verbiage.** We now have an example where every observation begins with a sensory verb and where all of the abstract language has been replaced with concrete nouns:

> As I arrived on the scene, I saw the man walking in the middle of the roadway. I heard him yelling at passing vehicles. I saw the man wave his hands above his head and jump up and down. I saw him step in front of cars. I saw cars' brake lights as they stopped suddenly. I saw other cars swerve to avoid striking him. One vehicle had to stop so suddenly that I heard its tires screeching.

There are many places in this example where it should be evident to readers which senses you used to make your observations. For instance, how else would you know the man was waving his hands above his head and jumping up and down except to see him? How else would you know that tires were screeching except to hear them?

The third rule states that you should eliminate any verbiage so obvious that your readers could not *misunderstand* the source of your observation. Read that sentence again carefully. It is a high bar to meet. Ensure you are confident that readers can't misunderstand what you've written before removing the language. Here's how the excerpt might read after removing the obvious verbiage (and doing some light editing):

> As I arrived on the scene, I saw the man walking in the middle of the roadway, and I heard him yelling at passing vehicles. He was waving his hands above his head and jumping up and down. At one point, he

stepped in front of oncoming traffic, suddenly causing a car to stop. Two other cars swerved to avoid striking him. One vehicle stopped so suddenly that its tires screeched.

Now we have a paragraph that uses sensory language by following each of the three rules discussed in this section. Take a moment to compare this paragraph to the original example in section 8.1.2.

Another type of obvious verbiage involves the use of filler phrases like "I noticed," "I could tell," and "I was able to." These phrases naturally lead your readers to wonder why you noticed, how you could tell, or what made you able to. Combining these filler phrases with sensory language can lead to awkward, wordy sentence constructions:

I noticed the smell of marijuana.

I could tell that I felt something in the suspect's pocket during the pat down.

When I knelt down, I was able to see the gun under the sofa.

To avoid this problem, follow the rules in section 8.1.1 to replace filler phrases with concrete language:

I smelled marijuana.

I felt a bulge in the suspect's pocket.

I knelt down and saw the gun under the sofa.

If writing from your senses is a new concept, it may take a little getting used to. As you begin writing this way, it can help to write out your sentences after applying each rule. Once you become more proficient, you will be able to evaluate each of your sentences in your head without writing out each iteration.

8.1.5   **Documenting observations captured on body camera.** Body cameras can be helpful tools for documentation. By reviewing body camera footage, you can slow down events and focus on details your brain may not have had time to process at the scene. There are pros and cons to being able to do this. One pro is that you can use your body camera to fill gaps in your memory. Another pro is that you can document the exact words spoken by suspects, victims, or witnesses.

One con is that you may observe things in the body camera footage that weren't possible or practical to notice on the scene but that may have altered your decision-making had you seen them. Another con is that body cameras capture images differently than the human eye. A typical body camera captures images within a 120–170° horizontal field of view, and everything within that field of view is within focus. On the other hand, the human eye has a 200–220° field of view but can only sharply focus on about 2–3° of that visual field in a given moment.[2]

Add to this the fact that stress further impacts your perception, and you can see how you may completely miss or misperceive something at the scene that was plainly observable on body camera, or how your body camera may have completely missed something that you saw with your natural eye. For example, you may have missed seeing a knife sitting on a table eight feet behind a suspect because you were focused on their hands, even though the knife was clearly visible on body camera footage. Or you

---

[2] See Boivin, R., Faubert, C., Gendron, A., & Poulin, B. (2020). Explaining the Body-Worn Camera Perspective Bias. *Journal of Qualitative Criminal Justice & Criminology.* https://doi.org/10.21428/88de04a1.bc4fdeda

may have reacted to movement in your peripheral vision when your body camera missed that same movement.

For these reasons, body camera footage should never be the primary source for your reports, but it can still provide valuable supplemental information. To effectively use body camera footage while writing your reports, follow these two rules:

1. *Write a draft without reviewing your body camera.* Before viewing your body camera footage, write a draft of your report based solely on your memory and notes. This will allow you to capture the incident without any unintentional influence from what you see (or think you see) in your body camera footage. After completing a first draft, review your body camera footage to ensure you included key information or to fill in precise details.

2. *Attribute the body camera footage when it shows something you do not remember.* When your body camera depicts something you can't honestly remember, let your readers know the source of the information you are presenting:

   > My body camera depicts Officer Klinger walking around the east side of the house.

   > My body camera captured Ms. Vigil clenching her fists five times.

The key point to remember when using body camera footage is that it is a documentation *tool*, not a replacement for a well-written description of events.

8.2 Describing Actions

8.2.1 **Write in action-reaction sequences.** If you are not describing observations, you are probably describing actions. As a police officer, you don't take arbitrary actions or make random decisions. Most of the time, your actions are actually *reactions* to the actions of others. If a suspect flees, you may give chase. If a witness lies to you, you may change your line of questioning. If the driver in front of you slams on their brakes, you may take evasive maneuvers. In each of these situations, the actions of another person influence your reactions. Thinking of police incidents as sequences of actions and reactions makes documenting them easier.

Writing in action-reaction sequences creates a chain of events that guides readers toward a logical conclusion. The first action causes a reaction, which then becomes the cause of the next action, and so forth.

Similar to documenting your observations, there are three rules to follow when documenting your actions:

1. Start with the actions of others.
2. Link your reactions.
3. Eliminate irrelevant actions or reactions.

8.2.2 **Start with the actions of others.** Action–reaction sequences start with the actions of another person. To continue the example from section 8.1.2, imagine that after seeing the man walking in traffic, you get on your cruiser's PA system and tell him to move out of the roadway. What happens next is explained in this report excerpt:

> After seeing the subject in the roadway, I told him to move using my PA system. I was pulling my cruiser to the side of the road when I saw him crouch down

and bang his head on the sidewalk. I grabbed his arms and forced him to lie down. I braced his head against the pavement with my hand while telling him to stop hitting his head.

The sequence of events in this example is muddled. Plus, some key actions are missing. *How did the subject get from the roadway to the sidewalk? How did you suddenly go from pulling your cruiser over to grabbing the subject's arms? Was grabbing the subject's arms the method you used to force him to lie down, or were you doing something else* and *grabbing his arms?*

Let's help clarify the events in this paragraph by listing the actions of the subject:

1. He was standing in the roadway.
2. He crouched down.
3. He began banging his head on the sidewalk.
4. He lay down.

Extracting others' actions into a list forces you to do three things. First, it forces you to express each action in its simplest form. The subject did not crouch *and* bang his head; they were two separate actions. Second, it forces you to place the actions in sequence. The subject cannot do one thing *while* doing something else; one action must come before the other. Third, it forces you to identify missing actions. In our list, it's unclear that the subject left the roadway until you mention that he crouched down; let's fix this by adding an action to the list. We'll place any missing actions in brackets to remind ourselves that we may or may not want to include them in our final description.

1. He was standing in the roadway.

2. [He walked to the sidewalk.]

3. He crouched down.

4. He began banging his head on the sidewalk.

5. He lay down.

With this accurate list of the subject's actions,[3] you are now ready to link your reactions as the officer who responded to this incident.

8.2.3   **Link your reactions.** Once you have a list of someone's actions, you can link your reactions. Let's extract your reactions from the example. Just as you listed the other person's actions, break down your reactions into their simplest form, list them in sequence, and identify any missing reactions (shown here in brackets).

1. I told him to move using my PA system.

2. I pulled over my cruiser.

3. [I exited my cruiser.]

4. [I approached the subject.]

5. I grabbed his arms.

6. I forced him to lie down.

7. I braced his head against the pavement with my hand.

8. I told him to stop hitting his head.

Now that you have a list of your reactions, you need to link them to your subject's actions. An easy way to do this is to say, "They did *X*; therefore, I did *Y*."

---

[3] You have probably noticed that each of the subject's actions are technically your *observations* about his actions, so don't forget to follow the rules for describing observations in section 8.1.

1. He was standing in the roadway;

    therefore, I told him to move using my PA system.

2. [He walked to the sidewalk];

    therefore, I pulled over my cruiser.

3. He crouched down;

    [*therefore*, I exited my cruiser.]

    [*therefore*, I approached the subject.]

4. He began banging his head on the sidewalk;

    therefore, I grabbed his arms.

    therefore, I forced him to lie down.

    therefore, I braced his head against the pavement with my hand.

    therefore, I told him to stop hitting his head.

You'll notice that more than one of your reactions is sometimes linked to a person's action. This is fine if the reactions are closely related, as with list item #3 (i.e., exiting your cruiser and approaching the subject); however, be careful that you don't combine too many reactions and risk having your readers question what caused you to react. The reactions listed under item #4 may cause your readers to ask:

*   Once you approached him, was he still banging his head, or had he stopped?

*   Did he comply once you grabbed his arms, or was he trying to escape your grasp?

*   By forcing him to lie down, didn't you place his head *closer* to the pavement? Why not just sit him up instead?

*   Did you give him verbal commands to stop hitting his head before or after you braced his head against the pavement?

When you face such questions, you probably have a gap in your action-reaction sequence. Usually, the gap comes because you have grouped too many of your reactions under a single action taken by the other person. Here's how the action-reaction sequence may look after reconsidering the questions posed by your readers (pay attention to #4–6):

1. He was standing in the roadway;

    therefore, I told him to move using my PA system.

2. [He walked to the sidewalk];

    therefore, I pulled over my cruiser.

3. He crouched down;

    [*therefore*, I exited my cruiser.]

    [*therefore*, I approached the subject.]

4. He began banging his head on the sidewalk;

    [*therefore*, I told him to stop hitting his head.]

    therefore, I grabbed his arms.

5. [He tried to pull away from me;]

    therefore, I forced him to lie down.

6. [He continued to bang his head against the pavement;]

    therefore, I told him to stop hitting his head.

    therefore, I braced his head against the pavement with my hand.

Notice how this revised sequence makes it clear why you took the actions you did instead of some of the alternatives your readers have asked about. Also, notice how considering your readers' questions helped you refine and reorder a few items in your list. Assuming this is a true accounting of events, considering your reactions closely may have helped you to remember that you told him to stop banging his head on two separate occasions, not just the one time implied by your initial report.

An easy test to determine if you are correctly articulating an action-reaction sequence is to pick any sentence that describes something you did and ask yourself, "Why did I do this?" You should be able to find the answer by identifying a sentence earlier in your report that contains the action that caused your reaction.

8.2.4   **Eliminate irrelevant actions.** After identifying every action and reaction within a sequence, you will probably find some actions or reactions that are so obvious they don't need to be stated or that are completely irrelevant to your incident.

For example, it's usually not relevant to mention that you exited your cruiser and closed the door behind you; however, if a suspect takes off running because he hears the click of your door closing, this fact becomes relevant because it forms part of an action-reaction sequence. Likewise, it's usually not relevant to mention that you activated your emergency equipment to conduct a traffic stop; however, if the suspect driver disregards your attempts to stop them, it may very well be relevant because it forms part of your action-reaction sequence. (For more information about determining if a fact is relevant, see Chapter 4.)

Now that we have identified a complete action-reaction sequence for the example incident in section 8.1.2, let's put it into paragraph form. You can do this by documenting the actions and reactions in the order you have listed them. As you do so, determine if each action or reaction is necessary to form a complete sequence. Pay special attention to see if the actions or reactions you bracketed are now relevant.

Here is what your revised paragraph may look like. The subject's actions are in boldface type. Your reactions are underlined.

After seeing the **subject in the roadway**, I used my PA system to tell him to move to the sidewalk. **He complied.** As I pulled over my cruiser, he **sat down on the sidewalk.** While I was walking up to him, he **began banging his head against the pavement.** I ran over to him. I grabbed him by both arms while telling him to stop hitting his head. **He tried to pull away from me,** so I pushed him into a prone position. **He began hitting his head again,** so I yelled at him to stop. I then braced his head against the pavement with my hand to prevent him from hurting himself further.

You probably noticed that this paragraph wasn't composed by merely putting the list of actions and reactions into paragraph form. Although each action and reaction appears in the paragraph, some are reworded or combined into compound sentences (see 11.1.3). Additionally, these actions and reactions were simplified when they appeared in list form; however, real-life actions can happen simultaneously, so it's okay to use words like *while* or *as* to describe this dynamic.

8.2.5   **Special considerations when describing actions.** The example of the man in the roadway contained a relatively simple action-reaction sequence. This made it easy to demonstrate how actions and reactions interact, but real-life situations may not always fit into so neat a formula. Here are a few variations to strict action-reaction sequencing.

Action-reaction groups. What if two action-reaction sequences happen simultaneously? Imagine you are conducting surveillance after a string of auto thefts at a local car dealership. While surveilling after hours, you see two subjects enter the lot. Here's how you might document what you witnessed:

> I saw two subjects dressed in dark-colored hoodies walk onto the lot. Subject #1 approached the lot from Deerfield Drive. Subject #2 approached from North Crescent Street. Subject #1 began trying to open lockboxes on the windows of pickup trucks at the far west side of the lot. I radioed what I was seeing so a marked patrol unit could respond. Subject #2 began walking between cars on the east side of the lot. Subject #1 found a lockbox that was open, but there appeared to be no keys inside because the subject closed the box and continued searching. Subject #2 pulled an unknown device from their pocket and held it to each lockbox. At this time, a car drove past on Deerfield Drive, and both subjects ducked out of sight. After the car passed, Subject #1 began checking lockboxes again.

Although this is an acceptable action-reaction sequence, it may become confusing for readers because it bounces back and forth between the two subjects so frequently. In situations where two independent action-reaction sequences happen at the same time, you can group similar information and include a short sentence explaining that both sequences happened simultaneously (see 5.1.3 for another example):

> I saw two subjects dressed in dark-colored hoodies walk onto the lot. Subject #1 entered the lot from Deerfield Drive and began trying to open lockboxes on the windows of pickup trucks at the far west side of the lot. Subject #1 found a lockbox that was open,

but there appeared to be no keys inside because the subject closed the box and continued searching.

Simultaneous to these events, Subject #2 entered the lot from North Crescent Street and began walking between cars on the east side of the lot. Subject #2 pulled an unknown device from their pocket and held it to each lockbox.

During these events, a car drove past on Deerfield Drive. Both subjects ducked out of sight until the car was gone, and then they resumed their activities. I requested a marked patrol unit.

Extended actions or reactions. Some actions or reactions may take many sentences or paragraphs to explain. For example, when conducting an interview, you may ask the interviewee to tell you what happened. Their answer may take up multiple paragraphs. In such cases, don't feel obligated to break up their longer statement by constantly interjecting your follow-up questions unless they are especially relevant. Instead, begin the interviewee's statement with a simple phrase like, "She told me," and then allow their statement to flow unimpeded.

Not this:

I asked her what happened.

She said she had just gotten off work Tuesday night when she heard what sounded like gunshots.

I asked her why she thought they were gunshots.

She said she knew they were gunshots because she used to light off fireworks as a kid, and these noises did not sound like fireworks.

I asked her what happened next.

She said she turned around and saw a car speeding away.

But this:

> I asked her what happened. She told me she had just gotten off work Tuesday night when she heard what sounded like gunshots. She knew they were gunshots because she used to light off fireworks as a kid, and these noises did not sound like fireworks. After hearing these sounds, she saw a car speeding away.

8.3   Supporting Information

A third type of information that is neither an observation nor an action may appear in your reports. It is *supporting information*. Supporting information explicitly tells your readers why your observations were relevant or why your actions were reasonable. Supporting information comes in two varieties: *background information* and *conclusions*.

8.3.1   Background information.
Background information is information you knew before becoming involved in your incident that influenced your decisions while at the scene. This isn't pre-arrival information (see 6.2.2), which you typically learn after a call has been dispatched. This is information you bring with you based on your knowledge, training, or prior experience. Since these are the sources, background information is typically captured by the worn-out phrase "knowledge, training, and experience," as in:

> While speaking with Mr. Walker, he kept looking from side to side. Based on my knowledge, training, and experience, I placed him in handcuffs.

Your knowledge, training, or experience may very well have been important background information that influenced your decision to apply handcuffs. The problem is that your readers don't know what *specific* knowledge, training, or experience contributed to your decision. You are asking readers to accept the reasonableness of your actions based on your word alone.

To avoid this error, treat knowledge, training, and experience as distinct categories instead of a catchall phrase. When you are tempted to refer to your knowledge, training, or experience, begin the sentence with, "I knew from…" or similar language, and then describe your specific training and/or experience that led to this knowledge.

> During my conversation with Mr. Walker, he failed to keep eye contact with me and kept glancing over his shoulders. **I knew from** my prior interactions with Mr. Walker that he often fled from or fought with police. Additionally, **I knew, based on my training** in pre-assault indicators, that suspects often check their surroundings to look for escape routes before attempting to flee or to check for witnesses before attempting to assault an officer. Based on this information, I detained Mr. Walker in handcuffs.

8.3.2   **Conclusions.** Conclusions are judgments you make based on facts. The easier it is for readers to see the facts that led to your conclusions, the more reasonable your judgments will be. "The man was drunk" is a conclusion. You do not observe "drunk" with your senses; you observe several different factors that lead you to conclude someone was drunk. In an effective report, you must present enough of these factors so readers agree your conclusions are valid.

Not this:

> The man approached me, and he was obviously drunk. I placed him in handcuffs.

But this:

> When the man approached me, I saw that he had bloodshot eyes. I also smelled the odor of an alcoholic beverage coming from his person, and I heard that his speech was slurred. Based on this information, I concluded that he was drunk, and I detained him in handcuffs.

Conclusions help readers understand the results of your decision-making process. In the above example, the facts lead to the fairly obvious conclusion that the man was intoxicated. In other examples, however, it may be necessary to describe how you came to your conclusion more explicitly. Here is an example from a domestic violence case where the officer chose not to make an arrest:

> After my investigation, I determined that I did not have enough probable cause to make an arrest because:
>
> • Both parties had minor scratches on them.
>
> • Both parties had conflicting stories.
>
> • There were no independent witnesses.
>
> • Although both parties were still married, Ms. Chi had been living in an apartment across town for the past eight months and planned to return there tonight.

Notice how the word "conclusion" is never used in the above example; however, it is still clear to readers that this information presents the officer's rationale behind the decision not to arrest.

9. Describing People, Places, and Things

9.1   **Referring to People By Name**

   9.1.1   Generally

   9.1.2   Names on first and subsequent mentions

   9.1.3   Roles

   9.1.4   Titles

   9.1.5   Adults

   9.1.6   Juveniles

   9.1.7   Police officers

   9.1.8   Names discovered later in your investigation

   9.1.9   Duplicate names

   9.1.10 Supplemental information

   9.1.11 Nicknames

   9.1.12 Custom labels

9.2   **Describing People's Physical Characteristics**

   9.2.1   Generally

   9.2.2   Physical appearance

   9.2.3   Race and ethnicity

   9.2.4   Sex

   9.2.5   Age

   9.2.6   Height

   9.2.7   Weight

   9.2.8   Hair

   9.2.9   Eyes

   9.2.10 Scars, marks, and tattoos

9.2.11 Clothing
9.2.12 Disabilities and medical conditions

9.3   Describing Injuries
9.3.1 Generally
9.3.2 Severity
9.3.3 Type
9.3.4 Location

9.4   Documenting Verbal Statements
9.4.1 Generally
9.4.2 Deciding whether to quote or paraphrase
9.4.3 Documenting recorded statements
9.4.4 Accurately reflecting the context of statements
9.4.5 Paraphrasing
9.4.6 Accents
9.4.7 Slang
9.4.8 Mispronunciations
9.4.9 Wrong words and other errors
9.4.10 Filler words and pauses
9.4.11 Block and inline quotations

9.5   Describing Places
9.5.1 Generally
9.5.2 Addresses
9.5.3 Business names
9.5.4 Cardinal directions
9.5.5 Direction of travel
9.5.6 Relative positions
9.5.7 Reference points and landmarks
9.5.8 GPS coordinates
9.5.9 Virtual locations
9.5.10 Custom labels

9.6   Describing Things
9.6.1 Generally
9.6.2 Vehicles
9.6.3 Weapons
9.6.4 Documents and photographs
9.6.5 Digital evidence

9.6.6   Lost, damaged, or stolen property
9.6.7   Brand and product names
9.6.8   Items with similar descriptions
9.6.9   Evidence numbers

The most common things you will document in your police reports are the people involved, the statements people make, the places where the incident happens, and the evidence you observe or collect. This chapter provides guidelines for presenting this information in a clear, standardized format. Whether you adopt all or some of these guidelines, strive to be consistent. As readers grow accustomed to how you describe people, places, and things, they will be better able to find the information they are looking for.

9.1   Referring to People By Name

9.1.1   **Generally.** When referring to people, use their legal name unless you have a good reason not to. Legal names are preferable to custom labels, such as *Victim 1* or *Suspect A* (see 9.1.12), because such labels force readers to cross-reference other parts of your report to discover who you are referring to.

9.1.2   **Names on first and subsequent mentions.** The first time you mention a person, provide as much relevant information as required by your incident. On every subsequent mention, refer to the person by their salutation (*Mr.* or *Ms.*) or title, followed by their last name.

Format on the first mention:

ROLE, SALUTATION/TITLE FIRST NAME "NICKNAME" LAST NAME (SUPPLEMENTAL INFORMATION)

Format on subsequent mentions:

SALUTATION/TITLE LAST NAME

9.1.3 **Roles.** A person's role refers to the part a person plays in your incident. Typical roles in police reports include:

Suspect	Victim	Witness
Caller	Complainant	Subject[1]
Decedent	Prisoner	Arrestee

Include a person's role the first time you mention them. This helps readers anticipate what to expect from your interactions with this person. On subsequent mentions, identify a person by their salutation and last name.

First mention:

the complainant, Mr. Dwight Pearson

the suspect, Ms. Joy Banks

Subsequent mentions:

Mr. Pearson

Ms. Banks

---

[1] *Subject* is often used generically to refer to a person; however, some agencies use this term to refer to the subject of their investigation (i.e., their suspect).

9.1.4 **Titles.** Titles are official designations that describe people's employment position, education, or professional certification. On the first mention, include a person's title if it is relevant to your incident (see 14.7 for how to capitalize titles). On subsequent mentions, refer to the person by their title or salutation, followed by their last name. A good rule of thumb is to write the person's title throughout your report if you would refer to them by this title in speech. If you wouldn't, use the salutation *Mr.* or *Ms.*

> *First mention:*
>
> Superintendent Laurence Schmidt
>
> Project Manager Salvatore Cortez
>
> the suspect, Doctor Alison Park
>
> *Subsequent mentions:*
>
> Superintendent Schmidt
>
> Mr. Cortez
>
> Doctor Park *or* Dr. Park

9.1.5 **Adults.** Identify adults by their full name on the first mention. On subsequent mentions, refer to them by their title or salutation, followed by their last name.

> *First mention:*
>
> Mr. Christian Marsh
>
> Judge Seymour Grimes

Subsequent mentions:

Mr. Marsh

Judge Grimes

9.1.6   **Juveniles.** Identify juveniles by their full name on the first mention. On subsequent mentions, refer to juveniles by their first name only. In cases where it may be necessary to protect the juvenile's identity, refer to them by their initials or a custom label (see 9.1.12) throughout your entire report.

First mention:

the missing juvenile, Kenyatta Casteel

the victim, C.H.

a witness to this incident, Witness #1

Subsequent mentions:

Kenyatta

C.H.

Witness #1

9.1.7   **Police officers.** Identify police officers by rank or title, first initial, last name, and badge number on the first mention. On subsequent mentions, refer to them by their title and last name.

First mention:

Officer J. Wiley (#1402)

Detective B. Roberts (#982)

Subsequent mentions:

Officer Wiley

Detective Roberts

9.1.8   **Names discovered later in your investigation.** During some incidents, you may not learn a person's identity until later in your investigation, often after you have already interacted with them. Still, identify the person by their full name on the first mention, but precede their name with the words *later identified as,* and offset the entire phrase with commas.

the suspect, later identified as Ms. Carli Bachman

I found one of the victims, later identified as Mr. Rory Magee, slumped against the steering wheel.

9.1.9   **Duplicate names.** Occasionally, you will need to refer to two different people who share the same name. Designate a custom name for each adult that shares a salutation and last name or for each juvenile that shares a first name.

Mr. Andrew Phillips (hereafter "Andrew") and his brother, Mr. Alexander Phillips (hereafter "Alexander")

Ms. Neva Scott (hereafter "Ms. N. Scott") and Ms. Denisha Scott (hereafter "Ms. D. Scott")

Juveniles Bret Duval (hereafter "B. Duval") and Bret Hooper (hereafter "B. Hooper")

9.1.10 **Supplemental information.** If supplemental information is necessary to identify a person properly, place it in parentheses after their full name on the first mention.

> Ms. Rachael Bridges (DOB: 01/12/1997)

> Mr. Duane Tyler (B/M, 6'2", 130 lb., brown hair, blue eyes)

9.1.11 **Nicknames.** If a person's nickname or "street name" is important to your incident, include it in the first mention of the person's full name. Either insert the nickname in quotation marks between their first and last name or include it in parentheses, preceded by the abbreviation *aka.* (i.e., "also known as").

> *First mention:*

> one of the victims, Ms. Elizabeth "Shorty" Barrow

> the suspect, Mr. Timothy Herman (aka "Badger")

> *Subsequent mentions:*

> Ms. Barrow

> Mr. Herman

9.1.12 **Custom labels.** Custom labels may be necessary when you don't know a person's identity, when you wish to keep a person's identity confidential (see 9.1.6), or when a person's declared identity does not match their legal name (see 14.1.5). When establishing a custom label, use parentheses or set the name off with commas.

He described the suspect as a white male, 20–30 years old, 5'0"–5'5", 150–175 lb., wearing a red shirt and blue shorts (hereafter "Suspect #1").

Unknown Suspect #2

Confidential Informant #10-74

The victim, A.A., told me what happened.

Mr. Connor Egan, who self-identifies as Ms. Paige Egan (hereafter "Ms. Egan"), met me at headquarters.

9.2   Describing People's Physical Characteristics

9.2.1   **Generally.** You may need to describe someone's physical traits when their identity is unknown, when they match a lookout description, or when their physical characteristics are relevant to your incident. Avoid giving long physical descriptions for each person in your report as a matter of routine. When the physical description is extensive, separate it into its own paragraph.

9.2.2   **Physical appearance.** Physical appearance includes physical traits (height, weight, skin color, hair color, eye color, etc.); scars, marks, and tattoos; and clothing. Some disabilities or medical conditions may also manifest themselves physically. When describing people's physical appearance, stick to a standardized set of characteristics in a standardized order.

> *Format for describing physical appearance:*
>
> RACE ETHNICITY SEX, AGE, HEIGHT, WEIGHT, HAIR DESCRIPTION, EYE COLOR, SCARS, MARKS, AND TATTOOS, CLOTHING DESCRIPTION, ADDITIONAL INFORMATION.

Example:

The suspect is a white non-Hispanic male, 45–50 years old, 5′10″–6′2″, 150 lb., with short brown hair, green eyes, and a large birthmark on his right elbow. He was last seen wearing a green baseball cap, black hooded sweatshirt, blue jeans, and white New Balance shoes.

Be careful not to summarize a person's entire identity with one of their characteristics (see 14.1.4):

Not this:

An Asian

A disabled person

The tall blonde

But this:

An Asian male

A person with a disability

A tall woman with blonde hair

9.2.3   **Race and ethnicity.**[2] Race and ethnicity are two separate categories. *Race* refers to people with similar physical traits that are common with their shared ancestry. The six commonly-used categories of race are:

1. *White.* Those with ancestral origins in Europe, the Middle East, or North Africa.

---

[2] Information about race and ethnicity was derived from the United States Census Bureau, *About the Topic of Race,* https://www.census.gov/topics/population/race/about.html

2. *Black* or *African American.* Those with ancestral origins in the black racial groups of Africa.

3. *American Indian* or *Alaska Native.* Those with ancestral origins in North, Central, and South America.

4. *Asian.* Those with ancestral origins in the Far East, Southeast Asia, or the Indian subcontinent.

5. *Native Hawaiian* or *Other Pacific Islander.* Those with ancestral origins in Hawaii, Guam, Samoa, or other Pacific Islands.

6. *Other.* Those with ancestral origins not listed above.

Ethnicity refers to shared Spanish, Hispanic, or Latino cultural identity unrelated to physical traits. Someone's ethnicity is classified as *Hispanic, non-Hispanic,* or *unknown.*

If a person's official identification lists their race or ethnicity, use that information. If not, use your best judgment, the person's self-declaration, or the label *other* or *unknown.*

9.2.4   **Sex.** Sex describes a person's biological sex. Identify someone's sex as *male, female,* or *unknown.*

9.2.5   **Age.** Measure age in years for adults and children older than two years. Measure age in months for children under two years old. Hyphenate ages when they act as adjectives.

a 35-year-old male

a two-month-old infant

a male who is 35 years old

an infant who is two months old

9.2.6 **Height.** If you know someone's exact height, provide the measurement in feet and inches. Either spell out the words *feet*[3] and *inches*, use the abbreviations *ft.* and *in.*, or use an apostrophe in place of *feet* and quotation marks in place of *inches* (see 13.7.5 and 13.8.5).

> 6 feet 7 inches

> 6 ft. 7 in.

> 6'7"

If someone reports a height range to you, document it as reported, and attribute the source.

> Ms. Seaton told me he was 5'8" to 6'0" tall.

If you estimate someone's height, provide a range instead of using words like *about* or *approximately*. Add two inches in either direction to create the height range.

> *Not this:*

> about five feet tall

> *But this:*

> between 4'10" and 5'2"

9.2.7 **Weight.** If you know someone's exact weight, provide the measurement in pounds. Either spell out the word *pounds* or use the abbreviation *lb*.[4]

> 350 pounds

> 125 lb.

---

[3] Note that the word is *feet*, not *foot*.

[4] The abbreviation remains *lb.* whether it is one pound or many.

If someone reports a weight range to you, document it as reported, and attribute the source.

Mr. Herring said the victim was over 400 pounds.

If you estimate someone's weight, provide a range instead of using words like *about* or *approximately*. Add ten pounds in either direction to create the weight range.

The suspect appeared to be 230–250 pounds.

9.2.8   **Hair.** Hair has properties of *color*, *length*, and *style*. When describing natural hair colors, use one of the five basic colors:

black	blonde	gray
brown	red	

When necessary, describe how the hair is tinted or shaded:

light	bleached	highlights
medium	streaked	lowlights
dark	dyed	ombre

When describing dyed hair color, use colors that most readers can identify without looking up.

Not this:

chartreuse

puce

But this:

yellow-green

dark red

Describe hair length using measurements (in feet and inches) or by using body parts as reference points.

Her hair was 3–4 feet long.

buzzed haircut shorter than one-half-inch in length

shoulder-length hair

hair to the middle of his back

Length can also describe the absence of hair:

bald   front receding hairline

Describe hairstyles using their common name. If your readers are unlikely to know a hairstyle by its name, or if they can't find it with a quick internet search, provide a description instead. Here are a few common hairstyle names:

bob	cornrows	mohawk
bowl cut	crew cut	pixie cut
braid	dreadlocks	ponytail
bun	extensions	rattail
comb-over	flattop	updo

Don't forget about facial hair, which also has properties of color, length, and style.

dark brown handlebar mustache

closely-shaven chin-strap beard

gray soul patch

9.2.9   **Eyes.** *Color* is the basic property used to describe eyes. There are five basic eye colors:

amber   brown   hazel

blue   green

If further description is necessary, use plain language to describe distinct eye characteristics:

a lazy left eye   prominent eyeballs

9.2.10   **Scars, marks, and tattoos.** Scars and marks have properties of *size, shape,* and *location.* Tattoos have properties of *size, content,* and *location.* When identifying size, measure in inches or by using body parts as reference points.

scar extending from his hairline to his right eye

circular birthmark approximately two inches in diameter

tattoo of a leopard seal covering her entire right bicep

9.2.11   **Clothing.** It is natural to describe clothes from the top down because that is the way the eyes typically fall on a person; however, there is a benefit to describing clothing from the bottom up because shoes and pants tend to be more difficult to change quickly, and therefore may be a bigger help in identifying the person later. Choose the method that makes the most sense for your incident.

Format for describing clothing (top-down):

HAT SHIRT/JACKET PANTS, SHOES, ACCESSORIES

Format for describing clothing (bottom-up):

SHOES PANTS SHIRT/JACKET, HAT, ACCESSORIES

Example:

The missing female was last seen wearing red Adidas shoes, bright blue yoga pants, a black jacket, and a black knit cap. She wears a yellow-gold wedding band on her left ring finger.

9.2.12   **Disabilities and medical conditions.** If you know the technical term for a disability or medical condition, use it. If the term is unlikely to be understood by your readers, include a plain language description in parentheses.

Down syndrome   strabismus (cross-eyed)

If you don't know the proper name of a disability or medical condition, describe the physical effects if they are relevant to your incident.

He walks with a cane.

The subject limps with her left leg.

The suspect is missing his right arm.

9.3   Describing Injuries

9.3.1   **Generally.** Injuries have properties of *severity*, *type*, and *location*. Using overly technical terminology can confuse your readers, so describe injuries in a way that is consistent with your training and your readers' knowledge. Medical reports containing technical injury details can be included in your case file when needed. Avoid declaring a medical diagnosis unless you can cite its source. Instead, describe what you observe.

Not this:

Mr. Richards was having a heart attack.

But this:

Mr. Richards' son, Toby, told me his father was having a heart attack. I saw Mr. Richards lying unresponsive on the ground.

9.3.2 **Severity.** Injuries come in two severities: *life-threatening* and *non-life-threatening*. Beyond these two descriptions, describe the severity of the injury in plain English, including the source of the information.

Mr. Jones was transported to the hospital with a non-life-threatening laceration to his right middle finger. Medics told me that Mr. Jones may lose his finger.

9.3.3 **Type.** Although many technical medical terms exist to describe injuries, a few standard terms cover most injuries you will encounter. Unless you have specialized training, stick to these terms or their plain language equivalents.

1. *Blunt force trauma.* Injuries caused by impact with a solid surface or object. These injuries include:

   • *Abrasion.* A scrape.
   • *Contusion.* A bruise.

- *Laceration.* A ragged tearing of tissue (compare to *incision*).
- *Dislocation.* A joint that has been forced from its proper position.
- *Fracture.* A complete or partially broken bone.

2. *Penetrating injury.* Injuries caused by an object entering the body. These injuries include:

- *Gunshot.* A bullet or other projectile shot into the body.
- *Incision.* A cut caused by a sharp or pointed object. The wound is typically wider than it is deep.
- *Stab wound.* A puncture from a sharp or pointed object. The wound is typically deeper than it is wide.

3. *Other injuries.* Other injury types include:

- *Animal bite.* A wound caused by contact with an animal's teeth.
- *Burns.* Any injury to the skin or tissue caused by heat. Common heat sources include the sun, chemicals, fire, and electricity.
- *Electrical injuries.* Any injury caused by contact with high-voltage electricity.

9.3.4 **Location.** Use plain language to describe injury locations, and include a diagram with your report when more specificity is necessary. Stick to a consistent format when describing the location of injuries:

Format for describing injury locations:

front/back/left/right/center of BODY PART, ADDITIONAL INFORMATION

Keep in mind that injury locations should be described from the injured person's perspective (i.e., an injury on the left cheek refers to *their* left cheek).

palm-side of the hand

Mr. Jones had a small contusion on the middle of his right bicep.

Ms. Alexander had a deep laceration on the right side of her skull, a few inches above her ear.

9.4   Documenting Verbal Statements

9.4.1   **Generally.** Verbal statements come in three varieties: *full quotations*, *partial quotations*, and *paraphrases*. *Full quotations* express complete ideas or statements using the words of the person who made the statement. *Partial quotations* use certain words or phrases from the person making the statement but require your words to complete or clarify the statement's meaning. A *paraphrase* summarizes what someone else has said in your own words.

Example of a full quotation:

During my interview, the suspect said, "I did it. I robbed him. And then I told him I'd kill him if he moved, and that's when he took off running. And so I caught him and hit him with the bat till he stopped moving."

Example of a partial quotation:

During my interview with Mr. Hickman, he said he "hit him with the bat till he stopped moving."

Example of a paraphrase:

During my interview, the suspect told me he robbed and assaulted Mr. Barrett.

9.4.2 **Deciding whether to quote or paraphrase.** The decision to quote or paraphrase is largely determined by your particular incident, the content of a person's statements, and how well you captured the exact wording of those statements. There are serious ethical and legal implications that come with misquoting someone or guessing what they said. To avoid any problems, only quote someone's exact words if you can answer *yes* to all three of these questions:

1. *Is the content of the statement relevant?* If the content of the person's statement is *irrelevant* to your report, there is no need to quote or paraphrase; leave the statement out entirely.

2. *Are the precise words essential to convey meaning?* If the content of the person's statement is relevant, but their exact words are not essential to convey their intended meaning, then paraphrase what they said.

3. *Can you write the words exactly as they were spoken?* If a person's statement is relevant *and* their precise words are essential *and* you can record the exact words as they were spoken, then consider using a full or partial quotation; however, if a person's statement is relevant *and* their precise words are essential, *but* you cannot write the words exactly as they were spoken, you have no other choice but to paraphrase.

9.4.3 **Documenting recorded statements.** Body cameras, dash cameras, digital recorders, cell phones, and similar devices can be invaluable tools in capturing verbal statements. There is no excuse for sloppily documenting someone's statement when you have access to a verbatim recording. If your report misrepresents someone's statements, intentionally or unintentionally, it is simple for an attorney to discredit you by comparing the recording to your written report.

Recorded statements carry with them the temptation to over-quote. Before taking the time to transcribe someone's statement, make sure you have established the need to use their exact words (see 9.4.2). If you decide that a verbatim quote is necessary, listen to the recording after you have finished typing to ensure that you have documented exactly what was said. You'd be amazed how often your brain fills in words that weren't actually said.

When documenting short recorded statements that you have captured on the street, it's usually not necessary to note that you have transcribed the statement from a recording; however, when the statement is lengthy, or the existence of the recording is important to your incident (such as with a confession), include a brief statement to explain how the statement was captured:

This statement was captured on body camera.

I recorded this interview using my department-issued digital recorder.

9.4.4 **Accurately reflecting the context of statements.** Whether you decide to quote or paraphrase, it is essential that you accurately represent the context in which the statement was made. If a suspect sarcastically says, "Yeah, I did it," including this statement as a sincere confession would be unethical.

Likewise, if the suspect says, "I didn't do it, but if I did it, I'd be sure to use a baseball bat," it would be unethical to imply guilt by only including the partial quotation,

"If I did it, I'd be sure to use a baseball bat." (Note: the suspect may still be guilty, but misrepresenting this quote isn't the proper way to prove it.)

Similarly, suppose a subject gives a statement while severely intoxicated, emotionally distressed, or otherwise not fully cognizant. In that case, the statement may still be valid, but it must be accompanied by a brief description of the context in which it was given if you are to present the statement objectively.

9.4.5   **Paraphrasing.** Since a paraphrase is someone else's statement written in your own words, don't use quotation marks. Begin with a short introductory phrase and then include the paraphrase as part of the normal flow of your writing:

> She said she was driving eastbound on 16th Avenue from C Street when she saw a man collapse on the sidewalk.

When paraphrasing multiple statements from the same person, don't unnecessarily repeat phrases like "she said" and "he told me" (see 8.2.5).

Not this:

> She said she was driving eastbound on 16th Avenue from C Street when she saw a man collapse on the sidewalk. She said she thought the man was having a medical emergency. She said she pulled her car over and began to render aid. She said she noticed a gun on the sidewalk when she flipped the man over.

But this:

She said she was driving eastbound on 16th Avenue from C Street when she saw a man collapse on the sidewalk. She thought the man was having a medical emergency, so she pulled her car over and began to render aid. When she flipped the man over, she noticed a gun on the sidewalk.

Note that if your paraphrase spans multiple paragraphs, you *should* begin each paragraph with "she said," "he told me," or a similar phrase to signal to readers that you are still paraphrasing someone else's account.

If you must paraphrase a lot of information, consider using bullet points to capture the most important details concisely (see 14.5.4):

Ms. Flores told me:

- She closed the bar at 3:00 a.m.

- When she came to the parking lot, her car was the only one there.

- She didn't notice anyone on the sidewalk or the streets when she left the parking lot.

9.4.6   **Accents.** Accents are unique pronunciations based on someone's geographic or social origins. The most common way to capture accents in quoted speech is to drop letters or intentionally misspell words. This is almost always unnecessary and distracting. If the person's accent is essential to your case, tell your readers directly, and then write any quoted statements using standard spellings.

Not this:

"I can't take 'er to the 'ospital."

"Ain't you jus' the cutest thang."

But this:

He spoke with a British accent. He said, "I can't take her to the hospital."

"Ain't you just the cutest thing," she said with a mock Southern accent.

9.4.7   **Slang.** When a slang word is relevant to your incident, include it in quotation marks, followed by a brief explanation of the word's meaning.

They told me they were both "sick." ["Sick" is a term commonly used by drug users who are experiencing withdrawal symptoms.]

9.4.8   **Mispronunciations.** Pronunciation describes how a word sounds when spoken. Trying to capture mispronunciations in writing is usually irrelevant since the word's spelling remains the same. For example, the written word *especially* remains the same regardless of whether someone pronounces it *ess-PESH-all-ee* or *ecks-PESH-all-ee*.

As with accents, trying to capture nuances of pronunciation in your reports is usually unnecessary and distracting. If, however, a specific pronunciation is necessary to establish an M.O. or is otherwise relevant to your incident, write out the pronunciation phonetically (as demonstrated in the previous paragraph).

9.4.9   **Wrong words and other errors.** If someone accidentally uses a wrong word—such as saying "seminary" instead of "cemetery"—and they correct themselves, then include the word they originally intended. If they do not correct themselves, and if you must directly quote them, then include the wrong word to maintain accuracy, but also include a comment in brackets so your readers know the mistake was not an error on your part.

> Ms. Walker said, "I would never cheat on my husband. I am completely monotonous [Ms. Walker likely meant 'monogamous']."

If you are quoting written source material (e.g., a ransom note, a threatening letter, corporate documents) and the quoted material includes a grammar or spelling error, quote the material exactly as it is written, but follow it with the Latin abbreviation *sic*[5] in square brackets so readers know you did not make a transcription error.

> The anonymous letter stated, "Your day is coming. Be careful. Your [sic] going to be sorry."

9.4.10 **Filler words and pauses.** Only include pauses and filler words like *ah*, *um*, *like*, and *so* if you are generating an official transcript or if including these words or pauses is needed to show hesitation or uncertainty on the part of the person you are quoting. In the latter case, it is usually better to explain the reason for the uncertainty and quote the person without fillers.

> He told me, "I'm going home," but he paused for at least five seconds between each word as he struggled not to fall back asleep.

9.4.11 **Block and inline quotations.** *Block* and *inline* refer to the formatting of a quotation within your report. Block quotations are full quotations set off as their own paragraph

---

[5] The abbreviation *sic* stands for the Latin phrase *sic erat scriptum*, which is translated "thus was it written."

and left-indented. Here is the example from section 9.4.1 as a block quotation:

> During my interview, the suspect said,
>
> > "I did it. I robbed him. And then I told him I'd kill him if he moved, and that's when he took off running. And so I caught him and hit him with the bat till he stopped moving."

The choice to use a block quotation is purely a stylistic one. It is often visually helpful to use block quotations when full quotations span three or more lines, but do what makes sense to you and adds clarity for your readers.

Inline quotations are full or partial quotations within your text's normal flow.

> During my interview with John, he said Andrew was "a slob."

Enclose block and inline quotations in quotation marks to eliminate any confusion that this is a direct quotation.

9.5   Describing Places

9.5.1   **Generally.** Accurately describing places helps your readers know exactly where events took place. Such information may be necessary to properly document crime scenes, conduct follow-up investigations, or eliminate reasonable doubt at trial. The type of incident determines how specific you must be when describing places. For most incidents, the street address and, if applicable, business name will suffice. For other incidents, giving room locations, floor numbers, landmarks, GPS coordinates, or other specific details may be necessary.

9.5.2   **Addresses.** Addresses are the simplest and most universal way to document locations. On the first mention of a location, include the full address without the zip code. On subsequent mentions, refer to the location by its proper name (see 9.5.3) or common name (e.g., "the crime scene," "police headquarters").

Address format:[6]

BUILDING NUMBER PREDIRECTIONAL STREET NAME STREET TYPE

POSTDIRECTIONAL, UNIT TYPE UNIT IDENTIFIER, CITY, STATE

Examples:

65 Center Road, Ottawa, IL

65 Center Road, Apt. 3B, Ottawa, IL

65 N Center Road, Apt. 3B, Ottawa, IL

65 N Center Road E, Apt. 3B, Ottawa, IL

9.5.3   **Business names.** On the first mention, include the business name followed by the full address in parentheses. On subsequent mentions, refer to the business by its proper name only.

First mention:

7-Eleven (79 E Goldfield Lane, Austin, TX)

McDonald's (285 River Drive, Chicago, IL)

---

[6] Adapted from the United States Postal Service, *Publication 28—Postal Addressing Standards,* https://pe.usps.com/text/pub28/28c2_012.htm.

Subsequent mentions:

7-Eleven

McDonald's

9.5.4   **Cardinal directions.** Cardinal directions are the four main points shown on a compass: *north*, *east*, *south*, and *west*. Since cardinal directions don't change relative to the observer's perspective, they are a universal way to describe someone's or something's position or direction of travel. Cardinal directions always require a reference point (see 9.5.7). Something cannot be *north*; it must be *north of* something else.

Not this:

I found a spent shell casing toward the east

But this:

I found a spent shell casing on the east side of PetSmart.

9.5.5   **Direction of travel.** When indicating a person's or vehicle's direction of travel, use cardinal directions (see 9.5.4) or relative positions (see 9.5.6) to indicate not only which direction the person or vehicle was going but also where the person or vehicle was going *from*.

Not this:

The vehicle fled north.

The suspect turned down the left hallway.

But this:

The vehicle fled north from 1123 Cedar Road.

The suspect entered the business and turned left down the first hallway.

9.5.6   **Relative positions.** Relative positions describe something's position relative to something else. Words like *up, down, left, right, above, below, in front of, behind, over,* and *under* all describe relative positions. Because relative positions change based on the observer's perspective, you must always include a reference point (see 9.5.7) for a relative position to make sense.

Not this:

The stolen Camry was parked to the left of the Camaro.

The knife lay on the floor to the right of the body.

But this:

When facing the business, the stolen Camry was parked to the left of the Camaro.

The knife lay on the floor next to the victim's right arm.

9.5.7   **Reference points and landmarks.** Reference points are fixed objects used to describe the position of something else. Landmarks are recognizable fixed objects or geographical features, such as the Space Needle, the school flag pole, or the historic oak tree in the middle of the town square. When using landmarks or reference points, combine them with a measurement and either a cardinal direction (see 9.5.4) or a relative position (see 9.5.6).

> At the bottom of the driveway is a concrete post with a chain attached. I found a red leather glove on the grass approximately three feet east of this post.

9.5.8   **GPS coordinates.** The United States Global Positioning System (GPS) is a satellite network used to pinpoint exact locations. GPS coordinates identify something's location based on its distance from the equator and the prime meridian.[7] These coordinates are most commonly measured in degrees, minutes, and seconds, or in decimal degrees. When including GPS coordinates, remain consistent in your formatting.

Degrees, Minutes, and Seconds:

32 08'59.96" N, 110 50'09.03"W

Decimal Degrees:

37.563936, -116.85123

9.5.9   **Virtual locations.** Virtual locations include websites, chatrooms, computer servers, and social media groups. Since the names, URLs, IP addresses, etc., of many virtual locations can be easily changed, describe a virtual location in as much detail as possible on the first mention, including the date you accessed it. On subsequent mentions, use an abbreviated description.

---

7 The equator is the imaginary east-west line that divides the Earth into northern and southern hemispheres. The prime meridian is the imaginary north-south line that divides the Earth into eastern and western hemispheres.

Format for describing virtual locations:

LOCATION TYPE LOCATION NAME (UNIQUE IDENTIFIER), ACCESS
DATE, ACCESS METHOD

First mention:

Facebook group "Drive 4 Anarchy" (https://www.
facebook.com/groups/drive4anarchy), accessed
on 07 August 2023

The suspect's shared directory, "Summer Pics"
(\jonndix32\shared_files\photos\summer_private),
accessed on 05 July 2023 via an unprotected WiFi
connection.

Subsequent mentions:

Facebook group "Drive 4 Anarchy"

"Summer Pics" directory

9.5.10   **Custom labels.** In some situations, it may be beneficial to
rename locations for ease of reference. Suppose you are
documenting where evidence was collected in a three-bed-
room house. In that case, designate a custom label for
each bedroom rather than referring to the rooms as the
northeast corner bedroom, the *basement bedroom,* and so
forth. When using custom labels, keep your naming conventions consistent. For example, don't refer to the first
house as "House 1" and the second as "Residence 2."

Crime Scene One

Bedroom D

If your agency uses special terminology that is unlikely to be understood by outside readers, restate the terminology in plain language.

Not this:

I took position on the bravo side of the house.

But this:

I moved to the east side of the house.

9.6   Describing Things

9.6.1   **Generally.** On the first mention, describe the item in as much detail as possible. Use custom labels or abbreviated descriptions on subsequent mentions.

Format for describing items on first mention:

COLOR MAKE MODEL SERIAL NUMBER UNIQUE FEATURES/DAMAGE

First mention:

The stolen phone is a white Apple iPhone 14, serial number X0XX234XYXYX, with a cracked screen.

Subsequent mentions:

the stolen iPhone

the stolen iPhone 14 (X0XX234XYXYX)

9.6.2   **Vehicles.** On the first mention, provide a complete description of each vehicle. On subsequent mentions, identify the vehicle by its role in your incident and, if necessary, an abbreviated description.

Format for describing vehicles on first mention:

VEHICLE ROLE COLOR YEAR MAKE MODEL TAG VIN UNIQUE FEATURES/DAMAGE

First mention:

The stolen vehicle is a blue 2021 Toyota Camry with Utah tag 035ACE, VIN 5TFKV52134TRZ8UNP, and an after-market spoiler.

Subsequent mentions:

the stolen vehicle

the stolen Toyota Camry

9.6.3   **Weapons.** Weapons come in many shapes and varieties. Additionally, items not created as weapons (beer bottles, cinderblocks, baseball bats, tire irons, etc.) can be used as impromptu weapons. Provide as much detail about the weapon as possible on the first mention. On subsequent mentions, refer to the weapon using an abbreviated description.

Format for describing weapons on first mention:

COLOR MAKE MODEL TYPE CALIBER SERIAL NUMBER STATUS UNIQUE FEATURES/DAMAGE

First mention:

The recovered handgun is a black Glock 19 semi-automatic pistol chambered in 9 mm, serial number XAR184. The pistol was recovered with one 9 mm round in the chamber and fifteen 9 mm rounds in the magazine. The gun has a Trijicon RMR attached to the slide.

The stolen knife is a pink Spyderco folding knife with a 3″ blade, unknown model, and no serial number.

The suspect hit the victim with a loose brick that measured approximately 3.5″ wide by 2″ high by 7.5″ long.

Subsequent mentions:

the recovered handgun

the Glock 19

the stolen knife

the pink Spyderco knife

the brick

9.6.4   **Documents and photographs.** The purpose of referring to documents and photographs is 1) to explain how the document or photograph is relevant to your incident and 2) to point your readers to the original document or photograph if needed. A detailed description of documents and photographs is usually unnecessary. When referring to a document or photograph on the first mention, include a brief description of its content and location. On subsequent mentions, use an abbreviated description.

Format for describing documents and photographs on first mention:

TYPE/DESCRIPTION (IDENTIFYING NUMBERS; STORED LOCATION) SUMMARY OF CONTENTS

First mention:

the suspect's March 22, 2023 bank statement (account #57861321898; evidence #23423-04), which shows seventeen deposits of $1500 each

a photograph (attached to this report) depicting the suspect entering the surveilled location at 1153 hours on June 10, 2023

Subsequent mentions:

the March 22 bank statement

the photograph

9.6.5   **Digital evidence.** When describing digital evidence, include its content and the location where it is stored. Be as specific as needed for your readers to locate the original files at a later date.

300 images of child pornography on a 500TB hard drive, stored as evidence item #3

one PDF file containing fraudulent bank records, titled "BankRecords.pdf," stored on evidence.com

9.6.6   **Lost, damaged, or stolen property.** In addition to the basic details required for describing any property item, describe where and how the item was lost, damaged, or stolen. Include the item's value or the cost of the damages. When determining the monetary value of damages, make a good-faith estimate based on the statements of your victim, your knowledge, and publicly available information, such as reputable internet search results.

The victim estimated the damage to be $500.

According to internet search results for a similar model, the lost Rolex is valued at approximately $9700.

9.6.7   **Brand and product names.** When describing products, refer to them by their brand name if you know it, or, if you are unsure of the brand, use generic product names.

Examples with specific brand names:

The source of the fire was a box of Kleenex.

He stole three Red Bulls.

Examples with generic product names:

The source of the fire was a box of tissues.

He stole three energy drinks.

Be careful not to accidentally use brand names to replace generic terms. Here are a few familiar brand names and their generic equivalents:

Band-Aids	adhesive bandages
Chapstick	lip balm
Crock-Pot	slow cooker
Kleenex	tissue
Plexiglas	acrylic glass
Sharpie	permanent marker
Xerox	copy machine

9.6.8   **Items with similar descriptions.** If you describe two or more similar items, focus on what differentiates them. Describe each item in detail on the first mention, then designate a custom label for each item and use it on subsequent mentions.

> *First mention:*
>
> a black Gerber fixed-blade knife with a six-inch blade (hereafter "six-inch knife") and a black Gerber fixed-blade knife with a ten-inch blade (hereafter "ten-inch knife")
>
> *Subsequent mentions:*
>
> I located the six-inch knife in the safe and the ten-inch knife under the mattress.

9.6.9   **Evidence numbers.** If you describe an item that will be placed into evidence, consider appending its evidence number at each mention in your report. This is particularly useful when you have multiple similar items. It will also help readers see a clear chain of custody for each item throughout your report.

> white powder from Room A (#3451-01)
>
> white powder from Room B (#3451-02)
>
> white powder from Room C (#3451-03)

10. Describing Uses of Force

10.1   **Identifying Relevant Facts**

10.1.1   Defining *use of force*

10.1.2   Force and the Fourth Amendment

10.1.3   Legal justification for the seizure

10.1.4   Objective reasonableness and the Graham factors

10.1.5   Deadly force and the fleeing felon rule

10.1.6   Factors that contribute to the totality of the circumstances

10.1.7   State statutes and agency policy

10.1.8   T-Chart template for a use of force incident

10.2   **The Three-Part Use of Force Model**

10.2.1   Overview of the three-part model

10.2.2   Events preceding the use of force

10.2.3   Description of the use of force

10.2.4   Follow-up to the use of force

10.3   **Guidelines for Documenting Uses of Force**

10.3.1   Replace canned phrases with concrete language

10.3.2   Avoid words that imply gaps in your action-reaction sequences

10.3.3   Remember to include verbal commands

10.4   **Sample Use of Force Report**

10.4.1   Description of police incident

10.4.2   Sample use of force report

Uses of force expose officers to the possibility of physical injury, civil liability, citizen complaints, supervisor scrutiny, internal affairs investigations, and, in some cases, criminal prosecution. It's no wonder that the elevated stress levels that begin with use of force incidents often extend to the report writing process. Fortunately, writing use of force reports is fundamentally no different than writing reports about any other incident. Once you understand who your readers are and the questions they're likely to ask, you identify relevant facts and organize them into a logical report structure. You then use commonly accepted techniques to describe your observations and actions, and the people, places, and things involved in your incident.

Since these topics have been covered extensively in Chapters 1–9, we won't revisit them here. Instead, this chapter begins by describing the general facts your readers expect to see in your use of force reports. It then presents a three-part model to help you organize those facts. After that, it gives guidelines for documenting uses of force specifically. Finally, all this information is combined into a sample report about a use of force incident.

10.1   Identifying Relevant Facts

As explained in Chapter 4, there are two categories of facts: general facts and incident facts. This section will describe the general facts important to any use of force incident. The end of this section presents a T-Chart you can use as a starting place when determining the incident facts for your own real-life use of force incidents.

10.1.1   Defining *use of force*. There is no single definition of *use of force*, but it is generally understood as the "amount of effort required by police to compel compliance by an unwilling subject."[1] This definition contains four components you must address to properly document a use of force.

1. *Amount of effort.* You must describe what type and level of force you used.

2. *Required by police.* You must document the circumstances that made using force a reasonable option.

3. *To compel compliance.* You must explain what result you were attempting to achieve and what your legal authority was to do so.

4. *By an unwilling subject.* You must document what the suspect did that made you believe they were unwilling to comply with what you wanted them to do.

The three-part use of force model covered in section 10.2 covers all aspects of this definition.

10.1.2   **Force and the Fourth Amendment.** The Fourth Amendment to the United States Constitution protects citizens from unreasonable searches and seizures:

> *The right of the people to be secure in their persons,* houses, papers, and effects, *against unreasonable* searches and *seizures, shall not be violated...* (Emphasis added.)

Fourth Amendment seizures include any instances where police restrain an individual's freedom, including

---

[1] "Overview of Police Use of Force." National Institute of Justice. https://nij.ojp.gov/topics/articles/overview-police-use-force.

cases in which officers must use physical force.[2] But the Fourth Amendment only protects citizens against *unreasonable* seizures.[3] This means there are circumstances where the police may lawfully seize someone—including by using force—so long as they can show the seizure was *reasonable.*

Because of this, any discussion about whether or not the force used was reasonable must be preceded by proof that the seizure itself was reasonable. If you had no legal standing to seize an individual, any force you used to effect that seizure would be excessive and, hence, unreasonable under the Fourth Amendment.

What makes a seizure reasonable to begin with? According to the Warrant Clause of the Fourth Amendment, seizures are made reasonable when they are preceded by a warrant (e.g., an arrest warrant):

> …and no Warrants shall issue, but upon probable cause, supported by Oath or affirmation, and particularly describing the place to be searched, and the persons or things to be seized.

But what about times when officers cannot obtain a warrant? The United States Supreme Court recognizes that officers must often take "swift action predicated upon…on-the-spot observations."[4] For example, a police

---

[2] "Whenever an officer restrains the freedom of a person to walk away, he has seized that person." *Tennessee v. Garner*, 471 U.S. 1, 7 (1985); "*Terry v. Ohio*, 392 U.S. 1 (1968), and *Tennessee v. Garner*, 471 U.S. 1 (1985), required that excessive force claims arising out of investigatory stops be analyzed under the Fourth Amendment's 'objective reasonableness' standard." *Graham v. Connor*, 490 U.S. 386, 392 (1989).

[3] "What the Constitution forbids is not all searches and seizures, but unreasonable searches and seizures." *Elkins v. United States*, 364 U. S. 206, 222 (1960).

[4] *Terry v. Ohio*, 392 U.S. 1, 20 (1968)

officer who conducts a traffic stop has seized the vehicle's occupants for Fourth Amendment purposes. An officer who temporarily detains a robbery suspect pending an eyewitness identification has seized that suspect. Likewise, an officer who shoots a suspect after the suspect lunges at the officer with a knife has also seized that person. In none of these cases is the officer required (or able) to first obtain a warrant, yet in each of these cases, the seizure may still be reasonable. Determining the reasonableness of these seizures depends on a number of different factors, as explained in the next section.

10.1.3   **Legal justification for the seizure.** When officers restrain the liberty of a citizen without a warrant, they must demonstrate, at a minimum, that they have reasonable suspicion that the suspect has been, is currently, or is about to be involved in a crime. (In the parlance of the Supreme Court, officers must demonstrate that "criminal activity may be afoot"[5]).

This inference cannot be made on "inarticulate hunches." Instead, "the police officer must be able to point to specific and articulable facts which, taken together with rational inferences from those facts, reasonably warrant that intrusion"[6] on a citizen's Fourth Amendment rights.

What are these "specific and articulable facts"? The courts look at several different factors, including:

- What crime was being investigated
- The methods used to detain the suspect
- The length of the detention
- The time of day or night

---

[5] *Terry,* 392 U.S. at 30
[6] *Terry,* 392 U.S. at 21–22

- The suspect's furtive gestures or nervous behavior
- Whether the encounter took place in a high-crime or drug-trafficking area
- Whether there were recent crimes in the area
- Whether the suspect took headlong flight at the sight of police
- The suspect's proximity to the crime location
- The officer's knowledge of the suspect's criminal history
- The anonymous or corroborated nature of tips about the suspect
- Whether the suspect matched a lookout description or a wanted flyer

When documenting a Fourth Amendment seizure, the more factors you specifically articulate, the stronger your case will be that the seizure was reasonable. In evaluating all these factors, your ultimate goal is to show that "the facts available to the officer at the moment of the seizure…'warrant a man of reasonable caution in the belief' that the action taken was appropriate."[7]

Even after demonstrating proper legal standing to conduct a seizure, officers must also establish that the *manner* in which the seizure was carried out was reasonable.[8] It may have been lawful to detain a burglary suspect, for example, but not to strike him with a baton, tase him, or deploy a K-9.

10.1.4   Objective reasonableness and the Graham factors. To assess whether a particular use of force is reasonable, the

---

[7] *Terry*, 392 U.S. at 22

[8] "The 'reasonableness' of a particular seizure depends not only on *when* it is made, but also on *how* it is carried out." *Graham*, 490 U.S. at 386.

United States Supreme Court established the objective reasonableness standard in the 1989 case *Graham v. Connor*. The Court said:

> The "reasonableness" inquiry in an excessive force case is an objective one: the question is whether the officers' actions are "objectively reasonable" in light of the facts and circumstances confronting them, without regard to their underlying intent or motivation.

Because each use of force incident is unique, no set formula exists to determine reasonableness. Instead, reasonableness is determined through "a careful balancing of 'the nature and quality of the intrusion on the individual's Fourth Amendment interests' against the countervailing governmental interests at stake."[9]

To evaluate this balance, courts will pay "careful attention to the facts and circumstances of each particular case, including:

1. the severity of the crime at issue,
2. whether the suspect poses an immediate threat to the safety of the officers or others, and
3. whether he is actively resisting arrest or attempting to evade arrest by flight."[10]

These three criteria are known informally as the "Graham factors" or the "three-prong Graham test," and no police report is complete without including enough relevant facts to satisfy each of these factors.

10.1.5 **Deadly force and the fleeing felon rule.** The objective reasonableness standard also applies to deadly force inci-

---

[9] *Graham*, 490 U.S. at 396
[10] *Graham*, 490 U.S. at 396

dents; however, because "the intrusiveness of a seizure by means of deadly force is unmatched,"[11] the Supreme Court has imposed a higher legal standard by which its use is evaluated. In the 1985 Supreme Court case *Tennessee v. Garner*, the Court stated:

> Where the officer has probable cause to believe that the suspect poses a threat of serious physical harm, either to the officer or to others, it is not constitutionally unreasonable to prevent escape by using deadly force.

These criteria, informally referred to as the "fleeing felon rule," require that an officer demonstrate probable cause—a higher legal threshold than mere suspicion. If your report documents a deadly force incident, the relevant facts you include must meet this higher standard.

Note carefully the language used in the final clause of the above quotation: "it is not constitutionally unreasonable…." The Court did *not* say, "meet the proper criteria and deadly force is automatically considered reasonable"; they only said it is not an *un*reasonable option.

Ultimately, when determining if force, deadly or not, meets the reasonableness requirement of the Fourth Amendment, the courts "must balance the nature and quality of the intrusion on the individual's Fourth Amendment interests against the importance of the governmental interests alleged to justify the intrusion."[12] Since no two incidents are identical, every use of force will be viewed—and must be justified by the officer—in light of that incident's unique facts and circumstances.

---

[11] *Tennessee*, 471 U.S. at 9

[12] *United States v. Place*, 462 U.S. 696, 703 (1983) as quoted in *Tennessee v. Garner*, 471 U.S. 1, 8 (1985).

10.1.6   **Factors that contribute to the totality of the circumstances.**
The courts have never published a definitive list of all the
"facts and circumstances" they consider when determining
if a use of force is reasonable, but some of the factors they
may consider include:

- Whether the officer initiated the response or was re-
sponding to a call for service
- Whether the officer was ambushed
- Whether the officer was readily identifiable as an
officer (e.g., uniform vs. plain clothes, verbal
identification as a police officer)
- The suspect's disobedience to verbal commands
- The size and build of the suspect compared to the
officer
- The presence or use of weapons
- The mental state of the suspect
- Whether the suspect was under the influence of drugs
- Whether the suspect displayed pre-assault indicators
- The number of assailants
- The number of officers
- Whether the officer called for backup
- Injuries or exhaustion level of the officer
- Avenues of escape for the officer or the suspect
- The officer's prior knowledge or experience with the
suspect
- Whether the officer attempted to use de-escalation
measures

Not all of these facts and circumstances will be relevant
to every use of force report you write; the decision to
include or exclude any of this information will depend on

the nature of your unique incident. If your use of force is reasonable and your report is written effectively, your readers should come away with enough information to determine "whether the totality of the circumstances justifie[s] a particular sort of…seizure."[13]

10.1.7   **State statutes and agency policy.** Although federal law applies to all jurisdictions, state statutes and agency policies may be more restrictive. For example, your state may have a requirement that de-escalation measures be used before physical force. Or your agency policy may require you to summon a supervisor to a scene where the use of force is anticipated. When writing your reports, you should add these general facts to the list of relevant facts you'll need to include in your report. Your list will be customized to your state and agency, but here are some common factors that may be required:

- What less-lethal weapons were deployed or used
- Whether the officer checked the suspect for injuries
- What medical aid was rendered to the suspect
- Whether photographs were taken of the suspect's injuries
- Whether the suspect was transported to the hospital
- What witnesses were present, including other officers
- Whether a supervisor was requested and responded to the scene
- Whether the incident was captured on body camera

---

[13] *Graham v. Connor*, 490 U.S. 386, 396 (1989) quoting *Tennessee v. Garner*, 471 U.S. 1, 8–9 (1984).

10.1.8 **T-Chart template for a use of force incident**

This section provides a generic template that you can use in a use of force incident. Each general fact you should consider is listed in the left column. When writing a report for your own use of force incident, fill in the corresponding incident facts under the right-hand column.

Incident Synopsis

I responded to [describe legal justification for police presence]. The suspect [summarize suspect's actions that led to the use of force].

General Facts	Incident Facts
Reason for the initial seizure:	
elements of the crime being investigated	
reason to believe suspect is involved in the crime, including:	
• Time of day or night	
• Suspect's furtive gestures or nervous behavior	
• High-crime area	
• Proximity to crime location	
• Whether the suspect fled	
• Knowledge of suspect's criminal history	
• Anonymous or corroborated nature of tips about the suspect	
• Whether the suspect matched a lookout description or a wanted flyer	

Graham factors:

the severity of the crime

whether the suspect poses an immediate threat to the safety of the officers or others

whether the suspect is actively resisting arrest or attempting to evade arrest by flight

Deadly force criteria:

probable cause to believe the suspect poses a threat of serious physical harm

Circumstances contributing to the totality of the circumstances

Whether the officer initiated the response or was responding to a call for service

Whether the officer was ambushed

Whether the officer was readily identifiable as an officer (e.g., uniform vs. plain clothes, verbal identification as a police officer)

The suspect's disobedience to verbal commands

The size and build of the suspect compared to the officer

The presence or use of weapons

The mental state of the suspect

Whether the suspect was under the influence of drugs

Whether the suspect displayed pre-assault indicators

The number of assailants

The number of officers

Whether the officer called for backup

Injuries or exhaustion level of the officer

Avenues of escape for the officer or the suspect

The officer's prior knowledge or experience with the suspect

Whether the officer attempted to use de-escalation measures

State law and agency policies:

Use of less-lethal weapons

Aid rendered to the suspect

Documentation of suspect's injuries

De-escalation measures taken

Supervisor review of incident

Presence of witnesses

Availability of body camera recordings

10.2   The Three-Part Use of Force Model

10.2.1   **Overview of the three-part model.** The three-part use of force model allows you to organize the relevant facts of your incident in officer-chronological order under three broad headings. If you are using the *Five Parts of a Police Report Narrative*, the following subheadings should appear within the "Initial Investigation" section of your report (see 6.2.3):

1. Pre-arrival
2. Initial Investigation
   a. **Events preceding the use of force**
   b. **Description of the use of force**
   c. **Follow-up to the use of force**
3. Follow-Up Investigation
4. Administrative Actions
5. Case Disposition

Depending on your specific use of force incident, you may choose to use the exact wording of the three subheadings or choose wording better suited to your incident. Either way, the facts surrounding your use of force incident should appear in the same officer-chronological these subheadings imply.

10.2.2   **Events preceding the use of force.** In this section, describe the events leading up to the use of force, including your legal justification for interacting with the suspect, your decision to detain the suspect or take them into custody, and the initial resistance that began the use of force. Relevant facts in this section may include:

- The crime you were investigating
- How you came to be in the presence of the suspect
- Your legal justification for believing the suspect was involved in the crime
- Whether or not you were dressed in uniform
- Whether or not you announced yourself as a police officer
- Your initial contact with the suspect, including any verbal commands or attempts to restrain their movement
- A description of the environment you were in, including whether uninvolved citizens were present
- Your observations about the suspect, including their size, mannerisms, and any pre-assault indicators
- Your prior knowledge about the suspect

10.2.3   **Description of the use of force.** In this section, describe the precise sequence of events that occurred while using force, including the suspect's actions and your reactions to them. Relevant facts in this section may include:

- The action-reaction sequence of the physical altercation between you and the suspect
- The suspect's level of resistance
- The names of specific body parts on the suspect that you attempted to control
- The names of specific tactics you used to defend yourself and control the suspect
- Weapons the suspect used or attempted to use
- Weapons you used or attempted to use
- The position of your body in relation to the suspect
- Verbal commands you gave to the suspect
- Your communication with other officers on the scene
- Your radio communication
- Your attempts at de-escalation

10.2.4   **Follow-up to the use of force.** In this section, you describe what happened once the use of force was finished. Information in this section may include:

- Rendering aid
- Requesting medical personnel
- Requesting a supervisor
- Handcuffing the suspect
- Taking cover
- Calling for backup
- Establishing a crime scene

10.3   Guidelines for Documenting Uses of Force

10.3.1   **Replace canned phrases with concrete language.** Canned phrases are common expressions used to describe a frequent event. They're so generic they can apply to almost any use of force situation, which means they don't provide the detail readers need to understand what happened. Instead of canned phrases, use concrete language.

> *Not this*:
>
> I assisted him to the ground.
>
> He took a fighting stance.
>
> She approached me aggressively.
>
> I controlled his actions.
>
> I stopped the threat.
>
> *But this*:
>
> I performed an arm drag, bringing him into a facedown position on the ground.
>
> He moved his feet shoulder-width apart and raised his fists in front of his face.
>
> She walked toward me quickly, yelling and pointing her finger at me.
>
> I pinned his left arm to his side by grabbing him around the torso.
>
> I discharged my duty weapon twice, causing her to fall to the ground.

10.3.2 **Avoid words that imply gaps in your action-reaction sequences.** Gaps in your action-reaction sequences cause readers to question what information you have left out. A common red flag that indicates you may have left out information is the use of the words *eventually* or *until*:

> After grabbing his arms, I was *eventually* able to get him into handcuffs.

> I wrestled him *until* he presented his hands.

Words like *eventually* and *until* indicate the passage of time without explaining what happened during that time. Readers will naturally wonder what details you have left out. Instead of using such words, describe what happened.

> I grabbed his arms and pushed him against the wall of the building. I told him to place his hands behind his back, and he complied. I secured his hands with handcuffs, which I double-locked.

> I pulled his right hand behind his back and applied a handcuff. I told him to present his left hand two times. He ignored my commands. I pressed down on the handcuff to create pain compliance, and he put his left hand behind his back.

10.3.3 **Remember to include verbal commands.** Most officers are trained to issue verbal commands when using force. This has three benefits: 1) it tells the suspect what you expect them to do, 2) it broadcasts to the public that you are telling the suspect to do something and they are not complying, and 3) it forces you to breathe, which ensures your muscles get the oxygen they need to perform optimally.

The verbal commands you give during a use of force incident are just as important to document as the actions you take. Depending on the incident, it may be best to include verbal commands as part of your action-reaction sequences or to summarize them at the end of your use of force description.

Example of sequential statements:

I grabbed the suspect's right wrist. I felt him tense his arm. I told him to relax. He started to pull his arm away from me. I told him to stop resisting.

Example of a summary statement:

During this incident, I told the suspect no fewer than ten times to "stop resisting."

10.4   Sample Use of Force Report

10.4.1   **Description of police incident.** Imagine you are the officer responding to the incident described in this section. As you read the facts, consider how you might document this incident using the three-part model (see 10.2). Note that this incident description is written as you may tell a friend about it instead of in the style of an effective police report. In fact, it commits many of the errors discussed in this chapter. You may want to see how many errors you can identify and correct before reviewing the sample report included at the end of this chapter.

You are working a Friday evening detail in your local bar district when a citizen flags you down. She tells you that a male subject is outside one of the bars "trying to pick a fight" with people standing in line.

You mark out on the radio, ask for a backup unit, and approach the front of the bar to make sure no one is being actively assaulted. The bar is filled to capacity, and there's a line on the sidewalk to get in. It's here that you see the suspect. He's about 20 feet in front of you. He's six feet tall with an athletic build, and he's obviously intoxicated.

The suspect is screaming, stumbling up and down the sidewalk, and harassing the people waiting to get into the bar. As you approach, you see the suspect walk up to a male patron, yell something incomprehensible, and then chest-bump him. The citizen looks annoyed, but he's trying to keep his cool. The suspect then approaches a female patron and throws his arm around her shoulder. She's visibly uncomfortable. A bouncer is standing by the entrance to the bar, but besides waving you over, he isn't being much help.

You believe things will escalate if you wait for backup, so you decide to intervene. You announce your presence, and the suspect immediately turns and walks toward you. It's obvious your badge means nothing but a challenge to him.

He approaches you quickly, and you put out your hand to stop him. He swats your hand away. He yells something about his ex-girlfriend, but his speech is so slurred you can't make out anything else he's saying. You tell him he's under arrest for being drunk in public. He reaches out to push you on the shoulder, and you grab his arm to gain control. As soon as you do, the fight is on.

After struggling for a few seconds, you get him on the ground and eventually place him in handcuffs. You roll him into a seated position and notice that his hands and knees are bloodied from being scraped on the pavement. Fortunately, you are uninjured.

You summon medics and your supervisor to the scene. After they evaluate him and document his injuries, you transport him to the jail.

10.4.2   Sample use of force report

On 30 June 2023, at approximately 0035 hours, I was working an overtime detail in the 3500 block of Canal Street when I was flagged down by a citizen, who told me that a male subject was trying to "pick a fight" with patrons at Jack's Pub (3527 Canal Street).

INITIAL INVESTIGATION

Initial Observations of Suspect, Mr. Tommie Reyna

I requested a backup unit and responded on foot to Jack's Pub, where I saw a white male between 5'10" and 6'2" tall with an athletic build, later identified as Mr. Tommie Reyna, screaming loudly and stumbling down the sidewalk. I saw Mr. Reyna walking up to patrons waiting in line outside of Jack's Pub. He chest bumped a male subject standing in line. The male subject pushed him back. Mr. Reyna then put his arm around a female patron's shoulder, who ducked out of his grasp and stepped away. Based on both subjects' reactions, I concluded that they didn't want Mr. Reyna to touch them. As I continued approaching the scene, the Jack's Pub bouncer, Mr. Yeager, waved me over and pointed toward Mr. Reyna.

Events Preceding the Use of Force

I announced myself as a police officer and told Mr. Reyna to come talk to me. Immediately upon hearing me, Mr. Reyna walked quickly in my direction. Fearing that he would try to walk into me, I put my hand up to stop his progress. He swatted my hand away. He then yelled something incomprehensible, which may have included the word "ex-girlfriend," but his speech was so slurred it was impossible to understand him.

While he was yelling, I smelled the strong odor of an alcoholic beverage on his breath.

<u>Description of the Use of Force</u>

I told Mr. Reyna he was under arrest for public intoxication. He reached his right arm toward me and pushed me on my left shoulder. I grabbed his right arm with my right hand and told him again that he was under arrest. He pulled his arm toward his body. I grabbed his right arm with both hands to attempt to control him. Mr. Reyna walked backwards while trying to turn his body away from me. I responded by grabbing him around the torso with both arms and driving his body in a circular direction toward the ground. Mr. Reyna landed on the ground in a prone position. I straddled his back to maintain positional control. I told him to place both his hands behind his back.

He immediately complied. I handcuffed him and double-locked the handcuffs.

<u>Follow-up to the Use of Force</u>

I moved Mr. Reyna into a seated position and assessed him for injuries. I saw that both Mr. Reyna's palms and his right knee had minor abrasions ("road rash") from where he contacted the pavement. I summoned rescue and a supervisor to the scene.

Medics arrived on scene and offered to clean Mr. Reyna's abrasions, but he declined medical attention. Sergeant Finley arrived on the scene and photographed Mr. Reyna's scrapes (see her supplement report for more details).

I was not injured during this incident.

<u>Jail Transport</u>

I transported Mr. Reyna to the county jail, where he was held on charges of public intoxication and resisting arrest.

During this entire incident, I was dressed in full uniform and displaying my badge of authority.

ADMINISTRATIVE ACTIONS

Body camera activated.

Use of force report completed.

CASE DISPOSITION

Case cleared by arrest.

Part IV
Grammar, Punctuation, and Usage

G rammar concerns how words and sentences are combined to communicate ideas to your readers. Punctuation involves using special symbols that show the relationship between words and sentences. Usage describes how words and punctuation are employed in a commonly accepted manner.

Choices concerning grammar, punctuation, and usage come in two varieties: *right vs. wrong* and *good vs. better*. Ending your sentence with a comma falls under the first variety: it is wrong by any grammatical standard. But choosing whether to begin your sentence with the word *but* falls under the second variety: it is neither right nor wrong, but a matter of preference based on your style and the context of your writing.

You have likely been frustrated when one of your readers has presented their preference for a *good vs. better* decision as a choice of *right vs. wrong*. This often happens when you learn how to write reports according to one supervisor's standards, only to get a new supervisor and find out they have a completely different set of prefer- ences. The following chapters will help you understand how to distinguish between these two varieties and the rules that govern each choice.

Chapter 11 teaches you how to construct sentences according to the basic rules of English grammar. It is the most technical chapter in this book, but it will help you understand the rationale behind grammar decisions you are faced with. Chapter 12 explains how to fix errors that frequently break sentences. Chapter 13 reviews the rules of proper punctuation. Chapter 14 addresses questions of usage and formatting. Finally, Chapter 15 clears up the confusion between words that look or sound alike but have different meanings.

11. Basic Sentence Composition

11.1   What Makes a Sentence?

    11.1.1   Subject and predicate
    11.1.2   Independent and dependent clauses
    11.1.3   Sentence structures
    11.1.4   Sentence functions
    11.1.5   Parts of speech

11.2   Nouns

    11.2.1   Nouns generally
    11.2.2   Proper nouns and common nouns
    11.2.3   Count and non-count nouns
    11.2.4   Collective nouns

11.3   Verbs

    11.3.1   Verbs generally
    11.3.2   Verb forms
    11.3.3   Verb properties
    11.3.4   Verb tense
    11.3.5   Conjugating regular verbs in the past tense
    11.3.6   Conjugating regular verbs in the present tense
    11.3.7   Conjugating regular verbs in the future tense
    11.3.8   Conjugating irregular verbs
    11.3.9   Other verb tenses
    11.3.10 Verb person
    11.3.11 Verb mood
    11.3.12 Verb number
    11.3.13 Verb voice
    11.3.14 Example of regular verb conjugation: to arrive
    11.3.15 Example of irregular verb conjugation: to run

11.4   Adjectives

    11.4.1   Adjectives generally

11.4.2 Adjectives with comparisons

11.4.3 Compound adjectives

11.5 Adverbs

11.5.1 Adverbs generally

11.5.2 Adverb placement

11.6 Pronouns

11.6.1 Pronouns generally

11.6.2 Antecedents

11.6.3 Pronoun properties

11.6.4 Pronoun number

11.6.5 Pronoun person

11.6.6 Pronoun gender

11.6.7 Pronoun case

11.6.8 Pronoun chart

11.6.9 Interrogative pronouns

11.6.10 Relative pronouns

11.6.11 Demonstrative pronouns

11.7 Prepositions

11.7.1 Prepositions generally

11.7.2 Preposition placement within a sentence

11.8 Articles

11.8.1 Articles generally

11.8.2 Definite and indefinite articles

11.8.3 *A* vs. *an*

11.9 Conjunctions

11.9.1 Conjunctions generally

11.9.2 Coordinating conjunctions

11.9.3 Correlative conjunctions

11.9.4 Subordinating conjunctions

11.10 Interjections

11.10.1 Interjections generally

When you respond to a police incident, you take a series of actions that eventually lead to the conclusion of that incident. In your police report, you guide your readers through the relevant parts of your incident in a logical order. Sentences are grammatical vehicles that carry your readers, thought by thought, action by action, observation by observation, through your incident to the end of your report.

Your readers should see how the meaning of the first sentence leads into the second, the second into the third, and so forth. To do this, the simplest sentences are usually the most effective. Remember, effective police reports don't have to be poetic, but they must be clear. This chapter will help you construct clear sentences.[1]

11.1   What Makes a Sentence?

A sentence is a collection of words that conveys a complete thought. Sentences begin with a capitalized letter and end with a terminating punctuation mark (see 13.1.1, 13.5.1, and 13.6.1). Here is one of the simplest sentences we can write:

David ran.

Although this sentence contains only two words (and a period), it conveys a lot of information. Let's look at what the different parts of this sentence tell your readers.

11.1.1   Subject and predicate. Every sentence can be separated into two parts: the subject and the predicate. The subject, a noun, tells your readers who (or what) the sentence is

---

[1] This chapter provides a simplified review of technical grammar concepts. If you find the information in this chapter helpful, consider investing in a grammar reference that explores these topics in more depth.

about. The predicate tells your readers additional information about the subject. The predicate doesn't have to contain a lot of information, but it must contain a verb.[2]

David | ran.

David is the subject; *ran* is the verb and the predicate.

David | ran from the police.

David is the subject; *ran* is the verb; *ran from the police* is the predicate.

Without a verb, you don't have a complete sentence.

David | from the police.

Eliminating the verb *ran* makes this sentence incoherent.

Here are a few more examples of subjects and predicates:

I | interviewed the suspect.

The house | burned quickly.

She | was intoxicated.

Notice how each of the above sentences follows the same structure. The sentence begins with the subject, followed by the verb, followed by the remainder of the sentence (called the *sentence complement*). This *subject + verb (+ sentence complement)* construction is the standard pattern for all sentences in English. Although variations exist,

---

[2] Throughout section 11.1, a vertical line is used to separate the subject from the predicate. Unless otherwise indicated, the subject appears in boldface type, and the verb is underlined.

sticking to this basic sentence structure will make it clear who is doing what in each of your sentences.

11.1.2 **Independent and dependent clauses.** Up to this point, we have used the term *sentence* to describe a group of words that contains a subject and a predicate. A sentence that can stand alone is called an *independent clause*. A sentence that cannot stand alone is called a *dependent clause* (i.e., it depends on the sentence within which it is contained to give it meaning).

> **David** | ran from the police because he was guilty.
>
> *David ran from the police* is an independent clause; it can stand alone as its own sentence.
> *Because he was guilty* is a dependent clause; it cannot stand alone as its own sentence.

11.1.3 **Sentence structures.** Sentences have four possible structures. A sentence's structure is determined by its number of independent and dependent clauses. In the examples below, independent clauses are underlined; dependent clauses are contained within curly braces.

1. *Simple.* A simple sentence consists of one independent clause and zero dependent clauses.

   I responded to the scene.

2. *Compound.* A compound sentence consists of two independent clauses and zero dependent clauses.

   I responded to the scene, and I met with the victim.

3. *Complex.* A complex sentence consists of one independent clause and one or more dependent clauses.

I responded to the scene {using my lights and sirens}.

4. *Compound-complex.* A compound-complex sentence contains two independent clauses and one or more dependent clauses.

   {After I arrived on the scene}, <u>I approached the victim</u>, and <u>she immediately pointed to the man who assaulted her</u>.

11.1.4   **Sentence functions.** Sentences have four possible functions:

1. A *statement,* or *declarative sentence,* conveys information. It always ends in a period.

   David ran.

   I arrived on the scene.

2. A *question,* or *interrogative sentence,* seeks information. It always ends with a question mark.

   Did David run?

   How many people were on the scene?

3. A *directive,* or *imperative sentence,* tells someone to do something. It may end with an exclamation point or a period.

   Run, David!

   Don't take another step.

4. An *exclamation*, or *exclamatory sentence*, is a statement that conveys strong emotion. It always ends with an exclamation point.

> I can't believe David ran!

11.1.5 **Parts of speech.** Nouns and verbs form the basis of every sentence, but other words help give meaning and structure to your writing. Every word in a sentence performs a grammatical function known as its *part of speech*. There are nine parts of speech in the English language: noun, verb, adjective, adverb, pronoun, preposition, article, conjunction, and interjection. Many words can function as more than one part of speech, which can make things somewhat confusing. Let's look at parts of speech by adding some additional words to our example sentence:

> David ran from the slow police officer, but he was quickly tased.

11.2 Nouns

11.2.1 **Nouns generally.** A noun names a person, place, thing, or idea. There are two nouns in our example sentence:

> <u>David</u> ran from the slow <u>police officer</u>, but he was quickly tased.

11.2.2 **Proper nouns and common nouns.** A *proper noun* is the official name of a particular person, place, or thing. Capitalize proper nouns regardless of where they appear in a sentence.

> David Officer Landry Big Ben
>
> Seattle Monday Microsoft

A *common noun* is the opposite of a proper noun. It describes a generic person, place, or thing. It is not capitalized unless it begins a sentence.

man	police officer	clock
city	weekday	software

11.2.3 **Count and non-count nouns.** A *count noun* describes a discrete number of things that can be counted. For example, you could write "four bullets" because *bullet* is a count noun. Count nouns can be either plural or singular.

bullet/bullets	suitcase/suitcases
dollar/dollars	suggestion/suggestions

Non-count nouns describe things that cannot be counted. For example, you would never write "four ammunition." Non-count nouns don't have a separate plural form.

ammunition	luggage
money	advice

11.2.4 **Collective nouns.** Some nouns describe a group of individual things. These are called *collective nouns.* Collective nouns can be treated as singular or plural based on whether they refer to the group as a whole or to each member individually.

Singular.

The city council is meeting on Saturday.

Plural:

The city council are debating the issue.

The first example refers to the city council collectively, so it takes the singular verb *is*. The second example refers to the city council members as individuals, so it takes the plural verb *are*.

11.3   Verbs

11.3.1   **Verbs generally.** The verb is the action word of your sentence. It tells your readers what is going on with your subject. There are three verbs in our example sentence:

> David <u>ran</u> from the slow police officer, but he <u>was</u> quickly <u>tased</u>.

11.3.2   **Verb forms.** A verb with the word *to* in front of it is said to be in its *infinitive form*.

to arrest	to chase	to carry
to drive	to steal	to run

Removing *to* gives you the verb's *stem form* or *bare infinitive*. This is the form you would find in a dictionary.

arrest	chase	carry
drive	steal	run

Changing a verb's stem into the past tense (see 11.3.5 and 11.3.8) gives you its *past participle*.

arrested	chased	carried
drove	stole	ran

Adding *ing* to a verb's stem gives you its *present participle.*

arresting	chasing	carrying
driving	stealing	running

When a verb stem ends with *e*, you usually drop the *e* before adding *ing* (e.g., *chase/chasing*). Many times, the final consonant of the verb stem is doubled before adding *ing* (e.g., *run/running*).

11.3.3   **Verb properties.** Verbs have five properties: *tense, person, mood, number,* and *voice.* The process of changing a verb from its infinitive form to show each of these properties is called *conjugation.*

11.3.4   **Verb tense.** Events can occur in the past, the present, or the future. A verb's ability to express each of these time periods is known as its *tense.* Verbs that are conjugated according to standard conjugation rules are called *regular verbs.* Verbs that follow their own conjugation rules are called *irregular verbs.*

11.3.5   **Conjugating regular verbs in the past tense.** Add an *ed* to the verb stem to form the past tense of regular verbs. If the verb stem ends in an *e*, just add a *d*. If the verb stem ends in a *y*, change the *y* to an *i* and then add *ed.*

arrest/arrested

chase/chased

carry/carried

11.3.6 **Conjugating regular verbs in the present tense.** To form the present tense of regular verbs, use the verb stem unless the verb follows a person's name or the words *he*, *she*, or *it*. In those cases, add an *s* to the verb stem. But if the verb stem ends in an *o*, add an *es*. Or, if the verb stem ends in a *y*, change the *y* to an *i* and then add an *es*.

I arrest	he arrests
they go	it goes
I carry	she carries

11.3.7 **Conjugating regular verbs in the future tense.** Place the word *will* in front of the verb stem to form the future tense of regular verbs.

will arrest	will chase	will carry

11.3.8 **Conjugating irregular verbs.** Irregular verbs are conjugated differently in the past tense. You must either memorize these conjugations or consult a dictionary.

awake/awoke	catch/caught	drive/drove
lose/lost	run/ran	steal/stole

Some irregular verbs, like *to be,* have irregular forms for both the past and present tenses.

Singular	*Plural*

Past Tense

I was	we were
you were	you were
he/she/it was	they were

Present Tense

I am	we are
you are	you are
he/she/it is	they are

11.3.9   **Other verb tenses.** The past, present, and future tenses de-scribed thus far are called the *simple* past, present, and future tenses because they are the simplest way to express action. These tenses can be broken down into *perfect, progressive*, and *perfect-progressive* tenses (see 11.3.14 and 11.3.15 for examples of these tenses).

1. *Perfect tense* indicates that an action has been complet-ed. Form the perfect tense by combining *to have* with the verb's past participle.

Past-perfect

   had + [past participle]

Present-perfect

   have/has + [past participle]

Future-perfect

   will have + [past participle]

2. *Progressive tense* indicates that an action continues. Form the progressive tense by combining *to be* with the verb's present participle.

Past-progressive

was/were + [present participle]

Present-progressive

am/are/is + [present participle]

Future-progressive

will be + [present participle]

3. *Perfect-progressive tense* indicates that an action is, was, or will continue to happen, but the action is, was, or will be completed later. Form the perfect-progressive tense by combining *to have* with the word *been* and the verb's present participle.

Past-perfect progressive

had + *been* + [present participle]

Present-perfect progressive

have/has + *been* + [present participle]

Future-perfect progressive

will have + *been* + [present participle]

11.3.10 **Verb person.** *Person* indicates who is performing the action of the verb. In the *first person*, the speaker (or the writer) performs the action. In the *second person*, the person spoken to (or the reader) performs the action. In the *third person*, the person or thing spoken about performs the action (also see 7.1).

I <u>run</u>.

This sentence is in the first person because the writer is speaking about himself or herself performing the action.

You <u>run</u>.

This sentence is in the second person because the writer is speaking about the reader performing the action.

David <u>runs</u>.

This sentence is in the third person because the writer is speaking about David performing the action.

11.3.11 **Verb mood.** Mood indicates how the verb expresses action. The *indicative* mood is used to state a fact or ask a question. The *imperative* mood is used to give a command. The *subjunctive* mood is used to express a wish or desire. The indicative mood is used most frequently in police reports; the subjunctive mood is used least frequently.

David <u>ran</u>.

The indicative mood makes a statement.

<u>Run</u>, David.

The imperative mood issues a command.

If I <u>were</u> David, I <u>would run</u>.

The subjunctive mood states a wish or desire.

11.3.12 **Verb number.** *Number* indicates whether a verb is singular or plural. Verbs only change their number in the present tense third-person singular indicative form, indicated by the underlined verb below.

	Singular	Plural
First Person	I drive	we drive
Second Person	you drive	you drive
Third Person	he/she/it <u>drives</u>	they drive

11.3.13   **Verb voice.** Certain verbs transmit their action to an object. These are called *transitive verbs*, and the object they transmit their action to is their *direct object*. Verbs like *ask, cut, kick, punch, use,* and *warn* are examples of transitive verbs. Other verbs don't require a direct object. These are called *intransitive verbs*. Verbs like *agree, arrive, fall, listen, move,* and *run* are examples of intransitive verbs.

In our example sentence—*David ran*—we don't need to know anything else about where David ran or whom he ran to or from. The sentence makes grammatical sense the way it is. If we changed the verb to a transitive verb, however, we would need to include a direct object for the sentence to make grammatical sense.

> David <u>punched</u>
>
> This sentence is missing a direct object, leaving us to wonder who or what David punched. Notice how this sentence is not complete without the direct object.

> David <u>punched</u> the wall.
>
> *The wall* is the direct object of *punched*. Since *punched* requires a direct object, it is a transitive verb.

Voice shows a transitive verb's relationship to the subject of the sentence. If the subject of the verb is doing the action, the voice is *active*. If the subject of the verb is receiving the action, the voice is *passive*. Active voice is preferable in police reports (see 7.5).

> David <u>punched</u> the wall.
>
> This sentence uses the active voice. The subject (*David*) performed the action (*punched*).

> The wall <u>was punched</u> by David.
>
> This sentence uses the passive voice. The subject (*the wall*) received the action (*was punched*).

If you are wondering if your sentence is written in the active or passive voice, look for a conjugated form of *to be* with the verb's past participle (e.g., *was + punched*). This combination of a helping verb—*be, do, have*—plus a past participle is an example of a *verb phrase*.

11.3.14   **Example of regular verb conjugation:** *to arrive*

Singular   *Plural*

Past Tense

I arrived   we arrived

you arrived   you arrived

he/she/it arrived   they arrived

Past-perfect Tense

I had arrived   we had arrived

you had arrived   you had arrived

he/she/it had arrived   they had arrived

Past-progressive Tense

I was arriving   we were arriving

you were arriving   you were arriving

he/she/it was arriving   they were arriving

Past-perfect Progressive Tense

I had been arriving   we had been arriving

you had been arriving   you had been arriving

he/she/it had been arriving   they had been arriving

Present Tense

I arrive   we arrive

you arrive   you arrive

he/she/it arrives   they arrive

Singular	Plural

Present-perfect Tense

I have arrived	we have arrived
you have arrived	you have arrived
he/she/it has arrived	they have arrived

Present-progressive Tense

I am arriving	we are arriving
you are arriving	you are arriving
he/she/it is arriving	they are arriving

Present-perfect Progressive Tense

I have been arriving	we have been arriving
you have been arriving	you have been arriving
he/she/it has been arriving	they have been arriving

Future Tense

I will arrive	we will arrive
you will arrive	you will arrive
he/she/it will arrive	they will arrive

Future-perfect Tense

I will have arrived	we will have arrived
you will have arrived	you will have arrived
he/she/it will have arrived	they will have arrived

Future-progressive Tense

I will be arriving	we will be arriving
you will be arriving	you will be arriving
he/she/it will be arriving	they will be arriving

Future-perfect Progressive Tense

I will have been arriving	we will have been arriving
you will have been arriving	you will have been arriving
he/she/it will have been arriving	they will have been arriving

11.3.15   Example of irregular verb conjugation: *to run*

Singular   *Plural*

Past Tense

I ran   we ran

you ran   you ran

he/she/it ran   they ran

Past-perfect Tense

I had run   we had run

you had run   you had run

he/she/it had run   they had run

Past-progressive Tense

I was running   we were running

you were running   you were running

he/she/it was running   they were running

Past-perfect Progressive Tense

I had been running   we had been running

you had been running   you had been running

he/she/it had been running   they had been running

Present Tense

I run   we run

you run   you run

he/she/it runs   they run

Present-perfect Tense

I have run   we have run

you have run   you have run

he/she/it has run   they have run

Singular	*Plural*

Present-progressive Tense

I am running	we are running
you are running	you are running
he/she/it is running	they are running

Present-perfect Progressive Tense

I have been running	we have been running
you have been running	you have been running
he/she/it has been running	they have been running

Future Tense

I will run	we will run
you will run	you will run
he/she/it will run	they will run

Future-perfect Tense

I will have run	we will have run
you will have run	you will have run
he/she/it will have run	they will have run

Future-progressive Tense

I will be running	we will be running
you will be running	you will be running
he/she/it will be running	they will be running

Future-perfect Progressive Tense

I will have been running	we will have been running
you will have been running	you will have been running
he/she/it will have been running	they will have been running

11.4 Adjectives

11.4.1 **Adjectives generally.** An adjective is a describing word. It modifies a noun or a pronoun. There is one adjective in our example sentence:

> David ran from the <u>slow</u> police officer, but he was quickly tased.

The adjective *slow* describes, or modifies, the noun police officer. An adjective usually comes before the word it modifies.

11.4.2 **Adjectives with comparisons.** Adjectives can be used to make comparisons between two or more nouns. The adjective *slower*, for example, indicates the relative speed between two people or objects. If the adjective were *slowest*, it would tell your readers that there were at least three people or objects, each faster than the one you described.

For many adjectives, you add *er* or *est* to the end to show comparisons. But if the adjective has two or more syllables, you usually precede it with the word *more* or *most* instead of adding an ending.

> faster
>
> happiest
>
> longest
>
> more difficult
>
> more aggressive
>
> most suspicious

11.4.3   **Compound adjectives.** When two or more words function as a single adjective, place a hyphen between each word.

> broken-down vehicle
>
> green-eyed child
>
> hard-to-find building
>
> *But:*
>
> a vehicle that was broken down
>
> a missing child with green eyes
>
> a building that is hard to find

11.5   Adverbs

11.5.1   **Adverbs generally.** Like an adjective, an adverb is also a describing word. It modifies a verb, an adjective, or another adverb. There is one adverb in our example sentence:

> David ran from the slow police officer, but he was <u>quickly</u> tased.

The adverb *quickly* modifies the verb phrase *was tased*. Adverbs sometimes, but not always, end in *ly*.

fortunately	loudly	quite
impatiently	toward	never
angrily	rather	very

11.5.2   **Adverb placement.** The position of the adverb can change the meaning of your sentence. For clarity, keep the adverb close to the word it modifies.

> Rebecca had <u>only</u> superficial wounds.

> <u>Only</u> Rebecca had superficial wounds.

The first example suggests that Rebecca was wounded, and all her wounds were superficial. The second example suggests that multiple people were wounded, and only Rebecca's wounds were superficial (presumably, the other people's injuries were much worse).

11.6   Pronouns

11.6.1   **Pronouns generally.** A pronoun replaces a noun. In our example sentence, the pronoun *he* stands in place of the proper noun *David*.

> David ran from the slow police officer, but <u>he</u> was quickly tased.

Pronouns allow you to avoid repetition. Without the pronoun, our example sentence would read:

> David ran from the slow police officer, but David was quickly tased.

As we continued our report, the use of *David* would grow repetitive and distracting:

> David ran from the slow police officer, but David was quickly tased. David fell to the ground, where David sustained an injury to David's knee.

11.6.2   **Antecedents.** The noun that the pronoun refers to is called its *antecedent*. In the following examples, the pronoun appears in boldface type; its antecedent is underlined.

> <u>Mr. Sands</u> gave me **his** license.

> <u>The suspects</u> placed **their** hands on the wall.

11.6.3   **Pronoun properties.** Pronouns have properties of *number, person, gender,* and *case*. A pronoun must agree with its antecedent in number, person, and gender.

11.6.4   **Pronoun number.** *Number* determines whether the pronoun is singular or plural. A singular antecedent requires a singular pronoun, and a plural antecedent requires a plural pronoun.

> The <u>vehicle</u> was missing <u>its</u> keys.

> The <u>vehicles</u> were missing <u>their</u> keys.

11.6.5   **Pronoun person.** *Person* determines who the pronoun refers to. *First-person* pronouns refer to the speaker (or the writer). *Second-person* pronouns refer to the person spoken to (or the reader). *Third-person* pronouns refer to the person or thing being spoken about.

> *First-person*:

> <u>I</u> arrived on the scene.

> <u>We</u> located the suspect.

> *Second-person*:

> "<u>You</u> need to sit down."

Third-person:

<u>She</u> couldn't describe the vehicle.

<u>It</u> was damaged beyond repair.

<u>They</u> refused to cooperate.

11.6.6   **Pronoun gender.** *Gender* determines whether the pronoun refers to a male, female, or gender-neutral antecedent.

<u>Mr. Huê</u> forgot to lock <u>his</u> car.

<u>Ms. Hughes</u> had a knife in <u>her</u> pocket.

The <u>gun</u> had one round in <u>its</u> chamber.

11.6.7   **Pronoun case.** *Case* determines the pronoun's function within a sentence. A pronoun can serve as a subject or object. It can indicate possession (*possessive pronoun*). Or it can indicate that the verb's action applies to the sentence's subject (*reflexive pronoun*).

Subjective case:

<u>I</u> dusted for fingerprints.

Objective case:

The juveniles ran from <u>me</u>.

Possessive case:

Ms. Barbosa dropped <u>her</u> license.

Reflexive case:

Mr. Amir stopped the robbery <u>himself</u>.

11.6.8 **Pronoun chart**

Personal Pronouns

	Singular	**Plural**
First Person		
Subjective	I	we
Objective	me	us
Possessive	my mine	our ours
Reflexive	myself	ourselves
Second Person		
Subjective	you	you
Objective	you	you
Possessive	your yours	your yours
Reflexive	yourself	yourselves
Third Person		
Subjective	he, she it, one	they
Objective	him, her it, one	them
Possessive	his, her, hers its, one's	their theirs
Reflexive	himself, herself itself, oneself	themselves

11.6.9   **Interrogative pronouns.** *Interrogative pronouns* are used in questions. They don't have an antecedent.

who   what   which

whom   whose

<u>What</u> evidence was crucial in solving the case?

11.6.10   **Relative pronouns.** *Relative pronouns* introduce a dependent clause and connect it (or show how it *relates*) to an independent clause. Although many relative pronouns are the same words as interrogative pronouns, the difference is in how they are used. Relative pronouns are used to give more information about a noun or pronoun mentioned earlier in the sentence.

who   what   which

whom   whose   that

The officer found <u>a shoe</u> **that** proved crucial in solving the case.

11.6.11   **Demonstrative pronouns.** *Demonstrative pronouns* refer directly to their antecedent.

this   that   these

those

I'll catch her if <u>she drives this way again</u>, but I doubt **that** will happen.

11.7 Prepositions

11.7.1 **Prepositions generally.** A preposition shows the relationship between a noun or pronoun and another word in your sentence. There is one preposition in our example sentence.

> David ran <u>from</u> the slow police officer, but he was quickly tased.

In this example, the preposition *from* shows the relationship between David's act of running and the location of the police officer. Consider how changing the preposition changes the entire meaning of the sentence:

> David ran <u>to</u> the slow police officer.

> David ran <u>past</u> the slow police officer.

> David ran <u>over</u> the slow police officer.

Prepositions must always be linked to a noun or pronoun (known as the preposition's *object*). In the example sentences above, the slow police officer is the object of the preposition. If we remove the object, the sentences no longer make sense.

> David ran <u>to</u>

> David ran <u>past</u>

> David ran <u>over</u>

11.7.2 **Preposition placement within a sentence.** A preposition usually comes before its object, but it may also come after its object, such as when it appears at the end of a sentence.

The gun was <u>between</u> the sofa cushions.

It wasn't clear what she was looking <u>for</u>.

Some may argue that the second example should be rewritten so the preposition comes before its object, but the resulting sentence is unnecessarily awkward:

It wasn't clear for what she was looking.

Don't fall prey to constructing awkward sentences to follow the advice of not ending your sentences with a preposition.

11.8   Articles

11.8.1   **Articles generally.** An article shows whether a noun is specific or general. Our example sentence includes one article:

David ran from <u>the</u> slow police officer, but he was quickly tased.

11.8.2   **Definite and indefinite articles.** In the example sentence in 11.8.1, the word *the* is a *definite article* because it refers to a specific police officer who had been mentioned previously in the report. The words *a* and *an* are *indefinite articles* because they define something generally. If David ran from *a* slow police officer, your readers wouldn't know which officer David ran from specifically.

11.8.3   ***A* vs. *an*.** Use *a* when the word following begins with a consonant sound. When it begins with a vowel sound, use *an*.

a suspect

a university

an interview

an hour

11.9   Conjunctions

11.9.1   Conjunctions generally. A conjunction is a word that joins a phrase or sentence. There is one conjunction in our example sentence:

> David ran from the slow police officer, <u>but</u> he was quickly tased.

11.9.2   Coordinating conjunctions. *Coordinating conjunctions* join two statements of equal grammatical importance.

> I turned on my sirens, <u>and</u> the vehicle pulled over.
>
> I said he could leave <u>or</u> go to jail.

Common coordinating conjunctions include:

and	but	for
or/nor	so	yet

11.9.3   Correlative conjunctions. *Correlative conjunctions* are word pairs that join two statements of equal grammatical importance.

> She was <u>neither</u> sober <u>nor</u> compliant.
>
> <u>Either</u> sign the summons <u>or</u> get arrested.

Common correlative conjunctions include:

as many...as	both...and	either...or

neither...nor	not...but	not only...but also
rather...than	such...that	whether...or

11.9.4   **Subordinating conjunctions.** *Subordinating conjunctions* show that one statement depends on the other.

> <u>Once</u> you sign this form, I can release your property.

> Empty your hands <u>before</u> you exit the house.

Common subordinating conjunctions include:

after	because	before
if	once	since
till	when	whenever
where	wherever	while

11.10   Interjections

11.10.1   **Interjections generally.** Interjections express surprise or emotion. You probably won't use them often in your police reports; if you do, they would only be appropriate within a direct quotation. Our example sentence doesn't contain an interjection, but we can add one:

> <u>Wow!</u> David ran from the slow police officer, but he was quickly tased.

Here are some common interjections:

cool	hmm	nice
really	sure	ugh

12. Sentence Errors

12.1   Run-on Sentences
12.2   Tense Shifts
12.3   Subject-Verb Number Agreement
12.4   Pronoun-Antecedent Agreement
12.5   Pronoun-Antecedent Confusion
12.6   Misplaced and Dangling Modifiers

As discussed in the previous chapter, you have many factors to consider while constructing your sentences. Because of this, there are many possible ways that your sentences may become confusing, vague, or grammatically incorrect. This chapter discusses the most common sentence errors and how to fix them.

12.1   Run-on Sentences

Run-on sentences occur when two or more sentences are improperly presented as one. One type of run-on sentence is a *fused sentence*, which occurs when two complete sentences are joined without a conjunction or punctuation mark.

The suspect ran north he turned down the alley.

Fix a fused sentence by splitting the sentence into two separate sentences, or by adding a conjunction or proper punctuation.

The suspect ran north. He turned down the alley.

The suspect ran north; he turned down the alley.

The suspect ran north, and he turned down the alley.

The suspect ran north, but he turned down the alley.

Another type of run-on sentence is a *comma splice*. This happens when a comma joins two sentences without a conjunction.

I spoke to the victim, she told me she received a threatening email yesterday afternoon.

Fix a comma splice by splitting the sentence into two separate sentences, or by adding a conjunction or proper punctuation.

I spoke to the victim. She told me she received a threatening email yesterday afternoon.

I spoke to the victim; she told me she received a threatening email yesterday afternoon.

I spoke to the victim, and she told me she received a threatening email yesterday afternoon.

12.2   Tense Shifts

Tense shifts occur when a sentence or paragraph begins in one tense and shifts to another without a logical reason. Note the different verb tenses used in the underlined portions of these examples:

> After he <u>saw</u> the man with the knife, he <u>runs</u> away and <u>trips</u> on the curb.

> She <u>tells</u> me she <u>saw</u> the money on the ground and <u>picks</u> it up.

The first example shifts from the past tense to the present tense. The second example shifts from the present tense to the past tense and then back to the present tense. Since police reports are written mainly in the past tense, most tense shifts can be corrected by identifying each verb and changing it to the past tense. Notice how each of the underlined verbs is now in the past tense:

> After he <u>saw</u> the man with the knife, he <u>ran</u> away and <u>tripped</u> on the curb.

> She <u>told</u> me she <u>saw</u> the money on the ground and <u>picked</u> it up.

Tense shifts often indicate a sentence error, but they may be acceptable when done intentionally:

> He <u>said</u> he <u>will surrender</u> at noon tomorrow.

In this example, the subject of the sentence (*he*) makes a statement in the past (*said*) about something he will do in the future (*will surrender*).

12.3   Subject-Verb Number Agreement

Errors in subject-verb number agreement occur when a singular subject is used with a plural verb or vice versa. In these examples, notice how the subject (in boldface type) does not match the number of the verb (underlined).

> **They** <u>drops</u> the gun in a trashcan.

The **field test** <u>were</u> positive for cocaine.

To fix this error, first find the subject of the sentence and determine if it is singular or plural. Change the subject or verb to be singular or plural depending on the sentence's intended meaning.

She <u>drops</u> the gun in a trashcan.

The **field test** <u>was</u> positive for cocaine.

Misidentifying the subject of a sentence is a common cause of subject-verb disagreement. What is the subject of this sentence?

The box of bullets were on the desk.

If you believe the subject of the sentence to be *bullets*, then you may think this sentence is correct because both *bullets* and *were* are plural. But the true subject of this sentence is the box. The words *of bullets* tell us more information about the box, but they aren't the subject. Since *box* is singular, the correct verb is *was*.

The **box** of bullets <u>was</u> on the desk.

12.4   Pronoun-Antecedent Agreement

Errors in pronoun-antecedent agreement occur when a singular pronoun is used for a plural subject or vice versa.

Both girls had her shoes stolen.

Each of the cars had their window broken.

To fix this error, first identify the pronouns. Next, determine what word each pronoun refers to (i.e., its antecedent). In the first sentence, the pronoun *her* refers to the antecedent *both*. In the second sentence, the pronoun *their* refers to the antecedent *each*.

Both girls had her shoes stolen.

Each of the cars had their window broken.

Now, change the pronoun to match the number of its antecedent. In the first example, *both* is plural, so its pronoun must be plural also. In the second example, the singular *each* requires a singular pronoun. Use the table in section 11.6.8 to help you identify the proper pronoun.

Both girls had their shoes stolen.

Each of the cars had its window broken.

12.5   Pronoun-Antecedent Confusion

Pronoun-antecedent confusion occurs when it is unclear who or what the pronoun refers to.

Rebecca told Amy to destroy her drugs.

In this sentence, it is impossible to tell if *her* refers to Rebecca or Amy. To fix pronoun-antecedent confusion, add clarifying details or rewrite the sentence.

Rebecca told Amy to destroy her [Rebecca's] drugs.

Amy had two baggies of drugs; Rebecca told her to destroy them.

Rebecca told Amy to destroy the drugs in Amy's possession.

12.6 Misplaced and Dangling Modifiers

Modifiers are words that give more information about other words in a sentence. When a modifier appears to modify a word the writer did not intend, it is called a *misplaced modifier*. In this example, what word does *damaged* modify?

> I collected the damaged suspect's phone.

This example makes it sound like the suspect, not the phone, is damaged. To fix this, move the modifier next to the word it is intended to modify.

> I collected the suspect's damaged phone.

A *dangling modifier* occurs when the word it is intended to modify is missing from the sentence.

> Running from the bank, the gun was shot three times.

> Walking down the street, Mr. Artugo's wallet fell out of his pocket.

The first example makes it sound like the gun was running from the bank; the subject of the sentence is completely missing. The second example sounds like Mr. Artugo's wallet was walking down the street. The true subject of the sentence, Mr. Artugo, is mentioned only in its possessive form. To fix a dangling modifier, ensure the word the modifier refers to exists in the sentence.

> As the suspect ran from the bank, he shot his gun three times.

> While Mr. Artugo was walking down the street, his wallet fell out of his pocket.

13. Punctuation

13.1 Period (.)

13.1.1   Periods as terminating punctuation marks
13.1.2   Periods after indirect questions
13.1.3   Periods in abbreviations
13.1.4   Periods in initialisms and acronyms
13.1.5   Periods in lists
13.1.6   Periods in URLs and decimal numbers
13.1.7   Ellipses (…)

13.2 Comma (,)

13.2.1   Commas after introductory phrases
13.2.2   Commas with conjunctions
13.2.3   Commas with non-essential information
13.2.4   Commas with connecting adverbs
13.2.5   Commas in lists
13.2.6   Commas with direct quotations
13.2.7   Commas with addresses
13.2.8   Commas with dates
13.2.9   Commas with names

13.3 Semicolon (;)

13.3.1   Joining two sentences without a conjunction
13.3.2   Joining two sentences with a connecting adverb
13.3.3   Semicolons in lists

13.4 Colon (:)

13.4.1   Colons with lists
13.4.2   Joining two sentences without a conjunction
13.4.3   Colons with time

13.4.4   Colons with headings and subheadings

13.5   Question Mark (?)

13.5.1   Question marks with direct questions

13.6   Exclamation Point (!)

13.6.1   Exclamation points with direct quotations

13.7   Quotation Marks (" ")

13.7.1   Quotations marks with direct quotations
13.7.2   Quotation marks to refer to words.
13.7.3   Quotation marks with books, plays, etc
13.7.4   Quotation marks for names of vessels
13.7.5   Quotation marks with measurements
13.7.6   Quotation marks with other punctuation

13.8   Apostrophe (')

13.8.1   Apostrophes with possessive nouns
13.8.2   Apostrophes with possessive pronouns
13.8.3   Apostrophes with contractions
13.8.4   Apostrophes with plurals
13.8.5   Apostrophes with measurements

13.9   Hyphens and Dashes (- – —)

13.9.1   Difference between hyphens and dashes
13.9.2   Hyphens with compound words
13.9.3   Hyphens with prefixes
13.9.4   Hyphens with numbers
13.9.5   Hyphens when spelling out words
13.9.6   En dashes with number ranges
13.9.7   Em dashes to set off supplemental information
13.9.8   Em dashes to indicate a change in thought
13.9.9   Em dash with profanities

13.10 Parentheses (( ))

13.10.1 Parentheses with supplemental information
13.10.2 Parentheses with abbreviations and custom labels
13.10.3 Parentheses with numerals
13.10.4 Parentheses with numbered items in lists

13.11 Brackets ([ ])

    13.11.1 Brackets to add clarifying information

13.12 Slash (/)

    13.12.1 Slashes to indicate alternatives

    13.12.2 Slashes to replace the word *per*

    13.12.3 Slashes with dates

    13.12.4 Slashes in fractions

    13.12.5 Slashes with URLs

    13.12.6 Slashes with certain abbreviations

13.13 Spaces

    13.13.1 Different types of spaces

    13.13.2 Spaces after terminating punctuation marks

    13.13.3 Spaces after punctuation marks within a sentence

    13.13.4 Spaces with hyphens

    13.13.5 Spaces with dashes

    13.13.6 Spaces with headings

    13.13.7 Spaces before paragraphs

If sentences are the roads on which readers travel through your reports, then punctuation marks are the road signs: they let your readers know when to pause, how to merge ideas, and when to stay alert for important information. This chapter addresses the most common uses of punctuation marks in police reports. If you encounter a tricky punctuation situation not discussed in this chapter, consider if your sentence could be written more clearly. If you are confused by your punctuation, your readers will be too. When in doubt, revise and rewrite. There are few punctuation problems that can't be solved (or avoided altogether) by rewriting the sentence.

13.1 Period (.)

13.1.1 **Periods as terminating punctuation marks.** End every sentence not enclosed in quotation marks with a period. This rule is true for police reports but not necessarily for other types of writing. For example, in an email, you might ask a question directly to your reader and, therefore, end your sentence with a question mark. Or you may wish to express excitement by ending your sentence with an exclamation point. In police reports, you never ask your readers questions, and you maintain a professional, objective tone. This makes the period the only appropriate terminating punctuation mark for non-quotations.

> I spoke to the victim.

> I yelled at her to stop.

> He pointed the gun at the bank teller.

13.1.2 **Periods after indirect questions.** An indirect question is a question phrased as a statement. Use a period to terminate an indirect question (see 13.5.1 for direct questions).

> Ms. Chamberland asked if I wanted to fight her.

> The suspect asked Mr. Albright where the safe was.

13.1.3 **Periods in abbreviations.** Use a period at the end of most abbreviations that end with a lowercase letter.

> Ave.   Dr.

> Jr.   Ms.

> Inc.   etc.

But be aware of certain abbreviations where periods are typically omitted.

9 mm   50 mph

13.1.4   **Periods in initialisms and acronyms.** Do not use a period between letters in initialisms or acronyms (see 14.3) unless required for clarity. For example, the initialism for *United States* (U.S.) may be confused with the word *us* if the letters are not separated with periods.

SWAT   NCIC   PhD

U.S.   a.m.   p.m.

Some acronyms are in such common usage that they are treated as regular words, requiring neither periods nor capitalization.

scuba   radar   laser

13.1.5   **Periods in lists.** Use a period after each item in a list when the item itself is a complete sentence; otherwise, omit any punctuation.

I made three initial observations about the door:
- The wood on the doorframe was splintered.
- The deadbolt was still engaged.
- There was a distinct shoe impression next to the door handle.

The purse contained three items:
- one driver's license
- one pair of sunglasses
- one prescription pill bottle

13.1.6   **Periods in URLs and decimal numbers.** Use a period to separate the sections of a URL or decimal number. In these cases, the period is referred to as a *dot* or a *point*, respectively.

www.usdoj.gov   12.5 percent $30.45

13.1.7   **Ellipses (. . .).** An ellipsis, or series of three periods, indicates omitted information. The only plausible place for ellipses is within direct quotations, but you should avoid using them because your readers will question what information you omitted and why. Instead of ellipses, include the full quotation, partial quotation, or a paraphrase (see 9.4).

With an ellipsis:

Ms. Lacroix showed me the threatening email, which read, "I will come to your house . . . and I will kill you and your family."

Better alternatives:

Ms. Lacroix showed me the threatening email, which read, "I will come to your house, which I know is the house that is rightfully mine, and I will kill you and your family."

Ms. Lacroix showed me an email in which the suspect threatened to come to her house and "kill you and your family."

Ms. Lacroix showed me an email in which the suspect threatened to kill her and her family. He also claimed that the house rightfully belonged to him.

13.2   Comma (,)

13.2.1   **Commas after introductory phrases.** A phrase is two or more words that do not function as a complete sentence. Use a comma after an introductory phrase.

> Upon my arrival, I spoke with the victim.

> After searching the backyard, I turned my attention to the house.

13.2.2   **Commas with conjunctions.** Use a comma when joining two sentences with a coordinating conjunction (*for, and, nor, but, or, yet, so*). Never use a comma to join two sentences without a conjunction, which is known as a comma splice (see 12.1).

> I searched under the bed, but the gun was not there.

> I spoke to three witnesses at the scene, and each denied seeing anyone enter the business.

You may omit the comma when the second sentence is short or when the subject is implied.

> She smacked him in the face and he cried.

> He took a drink and spat on the ground.

13.2.3   **Commas with non-essential information.** The terms *essential* and *non-essential*[1] describe the grammatical function of information in a sentence, not whether the information is essential to your police incident. *Essential information* is required for readers to correctly interpret the meaning of

---

[1] The technical terms are *restrictive* and *non-restrictive*.

your sentence, while *non-essential information* is not. Place a comma on each side of non-essential information.

> Ms. Casey said the burglar, who was wearing a ski mask, attacked her.

In the above example, the commas around "who was wearing a ski mask" signal that it is non-essential information. This sentence tells readers that there was one burglar and *that* burglar was wearing a mask. In other words, the burglar and Ms. Casey's attacker were the same person. This would not be true if the sentence were written:

> Ms. Casey said the burglar who was wearing a ski mask attacked her.

In this example, the phrase "who was wearing a ski mask" is not surrounded by commas, signaling to readers that it is essential information. This sentence tells readers there were multiple burglars, but the one wearing the mask attacked Ms. Casey.

13.2.4   **Commas with connecting adverbs.**[2] Words like *however, therefore, consequently,* and *subsequently* are used to link ideas within and between sentences. When a connecting adverb appears within a sentence, surround it with commas unless your sentence flows naturally without them.

> We did not discover the USB drive. We did, however, discover two laptop computers.

> We concluded, therefore, that Mr. Rangel was lying.

> We therefore concluded that Mr. Rangel was lying.

---

[2] Technically called *conjunctive adverbs.*

I arrested Ms. Clemons for arson and subsequently transported her to the county jail.

When a connecting adverb appears as the first word in a sentence, it usually links its sentence to the one before it (see 13.3.2), but *however*, when used as the first word in a sentence, can also mean "whichever way." When this is the case, don't follow it with a comma.

However the suspects rotated the safe, they could not fit it through the doorway.

13.2.5 **Commas in lists.** When a list of three or more items is written as part of a sentence, use commas to separate each item in the list.

She searched for her missing daughter in the living room, the bedroom, the playroom, and the kitchen.

I placed the sunglasses, the wallet, and the car keys into evidence.

The comma that appears before the final conjunction in these examples is called the Oxford comma, and its usage is debated. While some argue that the Oxford comma is unnecessary, using it will help you avoid confusing sentences such as:

I spoke with the victims, Ms. Hull and Mr. Costello.

You can interpret the above sentence in two ways:

1. The officer spoke with the two victims, whose names were Ms. Hull and Mr. Costello.

2. The officer spoke with the victims (who are unnamed) in addition to Ms. Hull and Mr. Costello (who may be witnesses, suspects, etc., but who were *not* the victims).

An Oxford comma would resolve the whole issue:

I spoke with the victims, Ms. Hull, and Mr. Costello.[3]

Here's another example of a sentence whose meaning has been obscured by the lack of an Oxford comma:

Evidence I collected included nail clippings, blood and seminal fluid.

Are readers to understand that the blood and seminal fluid were two separate items of evidence, or were they mixed? Again, the Oxford comma helps readers clarify that you collected three distinct items:

Evidence I collected included nail clippings, blood, and seminal fluid.

But what if the blood and seminal fluid *were* mixed? Then rephrasing the sentence would be the best choice:

I collected nail clippings and a liquid sample containing blood and seminal fluid.

13.2.6 **Commas with direct quotations.** Use a comma when introducing direct quotations with words like *said* or *stated*. Do not use a comma before direct quotations that flow naturally with the sentence.

---

[3] Opponents of the Oxford comma will note that you could safely omit the Oxford comma if you just reworked the sentence: "I spoke with Ms. Hull, Mr. Costello and the victims." This solution works here, but not for more complex examples. Better to adopt the Oxford comma full-time than trouble yourself with each possible scenario.

Mr. Daigle said, "I killed her."

Ms. Godfrey stated, "I knew the time was 3 a.m. because that's when I let my dogs out the back door."

Mr. Brice told me he "rage stole" the candy bar when he realized he didn't have enough money to buy it.

Ms. Poe said she would "come back to this despicable city and make everyone sorry."

13.2.7 **Commas with addresses.** Use commas to separate each part of an address.

Main Street Cafe, 127 Main Street, Fayetteville, GA

10025 37th Street, Apt. 1E, Rockville, MD

13.2.8 **Commas with dates.** When writing dates using the month–day–year format, insert a comma between the day of the month and the year. Omit the comma when using the day–month–year format.

May 5, 2008

28 August 2013

When including the day of the week, separate it from the rest of the date with a comma.

Wednesday, October 13, 2010

Tues., 19 Jan. 2016

13.2.9 **Commas with names.** When writing a person's name using the last-name–first-name format, insert a comma after the last name only. In all other cases, omit commas.

> Tang, Roxana

> Pitt, Justin Alexander Jr.

> George Slattery III

> Justin Alexander Pitt Jr.

13.3 Semicolon (;)

13.3.1 **Joining two sentences without a conjunction.** Use a semicolon to join two complete sentences related in meaning and not joined by a conjunction.

> I interviewed Ms. Tomlin; she denied any involvement.

> Mr. Hyatt held up the knife and began walking toward me; I drew my gun.

13.3.2 **Joining two sentences with a connecting adverb.** When two sentences are connected with adverbs like *therefore, however, consequently,* or *subsequently,* precede the word with a semicolon and follow it with a comma (see 13.2.4).

> We followed the vehicle for 30 miles on the highway; however, we lost sight of it when it crossed the bridge.

> I linked Mr. Braxton to four separate forgeries; consequently, I obtained a warrant for each offense.

13.3.3 **Semicolons in lists.** Separate items in a list with a semicolon when the items themselves contain commas. In cases like this, it may be clearer to put the list in block format (see 14.5.4 and 14.5.5).

> Similar threats have been reported in Boston, MA; Washington, D.C.; Columbus, OH; and Miami, FL.

13.4   Colon (:)

13.4.1   **Colons with lists.** Use a colon to introduce an inline list (see 14.5.2 and 14.5.3) when introductory words such as *namely, such as, including* or *which included* do not appear.

> I returned the victim's property: a black purse, a wallet, and car keys.
>
> I returned the victim's property, which included a black purse, a wallet, and car keys.

Use a colon to introduce an inline list when it follows *as follows, the following*, or similar words.

> I discovered the following: a knife, brass knuckles, and a U.S. passport.

Always use a colon to introduce a list in block format (see 14.5.4 and 14.5.5).

> I gave the victim back her property, which included:
> - a black purse
> - a wallet
> - car keys

13.4.2   **Joining two sentences without a conjunction.** Like a semicolon, a colon can connect two sentences related in meaning and not joined by a conjunction. A colon draws more attention to itself than a semicolon, so reserve it for times when the second sentence explains or adds detail to the first.

> Mr. Dugan found his vehicle parked in the far corner of the parking lot: it had not been stolen.

> Toward the end of the interview, Ms. Rauch confessed to the child abduction: "I did it because I thought I would get away with it," she said.

13.4.3   **Colons with time.** When writing times in standard format, insert a colon between the hours and the minutes. When using military/international format, omit the colon.

> 3:30 a.m.   1545 hours

13.4.4   **Colons with headings and subheadings.** Headings and subheadings signal a change in topic. Since they are already set off from the rest of your text, do not follow them with a colon (see 6.1.2).

13.5   Question Mark (?)

13.5.1   **Question marks with direct questions.** In police reports, direct questions only occur within quotation marks (see 13.7.1). End direct questions with a question mark. End indirect questions with a period (see 13.1.2).

> Before he attacked her, he asked, "Which way is the subway?"

> Before he attacked her, he asked her which way the subway was.

13.6   Exclamation Point (!)

13.6.1   **Exclamation points with direct quotations.** Use an exclamation point in direct quotations that indicate commands or other forceful language. Never use exclamation points outside of direct quotations.

> I yelled, "Police! Don't move!"

> I heard her screaming, "Help! Help! Help!"

13.7   Quotation Marks (" ")

13.7.1   **Quotation marks with direct quotations.** Use quotation marks around quotations where the wording is recorded exactly as it was spoken (i.e., a *direct quotation*). Never use quotation marks around paraphrased statements.

> Ms. Hutson said, "I never felt such a hard punch in my life."

> Ms. Hutson told me she had never been punched so hard in her life.

> Mr. Grant said he was "mad blitzed" when he committed the assault.

> Mr. Grant told me he was high on drugs when he committed the assault.

13.7.2   **Quotation marks to refer to words.** Use quotation marks when referring to a word itself instead of the meaning of the word.

> The USB drive was labeled "favorite pictures."

The suspect used the word "epiphany" five times.

13.7.3 **Quotation marks with books, plays, etc.** Use quotation marks when referring to titles of books, plays, magazines, works of art, television shows, etc.

I saw multiple copies of "Soldier of Fortune" magazine on the passenger seat.

The anonymous caller threatened to bomb the theater during the 3 p.m. showing of "Wicked."

13.7.4 **Quotation marks for names of vessels.** Use quotation marks when referring to names of boats, airplanes, and other vessels.

Pursuant to our search warrant, we seized Ms. Starling's deck boat, the "Above Board."

13.7.5 **Quotation marks with measurements.** When writing measurements using numerals, use a quotation mark to stand in place of the word *inches*.[4]

3'6" (three feet, six inches)

13.7.6 **Quotation marks with other punctuation.** When periods, question marks, or exclamation points are required at the

---

[4] Technically, the marks appearing after feet (') and inches (") are not apostrophes or quotation marks at all; they are special characters called *prime marks* (a single prime mark indicates feet; a double prime mark indicates inches). Keyboards don't contain a prime mark key, so inserting it into your police reports can be a hassle. Save yourself the trouble and use an apostrophe or quotation mark. Your readers aren't likely to misunderstand your measurements or even notice (much less care) that you didn't use the technical symbol.

end of a quotation, always place them inside the closing quotation mark.

> He said, "I couldn't help myself."

> Ms. Chamberland said, "You want to fight me?"

> I yelled, "Police! Stop!"

Always place commas inside quotation marks, even when separating quoted items in a list.

> I located the subject known as "Snarky," but I lacked reasonable suspicion to detain him.

> I collected the boxes labeled "Archived Documents," "For Destruction," and "2022 Tax Documents."

Always place semicolons and colons outside quotation marks.

> She told me, "When you leave, I am going to kill myself"; therefore, I took her into custody for a mental health evaluation.

13.8 Apostrophe (')

13.8.1 **Apostrophes with possessive nouns.** When a noun does not end with the letter *s*, make it possessive by adding an apostrophe *s*. When a noun ends with the letter *s*, add just an apostrophe.

> the victim's blanket

> Ms. Stevens' vehicle

13.8.2   **Apostrophes with possessive pronouns.** Possessive pronouns (see 11.6.7) already indicate possession. With the exception of *one's*, they never take an apostrophe.

> The dog ran back to its yard.

> Lab tests proved that the gloves were hers.

> He told me, "One must mind one's own business."

13.8.3   **Apostrophes with contractions.** A contraction combines two words into a single word by dropping one or more syllables or letters. Use an apostrophe to replace dropped letters or syllables in a contraction.

> She wouldn't drop the knife.

> I couldn't locate the victim.

Use apostrophes to replace letters dropped at the beginning or end of a word (but see 9.4.6 for documenting accents).

> He told me, "My girl ain't missin'."

> She said she punched him "just 'cause I wanted to."

13.8.4   **Apostrophes with plurals.** Although the general rule is that apostrophes never make a word plural, apostrophes may be used to indicate plural numerals or letters.

> He had three 6's tattooed on his chest.

> She said, "mind your p's and q's."

13.8.5   **Apostrophes with measurements.** When writing measurements using numerals, use an apostrophe to stand in place of the word *feet* (see footnote for 13.7.5).

> 6'2" (six feet, two inches)

13.9   Hyphens and Dashes (- – —)

13.9.1   **Difference between hyphens and dashes.** Even though they look similar, hyphens and dashes are different punctuation marks with distinct looks and functions.

> Hyphen   -
>
> En dash   –
>
> Em dash   —

13.9.2   **Hyphens with compound words.** Compound words are two or more words joined together physically or by common usage. Some compound words are always hyphenated:

> father-in-law
>
> six-pack
>
> u-turn
>
> ex-wife

Some words are only hyphenated when they are used as an adjective for a noun:

> up-to-date information
>
> short-term solution

But:

information that is up to date

a solution that will work in the short term

Closed compounds are compounds in such common usage that they have become one word.

sailboat   football   pothole

Open compounds are words that frequently appear together but don't require a hyphen:

high school   real estate   ice cream

living room   first aid   cell phone

Compound words can be tricky, so consult a dictionary if you need clarification on which type of compound you are dealing with.

13.9.3   **Hyphens with prefixes.** Use a hyphen to attach a prefix to a noun.

anti-police   neo-Nazi   pro-business

13.9.4   **Hyphens with numbers.** Use a hyphen to separate sections of Social Security, telephone, and other pre-formatted numbers.

078-05-1120   767-555-0187

13.9.5   **Hyphens when spelling out words.** Use a hyphen between letters when spelling out words.

The letters R-E-V-E-N-G-E were written on the wall.

13.9.6   **En dashes with number ranges.** Use an en dash when indicating number ranges. The en dash stands in place of the word *through* or *to* and includes the number following the dash.

>pages 7–12

>15–20 people

>She estimated the knife to be 10–15 inches long.

When using an en dash, don't precede the number range with the word *from* or *between*.

>15–20 people

>a knife 10–15 inches in length

>*But:*

>from 15 to 20 people

>a knife between 10 and 15 inches long

13.9.7   **Em dashes to set off supplemental information.** Like commas and parentheses, em dashes can set off supplemental information in a sentence. While parentheses understate the information, em dashes emphasize it. Place em dashes before and after the information you wish to set off.

>The suspect—a white female with bright red hair wearing a yellow jacket—matched the description on the lookout flyer.

13.9.8   **Em dashes to indicate a change in thought.** Use em dashes to indicate a sudden change in thought.

She identified Mr. Poirier—the same Mr. Poirier who has been identified in six other attacks—as the man who followed her home from work.

13.9.9   **Em dash with profanities.** Since the only appropriate place for profanity is direct quotations, it is often best to write out the profane word in full to maintain accuracy; however, in cases where policy or prudence guides you away from including the actual profanity, write the first letter followed by an em dash.

I asked if he needed help. He replied, "F— you."

13.10   Parentheses (( ))

13.10.1   **Parentheses with supplemental information.** Use parentheses to enclose information that clarifies or adds detail but is not essential to the sentence's meaning.

I returned to the initial crime scene (3551 Main Street).

Ms. Stephens (DOB: 10/16/1992, SSN: 219-09-9999) told me she didn't see what happened.

The case appears to be related to similar incidents in the area (see case #202303451).

13.10.2   **Parentheses with abbreviations and custom labels.** Use parentheses to indicate an abbreviation or custom label that will be used throughout the report.

Drug Enforcement Agency (DEA)

The juvenile, Sandra Marrs (hereafter "Sandra"), fled on foot as I approached her.

13.10.3   **Parentheses with numerals.** Use parentheses when including a numeral after a number that is spelled out.

> He stole fourteen (14) flatscreen televisions.

13.10.4   **Parentheses with numbered items in lists.** Use only a closing parentheses when numbering each list item in an in-line list. In cases like this, it may be clearer to rewrite the list in block format (see 14.5.5).

> He told me he could not have committed the shooting because 1) he was out of town at the time of the incident, 2) he did not need money, and 3) he "wouldn't have been stupid enough" to leave the gun at the crime scene.

13.11   Brackets ([ ])

13.11.1   **Brackets to add clarifying information.** Use brackets (also called square brackets) to enclose clarifications added by you as the author.

> She said she went to the party looking for "White Girl" ["White Girl" is slang for cocaine].

> Ms. Baer said that Ms. Latimer removed the jewelry from her [Ms. Latimer's] room.

13.12   Slash (/)

13.12.1   **Slashes to indicate alternatives.** You may use a slash to replace the word *or* when indicating alternatives, but writing out the word is often clearer.

> black/gray jacket   black or gray jacket

35/40 mph   35 or 40 mph

The above examples demonstrate potential problems with using a slash to indicate alternatives. Unless readers interpret the slash as you intended, they could read the first example as a black jacket containing some gray and the second as 35 mph in a 40 mph zone.

13.12.2   **Slashes to replace the word *per*.** You may use a slash to replace the word *per*, but writing out the word is often clearer.

$50/person $50 per person

three piercings/ear   three piercings per ear

13.12.3   **Slashes with dates.** Separate the sections of a numeric date with slashes. Keep in mind that other date formats are usually clearer (see 14.6.6).

05/14/2023

13.12.4   **Slashes in fractions.** You may separate the parts of a fraction with a slash, but writing out the hyphenated words may be clearer. If you use numerals, ensure your word processor does not replace the fraction with a fraction character (½) since this may not transfer correctly between records management systems.

1/2 ounce   one-half ounce

13.12.5   **Slashes with URLs.** Use slashes to separate the parts of the directory path in a URL.

www.justice.gov/hatecrimes/hate-crime-statistics

13.12.6   **Slashes with certain abbreviations.** Some abbreviations include slashes, but writing out the word completely is usually more clear and professional.

N/A	not applicable
w/	with
w/o	without
b/c	because

13.13   Spaces

13.13.1   **Different types of spaces.** Spaces are not technically punctuation marks, but, like punctuation marks, they help your readers navigate your writing. In police reports, spaces appear as *character spaces* (between words, at the ends of sentences, and after certain punctuation marks), as *line breaks* (before and after headings and paragraphs), and as *indents* (before lists and at the start of new paragraphs).

Create a character space by pressing the spacebar once. Create a line break by pressing the *enter* key once. Create a double line break by pressing the *enter* key twice. Create an indent by pressing the *tab* key once.

13.13.2   **Spaces after terminating punctuation marks.** Use one space, never two, after every complete sentence.

I interviewed Ms. Burk. She told me her son went missing at 1700 hours.

When a terminating punctuation mark is contained within quotation marks or parentheses, place the space after the closing punctuation mark.

Mr. Lombard punched his chest and yelled, "Shoot me!" I quickly repositioned myself behind cover.

I responded to the Family Diner located at 4562 Ash Place. (This location has since been closed, and the building has been torn down.) Once on scene, I spoke with the manager, Ms. Mona Jennings.

13.13.3   **Spaces after punctuation marks within a sentence.** Use one space after commas, semicolons, and colons (see examples in 13.2.1, 13.3.1, and 13.4.1).

13.13.4   **Spaces with hyphens.** When hyphenated words appear in a series, place a space after all but the last hyphen.

The man on the bicycle approached fourth- and fifth-graders at three different elementary schools.

The missing children were six-, eight-, and nine-years-old respectively.

13.13.5   **Spaces with dashes.** Do not place spaces around en dashes (see examples in 13.9.6). Either omit spaces around em dashes or place a space on each side of the em dash. Whichever you choose, be sure to remain consistent.

13.13.6   **Spaces with headings.** Add a double line break before a heading. Add a single line break after a heading (see examples in 20.3).

13.13.7   **Spaces before paragraphs.** Add a double line break between paragraphs (see examples in 20.3). Alternatively, you may add a single line break before a paragraph and indent its first line, but this technique is more rare.

14. Usage and Formatting

14.1 Bias-Free Language

   14.1.1   Bias generally

   14.1.2   Stereotypes

   14.1.3   Offensive terms

   14.1.4   Person-first language

   14.1.5   Gendered language

14.2 Jargon

   14.2.1   Jargon generally

   14.2.2   Only use jargon you are certain your readers will understand

   14.2.3   If you can't avoid jargon, explain it first

14.3 Abbreviations

   14.3.1   Abbreviations generally

   14.3.2   Acronyms generally

   14.3.3   Initialisms generally

   14.3.4   Clipped words generally

   14.3.5   State abbreviations

14.4 Contractions

   14.4.1   Contractions generally

14.5 Lists

   14.5.1   Lists generally

   14.5.2   Inline unstyled lists

   14.5.3   Inline numbered lists

   14.5.4   Block bulleted lists

   14.5.5   Block numbered lists

14.6   Numbers

14.6.1   Numbers generally
14.6.2   Cardinal and ordinal numbers
14.6.3   Spelling out numbers
14.6.4   Number formats
14.6.5   Money and currency
14.6.6   Dates
14.6.7   Times
14.6.8   Fractions and decimals
14.6.9   Percentages
14.6.10 Weights and measures

14.7   Capitalization

14.7.1   Capitalization generally
14.7.2   Sentences
14.7.3   Proper nouns
14.7.4   Job titles and ranks
14.7.5   Nationalities
14.7.6   Cardinal directions
14.7.7   Seasons

14.8   Text Formatting

14.8.1   Text formatting generally
14.8.2   Italics, boldface, and underlined text
14.8.3   Text alignment
14.8.4   Fonts
14.8.5   Font size
14.8.6   Tables, graphs, and figures

Questions of usage are best answered by the author because usage concerns how an author chooses to combine words, phrases, and sentences to convey meaning. Since there are many ways to accomplish this, usage advice comes best in the form of guidelines rather than hard and fast rules. This chapter presents those guidelines along with some guidelines for formatting your police reports.

14.1   Bias-Free Language

14.1.1   **Bias generally.** While *bias* has a negative connotation that is usually linked to race, religion, sexual identity, and other protected classes, the word also describes the natural tendency all people have to interpret the world in a non-objective way. In short, bias is prejudice shaped by our experiences. *Implicit bias* is unintentional, while *explicit bias* is intentional.

If you see someone wearing ragged clothing and automatically assume they are unhoused,[1] you are expressing implicit bias. If you see a group of people of a certain race and make the conscious decision to investigate them based solely on this identity, you are expressing explicit bias. In police reports, as in policing, it is essential to avoid all types of bias.

Many police reports run into problems when the words and phrases used in the report imply bias where none exists. Using bias-free language, as described in this section, can help you avoid this error.

14.1.2   **Stereotypes.** Stereotypes are assumptions about individuals based on race, religion, sexual identity, or other characteristics. Stereotyping is harmful because it reduces individuals to generalizations drawn from their group. Whether or not these generalizations are accurate, relying on stereotypes shows your readers that your conclusions are based on generalized assumptions instead of specific facts.

To avoid stereotyping, focus on facts that apply to the individual(s) you are dealing with. For example, instead of assuming that all women are emotional or all men are ag-

---

[1] *Unhoused* or *houseless* are more acceptable terms than *homeless* to describe someone who does not have a fixed residence.

gressive, recognize that these stereotypes do not represent the full range of human experience.

14.1.3   **Offensive terms.** Offensive terms can perpetuate stereotypes. To avoid using offensive terms, familiarize yourself with language considered offensive or insensitive *from the perspective of the people you are referring to.*

> *Not this:*
>
> illegal alien
>
> crippled
>
> insane
>
> *But this:*
>
> undocumented immigrant
>
> a person with a disability
>
> a person in crisis

14.1.4   **Person-first language.** The easiest way to avoid stereotypes and offensive terms is to use person-first language, which acknowledges that a person is more than any one characteristic that describes them.

> *Not this:*
>
> a handicapped woman
>
> a homeless subject
>
> a wheelchair-bound man
>
> a drug addict

But this:

a person with a disability

a person who is currently unhoused

a person who uses a wheelchair

a person with a substance use disorder

As demonstrated above, beginning your sentences with the phrase "a person who/with" can help you present information in a person-centric way.

14.1.5   **Gendered language.** Gendered language assigns gender-specific words to people you are describing. For example, using the pronouns *he, him,* or *his* to refer to a man, or *she, her,* or *hers* to refer to a woman. If you know the gender of the person you are referring to, this isn't a problem:

She handed me her license.

I spoke to him by phone.

If you do not know the gender of a person, avoid defaulting to male-specific language:

Not this:

The masked suspect used his bag to break the window.

I requested that firemen respond to the scene.

But this:

The masked suspect used a bag to break the window.

The masked suspect used their bag to break the window.

I requested that firefighters respond to the scene.

You may have noticed that this section (and this book) occasionally uses what are technically plural pronouns—*they, them,* and *their*—to refer to a single person. This is an increasingly common practice in modern writing and is acceptable when you wish to adopt a gender-neutral term to describe an individual. Of course, *they, them,* and *their* are also still acceptable to describe groups of people.

Some people may prefer that you refer to them using pronouns that differ from those associated with their biological sex or government identification. In such cases, maintain consistency in how you refer to the person throughout your report, and notify your readers if you depart from standard conventions (see 9.1.12 and 11.6.6).

14.2   Jargon

14.2.1   **Jargon generally.** Jargon is specialized language used within a particular field or profession. Slang, abbreviations, and technical terms are all forms of jargon. If used correctly, jargon can help you communicate complex ideas quickly and accurately to a community of experts. If misused, jargon can confuse your message and alienate your readers. Consider the two guidelines in this section when determining if jargon is appropriate.

14.2.2   **Only use jargon you are certain your readers will understand.** Most of your readers will probably understand basic law enforcement terminology, but not all your readers work for your agency; therefore, stick to jargon that is shared widely between law enforcement agencies or is likely to be known to the general public:

10-4

arrest

ASAP

DUI/DWI

handcuff

Mirandize

frisk

Other jargon is less widely known. In these cases, consider if the plain language alternative would be clearer to your readers:

beat (patrol area)

bus (ambulance)

FI (field interview)

GOA (gone on arrival)

hook (tow truck; to arrest)

run code (respond with lights and sirens)

tech (crime scene technician; technology)

Remember that your readers may include a much broader audience than those who handle your reports (see Chapter 2). Unless you are certain your readers will understand your jargon, avoid using it. Or, if you can't avoid it, accompany it with an explanation.

14.2.3   **If you can't avoid jargon, explain it first.** Some jargon can't be avoided. For example, your agency probably has a preferred term to describe a printed document that notifies others about a wanted person. If you generate one of these documents, you will be expected to notate it in a report. Here are some common terms for such a document:

Wanted Flyer

Wanter Person Flyer

Wanted Poster

BOLO (Be on the Lookout)

Lookout Flyer

APB (All Points Bulletin)

ATL (Attempt to Locate)

Some of these terms are more commonly used than others. But if your agency has designated the term it wants to use, you don't have much choice but to use it too. When confronted with such a situation, either use the jargon and provide additional information in parentheses, or give a plain-language description and include the jargon in parentheses. Either way, be sure readers have enough information to deduce what the jargon means.

Option #1:

I created an ATL (attempt to locate) bulletin.

I completed form PD-1201b ("In-Custody/Arrest Documentation").

Option #2:

I created a flyer (ATL bulletin) with the suspect's information.

I completed the required arrest form (PD-1201b).

14.3   Abbreviations

14.3.1   **Abbreviations generally.** Abbreviations are shortened versions of words or phrases. There are three categories of abbreviations: *acronyms, initialisms,* and *clipped words.* It may be tempting to use abbreviations in your reports to save time or space. Usually, they have the opposite effect, forcing your readers to slow down to translate the abbreviations in their heads.

Not this:

The suspect was LSH WB on Baker Street. LSW a blue shirt.

But this:

The suspect was last seen heading westbound on Baker Street. She was last seen wearing a blue shirt.

Although the second example is a little longer, it is easier to read and less likely to be misinterpreted by your readers. If you insist on using abbreviations that are not in common usage, avoid abbreviations that have multiple interpretations:

c/o (care of; commanding officer; complaints of)

n/b (northbound; non-blocking; non-binary)

a/o (arresting/assigned officer; area of operation)

14.3.2   **Acronyms generally.** Acronyms are abbreviations where the first letter of each word is combined to form a new word. If the acronym may not be known to your readers, spell out the words fully on the first mention and place the acronym in parentheses. On subsequent mentions, use the acronym only.

First mention:

Automated Fingerprint Identification System (AFIS)

Subsequent mentions:

AFIS

Acronyms usually appear in all caps, but some acronyms are in such common usage that they function as regular nouns:

scuba (self-contained underwater breathing apparatus)

laser (light amplification by stimulated emission of radiation)

radar (radio detection and ranging)

14.3.3   **Initialisms generally.** Initialisms are abbreviations where the first letter of each word is combined into a new word, but each letter is pronounced separately. Normally, omit periods between letters in initialisms (but see also 13.1.4):

DUI

FBI

FTA

PD

14.3.4 **Clipped words generally.** Some abbreviations are formed by truncating, or clipping, parts of the word. Normally, spell out the word in its entirety unless the abbreviation is the more common usage. Be careful of abbreviations that can have multiple meanings.

> fridge (refrigerator)
>
> ad (advertisement)
>
> memo (memorandum)
>
> photo (photograph)
>
> fax (facsimile)
>
> vet (veterinarian *or* veteran)

14.3.5 **State abbreviations.** Either spell out the state name entirely or use the uppercase two-letter postal abbreviation. (See the table on the following page.)

State Abbreviations

Alabama	AL	Montana	MT
Alaska	AK	Nebraska	NE
Arizona	AZ	Nevada	NV
Arkansas	AR	New Hampshire	NH
California	CA		
Colorado	CO	New Jersey	NJ
Connecticut	CT	New Mexico	NM
Delaware	DE	New York	NY
District of Columbia	DC	North Carolina	NC
		North Dakota	ND
Florida	FL	Ohio	OH
Georgia	GA	Oklahoma	OK
Hawaii	HI	Oregon	OR
Idaho	ID	Pennsylvania	PA
Illinois	IL	Rhode Island	RI
Indiana	IN	South Carolina	SC
Iowa	IA	South Dakota	SD
Kansas	KS	Tennessee	TN
Kentucky	KY	Texas	TX
Louisiana	LA	Utah	UT
Maine	ME	Vermont	VT
Maryland	MD	Virgin Islands	VI
Massachusetts	MA	Virginia	VA
Michigan	MI	Washington	WA
Minnesota	MN	West Virginia	WV
Mississippi	MS	Wisconsin	WI
Missouri	MO	Wyoming	WY

14.4   Contractions

14.4.1   **Contractions generally.** Contractions are formed when two words are combined by dropping one or more syllables or letters. These syllables or letters are usually replaced by an apostrophe (see 13.8.3).

> can't (can not)
>
> haven't (have not)
>
> they're (they are)
>
> it's (it is)

If you've been told to avoid contractions in professional writing, disregard this advice. Using contractions makes your writing more conversational and approachable. Avoiding contractions will make your writing sound stuffy. Even so, it's still best to avoid non-standard contractions:

> must've (must have)
>
> there're (there are)
>
> ain't (am not; are not)
>
> gonna (going to)

14.5   Lists

14.5.1   **Lists generally.** Lists are an effective way to share related or sequential information. *Inline lists* appear as part of your paragraphs and flow within your sentences. *Block lists* are indented and separated from your paragraph by a double line break (see 13.13.1). Lists can be *numbered, bulleted,* or *unstyled,* depending on their location.

Types of Lists

List Format	List Style
Inline	Unstyled or Numbered
Block	Bulleted or Numbered

14.5.2   **Inline unstyled lists.** Inline unstyled lists are the most common type of list. These lists flow within your sentence and don't use numerals to indicate list items.

> I gave her a citation for speeding, driving without a license, and failing to signal a lane change.

> He turned over the gun, the wallet, and the mask.

14.5.3   **Inline numbered lists.** Inline numbered lists are the same as inline unstyled lists, except that numerals are used to separate list items. Use numbered lists when indicating sequences of events or when the total number of list items is important (see 13.10.4).

> I told him to 1) cancel his credit cards, 2) call his bank, and 3) file an online report.

> She hit him in five locations: 1) his chin, 2) his arm, 3) his cheek, 4) his temple, and 5) his right eye.

14.5.4   **Block bulleted lists.** Block lists are helpful when presenting more information than would naturally flow within a sentence or when the list items themselves are sentences. Bullets indicate to readers that the list items are presented in no particular order. A block bulleted list is set apart from the paragraph that precedes it with a double line break. Indent a block list from the left margin by pressing the *tab* key once before each list item.

> Although the witness accounts differed in a few areas, they agreed on the following facts:
> - The car was blue.
> - Two people occupied the car.
> - Neither of the car's occupants appeared to be over 25 years old.

Since some report writing software may not format the bullet character (•) correctly, you may also replace bullet points with hyphens.

14.5.5   **Block numbered lists.** Block numbered lists serve the same purpose as inline numbered lists but are useful when the list items are too lengthy to include as part of your sentence. Numbers indicate that your list items are in order of sequence or importance.

> I made the following observations:
> 1. The door was open.
> 2. Blood was on the doorframe.
> 3. The couch in the front room was overturned.

14.6   Numbers

14.6.1   **Numbers generally.** Numbers appear in police reports as addresses, phone numbers, ages, heights, weights, driver's license numbers, Social Security numbers, etc. When including numbers, triple-check that the number is recorded correctly. It's all too easy to mistype or transpose numerals when copying them from your notepad.

14.6.2   **Cardinal and ordinal numbers.** *Cardinal numbers* indicate quantity. *Ordinal numbers* indicate order.

> *Examples of cardinal numbers:*
>
> 0
>
> 1
>
> 29
>
> 510
>
> *Examples of ordinal numbers:*
>
> First   1st
>
> Second   2nd
>
> Third   3rd

14.6.3   **Spelling out numbers.** Generally, spell out whole numbers zero through nine. Use cardinal numbers for numbers 10 or higher.

> Three
>
> Eight
>
> 10
>
> 168

When numbers appear at the beginning of a sentence, spell them out or rewrite the sentence.

> One hundred people were inside the restaurant.
>
> The restaurant contained 100 people.

When spelling out numbers, it may also be helpful to follow the written-out number with the cardinal number in parentheses.

> I recovered three (3) guns, one (1) pair of gloves, and 100 glassine bags.

14.6.4   **Number formats.** When numbers adhere to a standardized format—telephone numbers, Social Security numbers, etc.—separate numerals with the appropriate punctuation marks (see 13.9.4):

> *Telephone numbers:*
>
> (415) 273-9164
>
> 415-273-9164
>
> *Social Security numbers:*
>
> 078-05-1120

For cardinal numbers with four or more digits, use a comma to separate groups of thousands.

> 2,977
>
> 13,458
>
> 525,600
>
> 2,542,358

14.6.5   **Money and currency.** A currency symbol (e.g., $, €, ¥) is usually the easiest way to distinguish between countries' currencies; however, many countries besides the United States of America use the dollar symbol ($) to denote their currency. If you are referring to United States dollars, you may generally omit the country designator; however, if there is any question about what currency you are referring to, include the country's currency code (see the table on the facing page).

When referring to large sums of money, write out the word *million* or *billion* instead of using abbreviations or including the necessary number of zeros.

Not this:

$100m

$2,500,000,000

But this:

$100 million

$2.5 billion

When referring to sums less than one million, write the amount out fully.

$100,000

$2,500

Currency Symbols and Formatting

Currency	Symbol	Formatting
United States Dollar	$	$1,234.56 US$1,234.56 1,234.56 USD
Canadian Dollar	$	Can$1,234.56 1,234.56 CAD
Mexican Peso	$	Mex$1,234.56 1,234.56 MXN
UK/Great Britain Pound	£	£1,234.56 GB£1,234.56 1,234.56 GBP
European Union Euro	€	Use a decimal to separate thousands and a comma to separate fractions. €1.234,56 1.234,56 EUR
Japanese Yen	¥	¥1,234.56 1,234.56 JPY

14.6.6 **Dates.** To avoid confusing the month number with the day of the month, use numerals for the day and spell out the month's name or abbreviation. Always use numerals for the year.

July 22, 2022

To further prevent confusion, consider separating the day and year with the name of the month:

22 July 2022

If you write a date with only numerals, use two numerals for the month, two for the day, and four for the year. Include leading zeros for single-digit months or days. Separate each set of numbers with a slash (see 13.12.3).

04/09/2002

11/26/2005

14.6.7 **Times.** Times can be expressed as *military time* or *standard time*. Military time (also called *international time* or *24-hour time*) is preferable in police reports because it eliminates confusion about whether the time occurred in the morning or the afternoon.

To format military time, use a four-digit number where the first two digits indicate the number of hours since midnight and the second two digits indicate the number of minutes since the start of the hour. Follow the number with a single space and the word *hours*. Do not separate the hours and minutes with a colon, space, or other punctuation.

1045 hours

2300 hours

Military time is always four digits. When the time occurs before ten o'clock in the morning, include leading zeros as part of the hour.

0039 hours

0922 hours

To format standard time, write the hour and minute separated by a colon and followed by a space and the abbreviation *a.m.* or *p.m.*, which indicates whether the time occurred before noon (a.m.) or from noon onward (p.m.).[2] Omit the leading zero for single-digit hours.

2:35 a.m.

10:05 p.m.

For maximum clarity, pair a time with its associated date:

13 December 2020 at 0517 hours

December 13, 2020, at 5:17 a.m.

Noon and midnight are easily confused when written as numerals, so consider using *noon* or *midnight* instead. When written as numerals, express noon as either *1200 hours* or *12:00 p.m.* Midnight is the first hour of the new day, so express it as either *0000 hours* or *12:00 a.m.*

14.6.8   **Fractions and decimals.** Fractions and decimals both indicate parts of a whole. Fractions may be written using numerals or hyphenated words. Decimals are always written

---

[2] The abbreviation *a.m.* stands for *ante meridiem,* which is Latin for "before midday"; *p.m.* stands for *post meridiem,* which is Latin for "after midday."

using numerals. When decimals are less than one, include a leading zero before the decimal point.

one-half	1/2	0.5
three-quarters	3/4	0.75

14.6.9   **Percentages.** Use numerals when writing percentages.

Not this:

seventy-five percent

two-and-one-half percent

But this:

75%

2.5%

14.6.10   **Weights and measures.** Weights and measures are formed by combining a fraction or decimal with the unit of measurement. When writing out measurements using hyphenated words, write out the amount and the full name of the unit of measurement. When using numerals, write the full name of the unit of measurement or its abbreviation. Separate the abbreviation from the numerals with a space and follow it with a period.

one-half pound

1/2 lb.

0.5 lb.

three-quarters of an ounce

three-quarter-ounce

3/4 oz.

0.75 oz.

14.7 Capitalization

14.7.1   **Capitalization generally.** Capital letters indicate proper nouns, the beginning of a sentence, or some abbreviations.

14.7.2   **Sentences.** Capitalize the first word in every sentence. Capitalize the first word in a direct quotation when the quotation itself forms a complete sentence.

> The suspects left the scene in a green vehicle.

> She said, "It's not like I shot him in the face."

> He told me he "will be gone a long time."

Don't capitalize the first word after a colon or semicolon.

> I presented the case to the magistrate: she declined to issue a warrant.

> I searched the vehicle; the pistol was under the driver's seat.

14.7.3   **Proper nouns.** Capitalize proper nouns regardless of where they appear in a sentence (see 11.2.2):

> I responded to Jerry's Fish Shop.

> the corner of Burton Street and Halifax Lane

> I pointed my Taser at him.

14.7.4 **Job titles and ranks.** Capitalize job titles and ranks when they appear as part of a person's name. Lowercase job titles and ranks when they are separate from a person's name.

> Chief Wakefield
>
> Sheriff Alley
>
> Citizens Against Drunk Driving President Loretta Sikes
>
> Oren Wakefield, chief of police
>
> Jasmine Alley, sheriff
>
> Loretta Sikes, Citizens Against Drunk Driving president
>
> the chief of police
>
> sergeant
>
> lieutenant

14.7.5 **Nationalities.** Capitalize country names, nationalities, and languages.

> visiting from England
>
> a Spanish man
>
> She used American Sign Language.

14.7.6 **Cardinal directions.** Don't capitalize the words *north, east, south, west, northeast, southwest,* etc., unless referring to the specific part of the country that goes by that name.

> The suspect ran north on Bell Avenue from Spring Street.

He is traveling through the deep South.

She said she wants to return to the Southwest.

14.7.7   **Seasons.** Don't capitalize *spring, fall, winter,* or *summer.*

There have been 13 auto thefts this fall.

14.8   Text Formatting

14.8.1   **Text formatting generally.** Most report writing software has only rudimentary text formatting features, and many systems that transmit and share reports don't correctly transfer formatting. For this reason, it's best to keep text formatting to a minimum and to never rely on formatting to help convey meaning.

14.8.2   **Italics, boldface, and underlined text.** Avoid emphasizing text with italics. Instead, place quotation marks around text that would have been italicized, such as names of creative works (see 13.7.3) or when referring to words themselves (see 13.7.2). Use boldface or underlined text for headings and subheadings only, never to emphasize words or phrases in the body of your reports. Alternatively, consider using all caps for headings and subheadings (see 6.1.2).

14.8.3   **Text alignment.** *Alignment* describes the text's relationship to the page's margins. Left-aligned text lines up with the page's left margin and has a ragged right edge. Right-aligned text lines up with the page's right margin and has a ragged left edge. Center-aligned text is centered between the left and right margins and has ragged left and right edges. The text of police reports, including headings, should be left-aligned.

14.8.4   **Fonts.** *Font* describes the design of text used in print or on the screen. Your police reporting software may not allow you to change the font, but if you have a choice, stick to a style that is well-known and widely supported. Here are just a few common fonts:

Arial	Helvetica	Times New Roman
Georgia	Tahoma	Verdana

14.8.5   **Font size.** *Font size* describes the size of the characters within a specific font style. The most common font size for body text is 11 or 12 points.[3] Choose one font size and maintain it throughout your report. Do not change font sizes to emphasize headings, subheadings, or other elements of your police reports.

14.8.6   **Tables, graphs, and figures.** Tables, graphs, figures, diagrams, and other visuals can be helpful supplements to your reports, but you should never rely on them to convey your basic description of the incident. If you wish to include any supplemental information, either attach it to your report or include it in your case file. Either way, include in your report a short description of the information and where readers can find it if they need to.

---

[3] A *point* measures the height of a font. One point equals about 1/72 of an inch.

15. Commonly Confused Words

The word pairs presented in this chapter are commonly confused or misused. Since the decision about which word to use largely depends on the context of your writing, basic spelling and grammar checkers may not alert you to possible errors in usage. This chapter is meant to demonstrate common uses of these words, not to offer every definition. For that purpose, consult a reputable dictionary.

A Lot/Allot

A lot means many. *Alot* is a common misspelling of *a lot*, which should always be two words.

> We have a lot of crashes at this intersection.

To[1] *allot* is to assign or distribute.

> I allotted fifteen minutes for each interview.

If you find yourself using *a lot*, well, a lot, you probably need to use more concrete language. "A lot of blood" isn't as clear as "a pool of blood approximately 12 inches in diameter."

---

[1] Words that are preceded by *to* indicate their function as a verb. Since police reports should be written in the past tense, many examples of verbs in this chapter are conjugated in the past tense.

Accept/Except

To *accept* is to receive or agree to something.

The suspect accepted the plea bargain.

Except indicates an exclusion or omission.

The burglar took all the clocks except the one in the hallway.

Adapt/Adopt

To *adapt* is to adjust or change based on circumstances.

She had to adapt her schedule to avoid her ex-husband.

To *adopt* is to take possession of or begin using something.

They adopted their daughter last July.

He adopted a friendlier manner once the handcuffs were on.

Advice/Advise

Advice is information you give to another person, usually in an attempt to help or influence them.

My advice was to keep walking and not look back.

Fastening your seatbelt is sound advice.

To *advise* is to give information, often in an official manner.

I advised him of his Miranda rights.

I advised her to step back or she would be arrested.

As a police officer acting in your official capacity, you advise people of their rights, advise them to leave the area, or advise them to appear in court. A citizen doesn't advise you of their name, advise you the bathroom is down the hall, or advise you that their dog Rufus jumped the fence and hightailed it down the street; they *tell* you these things.

Affect/Effect

To *affect* is to act upon something or someone.

Turning the stove's knob affects its temperature.

An *effect* is a result or consequence of some action.

The effect of touching a hot stove is third-degree burns.

Where these words get confusing is that *affect* is also a noun, used mainly in psychology, that describes someone's expression of emotion.

Despite the news of his son's death, the father had a blunted affect.

To add to the confusion, *effect* is also a verb commonly used in police work. To *effect* is to bring something about.

I effected the arrest.

You can avoid this confusion altogether by writing, "I placed him under arrest," or, even more simply, "I arrested him."

Aid/Aide

To *aid* means to give help or assistance.

first aid

rendering aid

aid and abet

An *aide* is a helper.

the teacher's aide

Neither of these should be confused with *AIDS*, an acronym that stands for acquired immunodeficiency syndrome, the life-threatening medical condition caused by the human immunodeficiency virus (HIV).

All Right/Alright

All right means satisfactory.

He felt all right.

Everything at the scene appeared all right.

Alright is an alternate, but less common, spelling. In informal writing, *alright* is all right, but in professional documents, such as police reports, it's best to stick with the two-word variant.

Allusion/Illusion/Allude/Elude

An *allusion* is an indirect reference to something else. An *illusion* is a deception or error in perception. To *allude* is to make an allusion. To *elude* is to avoid or escape.

If the woman you're speaking with at the scene of a robbery winks and says you may want to check out the guy in the alleyway, she's *alluding* to his involvement in the crime. If you enter the alleyway, find it empty, and turn around to see the woman jumping into a getaway car, you've just fallen for her *illusion*. And when you see the car disappear around the corner, you know she's *eluded* your capture. All of which is just a nice way of saying that you've been duped.

Alternate/Alternative

To *alternate* is to go back and forth between (usually) two different options.

> The traffic light alternated between red and green.

An *alternate* is a substitute.

> I took an alternate route.

You could just as correctly say, "I took an alternative route." While some would argue that the adjectives *alternate* and *alternative* have different meanings, the differences are so obscured in common usage that either is acceptable. One could even say that *alternate* is an acceptable alternative for *alternative*, and vice versa.

Among/Between

You may have been taught in school to use *between* when there are two items and *among* when there are many items:

> The married couple kept the secret between themselves.

> I couldn't find the victim's glasses among the broken beer bottles on the floor.

Unfortunately, actual usage isn't as straightforward. The following sentence contains three items, yet *between* sounds more natural than *among*:

> I couldn't choose between the pizza, sandwich, and fried chicken.

Since *among* and *between* are both used to distinguish one thing from two or more things, they are generally interchangeable, but trust your ear to tell you which is best.

If you intend to indicate something's placement in the middle of two items, then *between* is the clear choice.

> I located the suspect between the Waffle House and the 7-Eleven.[2]

This sentence makes it clear that the ne'er-do-well was located in the area between these two buildings. "I located the suspect among the Waffle House and the 7-Eleven" doesn't make much sense.

Appraise/Apprise

To *appraise* is to estimate the value of something.

> He appraised the ring at $4000.

To *apprise* is to inform, but in most cases, you'd do better just to *tell*.

> I apprised the commander of the situation.

---

[2] Note the correct spelling of the popular convenience store. It is not *7-11*.

I told the commander what happened.

Assure/Ensure/Insure

Although these three words are often—and correctly—used interchangeably, the following guidance will help you avoid confusion. Use *assure* when you are informing someone in a way that increases their confidence.

> I assured her she was safe now that the suspect was in custody.

> I assured him that the ambulance was on its way.

Use *ensure* to indicate a guarantee that something will happen.

> I ensured the handcuffs were double-locked.

Use *insure* for financial purposes.

> She insured her valuables against loss.

Baklava/Balaclava

Baklava is a Middle Eastern pastry filled with nuts and soaked in honey. A *balaclava* is a garment that covers every part of your head and neck except for your eyes.

> The thief removed his balaclava to eat the stolen baklava.

Bare/Bear

Bare means exposed or lacking a covering.

> I saw a bare bone when I examined the wound.

To *bare* is to expose.

> The dog bared its teeth.

To *bear* is to tolerate, sustain, carry, or proceed in a certain direction.

> She couldn't bear the abuse any longer.

> He refused to bear responsibility for his actions.

> He has the right to bear arms.

> Bear right at the detour sign.

A *bear* is a large, hairy animal.

> We discovered that a bear had eaten Rufus.

Blonde/Blond

Blonde and *blond* both refer to a gold, light yellow, or pale brown color, often in the context of human hair. Some people may tell you that *blonde* is reserved for females and *blond* for males, but the terms are interchangeable. Choose one, and remain consistent.

> The woman had blonde hair.

> The suspect was 5′6″ tall with blond hair and blue eyes.

Boarder/Border

A *boarder* lodges somewhere in exchange for money.

> The boarder stole everything when he left.

A *border* is a boundary, such as the line separating countries, states, counties, or private property.

> Crossing the Mexico-US border can be a dangerous journey.

> She cut down the pine trees on the east border of her property.

Brake/Break

To *brake* is to slow down. A *brake* is the object that causes the slowing.

> The driver braked the vehicle by pressing the brake pedal.

To *break* is to interrupt, split into pieces, or cause to malfunction.

> a break from work

> a glass that breaks

> a car that breaks down

Breath/Breathe

To *breathe* is to take oxygen into your lungs by inhaling and exhaling. A *breath* is the air that is inhaled or exhaled.

> Just breathe.

> Take a breath.

> He saw her stop breathing.

Buy/By

To *buy* is to purchase or to accept.

> She didn't see him buy the groceries.

> I didn't buy his story.

By indicates proximity, shows who performs an action, or tells how something is achieved.

> I parked my car by the fire hydrant.

> The letter was written by her ex-husband.

> You won't get by with that kind of effort.

Canvas/Canvass

Both spellings are interchangeable, but *canvas* is typically reserved for the closely woven fabric used for clothing, tents, boat sails, or oil paintings. *Canvass* is most often used to describe the act of going door-to-door to solicit opinions, orders, or information.

> A bear sliced open the tent canvas.

> We canvassed the neighborhood for witnesses.

Capital/Capitol

A *capital* is a city where the seat of government is located. A *capitol* is the building where a legislative body is housed. When referring to a specific capitol building, *capitol* should be capitalized.

> Richmond is the capital of Virginia.

The United States Capitol is closed for repairs.

Many state capitol buildings have gilded domes.

Carat/Karat/Caret/Carrot

A *carat* is a unit of weight used for precious stones. *Karat* and *carat* may both be used to describe the purity of gold.

A 12-carat diamond

24-karat gold

A *caret* (^) is the symbol used by your English teacher to indicate where you've left out a letter, word, or punctuation mark.

A *carrot* is an orange vegetable adored by Bugs Bunny and abhorred by small children.

Casual/Causal

Casual is relaxed or unconcerned.

Casual dress is appropriate for this occasion.

His attitude seemed far too casual given the grim circumstances.

Causal describes something that acted as a cause.

I found no causal factors for the fire.

Chord/Cord

A *chord* is three or more musical notes played together.

The jazz artist played many chords on the piano.

A *cord* is a long, flexible string or rope.

> They secured the Christmas tree to their car with a nylon cord.

> A short in the extension cord caused the fire.

Cite/Sight/Site

To *cite* is to officially call upon someone to appear before a court.

> I cited the woman for littering.

Sight is the ability to see or the thing that is seen.

> He lost his sight three years ago.

> Her family saw popular sights on vacation.

> He adjusted the sights of his rifle.

> The lost dog was quite a sight after being stuck in the brambles all night.

To *sight* is to observe.

> He sighted the target in the distance.

A *site* is a place or setting.

> the site of the disappearance

> the historic site

> our agency's website

Coarse/Course

Coarse means rough in texture or rude in demeanor.

> I scraped my elbow on the coarse wall.

> He spoke coarsely to his children.

A *course* is a route, a pathway, or a series of educational lessons.

> The vehicle took a roundabout course to get to its destination.

> The river follows a long, winding course down the mountain.

> I took a course in human behavior.

Complement/Compliment

A *complement* completes something else.

> Ketchup is a perfect complement to french fries.

A *compliment* is an expression of praise.

> She received many compliments on her high-profile arrest.

> I complimented his choice of shoes.

Something free is *complimentary*.

Conscience/Conscious

Your *conscience* is your inner moral compass.

He couldn't live with his guilty conscience any longer.

Conscious means aware or awake.

He was conscious and breathing.

She lost consciousness on the way to the hospital.

He wasn't conscious of his actions after the crash.

Consequently/Subsequently

Consequently means as a result of.

He is away on vacation; consequently, he will miss his court date.

Subsequently means following closely in time or order.

I saw the wanted subject sitting at the café, so I arrested him and subsequently took him to jail.

Continual/Continuous

Many will try to distinguish these two words, but they are interchangeable. The distinction often made is that *continual* means frequently recurring with short periods of interruption, while *continuous* means uninterrupted. Whichever word you choose, be consistent, and rely on your ear for specific use cases.

I saw continual foot traffic at the house.

I saw continuous foot traffic at the house.

Corps/Corpse

A *corps* is a group of people acting under a common direction.

> Marine Corps

> Peace Corps

A *corpse* is a dead body.

Counsel/Council

To *counsel* is to advise.

> She counseled her daughter to return home.

Your *counsel* is your attorney, who also provides you with *counsel*.

> Defense counsel was not present in the courtroom.

> His attorney provided the best counsel she could, but he still refused the plea deal.

A *council* is an advisory or formal legislative body that meets regularly.

> the town council

> the Chief's Advisory Council

Cue/Queue

A *cue* is a signal intended to begin an action.

> Upon receiving his cue from the lookout, the thief pried open the register.

A *cue* is also the long wooden stick with a felt tip used to play pool or initiate bar fights.

A *queue* is a line of people or objects waiting to be attended to.

> The bakery queue extended around the corner.

> I added the song to my queue.

Descent/Dissent/Decent

Descent is the act of moving downward.

> The trail has a descent of 800 feet.

> He fell during his descent of the stairwell.

Descent also refers to someone's origin or background.

> He is of Italian descent.

Dissent is an opinion that differs from common or official beliefs. To *dissent* is to differ in opinion.

> There were many voices of dissent at the town meeting.

> The judge dissented from the majority opinion.

Something is *decent* when it conforms to respectable standards and behaviors.

> Every child deserves to live in a decent home.

Dessert/Desert

Dessert is the sweet course you eat after dinner. A *desert* is an arid land with little vegetation. To *desert* is to abandon.

When the rain came, everyone deserted the beach.

The simple way to distinguish between *dessert* and *desert* is to remember that a dessert is sweeter than a desert, hence the reason *dessert* is spelled with an extra *s*.

Device/Devise

A *device* is something made for a specific purpose, especially a piece of mechanical or electronic equipment.

I use my cellular device to make phone calls.

She tossed the GPS device into the river.

To *devise* is to plan or invent something through careful thought.

He devised a plan for his escape.

Die/Dye

To *die* is to stop living. Figuratively, to *die* is to want something very much.

He died on a Tuesday.

She'd rather die than miss the concert.

Dye is the chemical used to change the color of fabric, hair, or other material. To *dye* is to change the color of something using a dye.

tie-dye

He dyed his hair to evade detection.

Disassociate/Dissociate

Disassociate and *dissociate* both mean to cease associating, but *dissociate* is the more common spelling.

> Once the school board learned of the criminal charges, they dissociated themselves from the teacher.

Discreet/Discrete

A *discreet* person is careful, prudent, or private.

> He was discreet about what he did at work.

> My discreet outfit helped me blend into the crowd.

> The shoplifter tried to be discreet, but security cameras still caught her in the act.

Things that are separate and distinct are *discrete*.

> The aggravated assault and the overdue child support payments were discrete issues.

Disinterested/Uninterested

Someone is *disinterested* when they are impartial (i.e., they don't have a vested interest in a matter; i.e., they don't have a dog in the fight). Someone is *uninterested* when they couldn't care less. You want your judge to be disinterested. You want the cop sitting on the side of the road to be uninterested when you drive by at twenty over the speed limit.

Dual/Duel

Dual means consisting of two parts or elements.

> dual citizenship

> dual purpose

A *duel* is a long-illegal contest between two people using deadly weapons. To *duel* is to engage in a duel.

Eminent/Imminent

Something *eminent* is noteworthy or prominent.

> an eminent guest

Something *imminent* is impending or ready to happen.

> We are in imminent danger of being hit by a hurricane.

> imminent threat of serious bodily injury or death

Envelop/Envelope

To *envelop* is to wrap up, cover, or surround.

> The mother enveloped her baby in a blanket.

An *envelope* is a folded paper container used to mail letters.

Evoke/Invoke

To *evoke* is to call forth, as with memories or emotions.

> The smell of cut grass evokes memories of my childhood.

To *invoke* is to call upon, usually in reference to a law, a right, or authority.

> He invoked his Fifth Amendment right.

> After being accused of murder, she invoked her right to an attorney.

Exercise/Exorcise

Exercise is the act of physical exertion that most of us would benefit from doing more regularly. To *exercise* is to engage in physical activity, but it can also refer to the act of using something generally.

> She exercised her First Amendment right by joining the protest.

> He exercised his authority by firing the employee.

To *exorcise* is to drive out an evil spirit from a person or place.

Explicit/Implicit

When something is *explicit*, it is definite and unambiguous.

> She made explicit her message that she no longer wanted to speak with me.

Swear words and certain sexual materials adopt the term *explicit* because they are unambiguous in their meaning and expression.

Quite the opposite of explicit, *implicit* refers to something implied or understood only because of its relationship to something else.

> She didn't explicitly say he could borrow the car, but handing him the car keys sent an implicit message.

Fair/Fare

Something is *fair* when it is done by the rules.

> The verdict was harsh but fair.

Fair can also mean light or blond, such as someone with a fair complexion.

A *fair* is a public event where you can find farm animals, carnival games, hot dogs, nauseating rides, and screaming children all in one location.

A *fare* refers to the money passengers pay for transportation or to the passengers themselves.

> He refused to pay the bus fare.

> The taxi driver picked up his fare on the corner.

Fare can also refer to a particular type of food.

> The restaurant has fancy decor and expensive fare.

> I only eat vegan fare.

To *fare* is to get along in a particular situation.

> The sheriff fared poorly in this election.

Farther/Further

Although both words are often used interchangeably, *farther* should be reserved for describing physical distance, while *further* should be used for differences of degree or quantity.

The bank is farther than the grocery store.

We settled the argument without further discussion.

To *further* is to advance.

This promotion will further my career.

Faze/Phase

To *faze* is to disturb.

Getting hit by the car didn't seem to faze him.

A *phase* is a stage.

She completed the second phase of her training.

Flair/Flare

Flair describes a certain level of stylishness or ability.

She dressed with flair.

He has a flair for photography.

A *flare* is a sudden burst of light or a device that causes the burst of light. To *flare* is to burn with sudden intensity.

I saw the flare from the explosion.

I lit a road flare.

The fire flared when he added lighter fluid.

Flier/Flyer

Flier and *flyer* can both be used to refer to someone who flies and to the paper handout advertising an event or product.

> She is a nervous flier.

> frequent-flyer

> She recognized him from the missing person flyer.

Forego/Forgo

Forego means to go before.

> Dinner foregoes dessert.

> Probable cause foregoes a warrant.

Forgo means to go without.

> I'll forgo dessert because I'm on a diet.

> For some crimes, you can forgo a written warrant.

You can remember that *forgo* means to go without because *forgo* "goes without" the letter *e*.

Formally/Formerly

Formally means officially or in accordance with proper etiquette.

> The detective formally announced her retirement on Monday.

> Dress formally for the annual awards banquet.

Formerly refers to things in the past.

His new wife was formerly his ex-wife's best friend.

Forth/Fourth

Forth means onward from a given point.

From that day forth, we were best friends.

Fourth is the ordinal of the number four.

He is in the fourth grade.

Hangar/Hanger

A *hangar* houses airplanes. A *hanger* suspends your clothes from the rod in your closet. A person who hangs things, such as windows or doors, is also a *hanger*. Someone who hangs another person until dead is a hangman, an executioner, or a murderer.

Hanged/Hung

Hanged and *hung* are both the past tense of to *hang*. *Hanged* is reserved for those times when a person is suspended by a rope around the neck. *Hung* is used for everything else that might reasonably be hung, such as picture frames, potted plants, televisions, etc. Someone allowed to be criticized unfairly has been "hung out to dry."

Home In/Hone

To *home in* is to find or get closer to.

I homed in on my opponent's weakness.

To *hone* is to sharpen, whether it be a metal blade or a particular skill. You don't *hone in* on anything.

> He honed the knife.

> I honed my public speaking skills.

Imply/Infer

To *imply* is to make a suggestion without explicitly stating something.

> His body language implied he was done talking.

To *infer* is to make a conclusion based on information that is not explicitly stated.

> Based on her statements, I inferred that she had dementia.

The easy way to keep these two words straight is by remembering that implying comes from the person giving the information, while inferring happens from the person receiving it.

Internment/Interment

Internment is the act of confining someone, usually during wartime.

> During World War II, the internment of Japanese Americans was widespread.

Interment is the act of burial.

> A person's interment happens within a few days of their death.

Later/Latter

Later refers to time; *latter* refers to a sequence, specifically to the last of two items.

I will call him later.

She could either accept the plea deal or go to trial; she chose the latter.

I collected the victim's pants and shirt, the latter of which was covered in blood.

Lay/Lie

Lay and *lie* are two of the more infamous culprits in the world of usage errors. The simple rule is easy enough: to *lay* is to put or to place; to *lie* is to recline. The key here is that *lay* requires you to specify what exactly is put or placed (i.e., a direct object), while *lie* does not.

"Lay down the knife!"

The man lays his blanket on the grass.

now I lay me down to sleep

She is going to lie down.

The man is lying on his blanket.

In the first two examples, the knife and the blanket are the objects being placed down (*laid* down, as it were). In the third example, the person places himself or herself down to sleep. In the final two examples, nothing is being placed by anyone: both people are entering a state of repose.

Things get confusing when you conjugate these verbs because the past participle of *lay* is *laid*, and the past participle of *lie* is *lay*. If all this makes you dizzy (go lie down), keep the following charts nearby when you have to conjugate these verbs.

Of course, nothing here is to be confused with *lie*, in the sense of telling a falsehood or omitting the truth. In this case, one *lies* or *is lying* (present), *lied* (past), *will lie* (future), and *had/has/will have lied* (perfect).

Conjugations of "to Lay"

	Simple	Progressive	Perfect
Past			
I		was laying	
he/she/it	laid		had laid
you/we/they		were laying	
Present			
I		am laying	
you/we/they	lay	are laying	have laid
he/she/it	lays	is laying	has laid
Future			
I			
you/we/they	will lay	will be laying	will have laid
he/she/it			

Conjugations of "to Lie"

Past	Simple	Progressive	Perfect
I	lay/lied	was lying	had lain/lied
he/she/it			
you/we/they		were lying	
Present			
I	lie	am lying	have lain/lied
you/we/they		are lying	
he/she/it	lies	is lying	has lain/lied
Future			
I	will lie	will be lying	will have lain/lied
you/we/they			
he/she/it			

Lead/Led

To *lead* is to guide the course of another, whether by influence or physical means. *Led* is the past tense of *lead*.

She leads the company.

He led the dog to the backyard.

Lead is the chemical element used in batteries, ammunition, and some paints.

lead exposure

lead poisoning

Lightening/Lightning

Lightening is the act of making something lighter.

> He is lightening his hair color.

> lightening the load in the vehicle

Lightning is the electrical discharge that occurs during thunderstorms.

Loose/Lose

Loose is the opposite of tight.

> My pants are too loose.

> A loose bolt caused the crash.

To *lose* is to fail to win or maintain, to misplace, or to rid oneself of something. To distinguish these words, remember that *lose* has lost its second *o*.

> She will lose the custody dispute.

> He tends to lose his balance.

> I always lose my phone.

> I'd like to lose 20 pounds.

Maybe/May Be

Maybe is synonymous with *perhaps* or *possibly*.

> Maybe I'll go to work, or maybe I won't.

The verb phrase *may be* is synonymous with *might be*.

She may be in town Sunday for an interview.

Miner/Minor

A *miner* works in a mine. A *minor* is someone who is under the legal age of adulthood. Something *minor* is of lesser importance.

charged as a minor

a minor setback

Mucous/Mucus

Mucous and *mucus* both deal with the thick liquid that forms inside your nose when you have allergies or a cold. *Mucous* is an adjective.

He had an inflamed mucous membrane.

Mucus is a noun.

My excess mucus made me realize I was sick.

Ordinance/Ordnance

An *ordinance* is a law, usually in the form of a municipal regulation.

A local ordinance prohibits riding skateboards on sidewalks.

Ordnance refers to military weapons and ammunition.

The military base has bombs, missiles, and other ordnance.

Passed/Past

Passed is the past tense of the verb to *pass.*

She passed the ball.

He passed the exam.

I passed the slow-moving vehicle.

Past refers to the time period before the present moment or to relative locations.

Leave the disagreement in the past.

the tree just past the horse stables

Patience/Patients

Patience is your ability to wait or endure hardship. It is what "wears thin" when you become irritated. *Patients* are the people in the reception area waiting to see the doctor, an activity which, incidentally, requires patience.

Peace/Piece

Peace is the absence of war (or any lesser conflict). A *piece* is part of a whole, such as a piece of pie.

Peak/Peek/Pique

A *peak* is a mountaintop or pinnacle. To *peak* is to reach the highest point in time or value. (Counterintuitively, reaching the top of a mountain is not usually referred to as *peaking* but as *summiting* or, less formally, *bagging a peak.*)

The actor peaked at a young age.

I am currently at my peak fitness.

To *peek* is to look quickly and secretly.

I peeked into the window.

To *pique* is to create interest, curiosity, or irritation.

The anonymous letter piqued my curiosity.

Her rejection piqued him.

Pedal/Peddle

A *pedal* is a foot-operated lever used to operate a bicycle, car, or other vehicle. To *pedal* is to work the pedals.

He pedaled vigorously to escape the charging dog.

To *peddle* is to sell something from place to place.

They peddled stolen stereo equipment from the back of their van.

Personal/Personnel

Personal means private or individual, as in "personal space." *Personnel* are the people who are employed by an organization.

Plain/Plane

Something is *plain* when it is simple or ordinary, which makes it clear why a large, flat area of land with no trees is also called a *plain*.

It was plain to me.

plain black wallet

Plane is short for *airplane*. It is also the name of one of several instruments used to smooth and shape wood.

Pore/Pour/Poor

A *pore* is a small opening in your skin. To *pore* is to read or study carefully.

He pored over case law in preparation for his exam.

To *pour* is to dispense a substance, usually a liquid.

She poured the poison down the drain.

To be *poor* is to be needy, impoverished, inadequate, or inferior.

The poor dog needed a bath.

Welfare assists those in poor circumstances.

She gave a poor excuse for being late to work.

His test results were too poor to qualify him for the SWAT team.

Precede/Proceed

To *precede* is to come before.

She preceded me into the room.

To *proceed* is to continue or begin again.

The detective proceeded with the investigation.

After securing the permits, construction proceeded.

Prescribe/Proscribe

To *prescribe* is to authorize the use of, such as in the form of a medical prescription. To *proscribe* is to forbid, especially by law.

> Felons are proscribed from owning firearms.

Presence/Present/Presents

Presence is the state of existing, occurring, or being present.

> Don't smoke in the presence of children.

> Your presence is requested.

> He noted each student's presence in class.

To *present* is to award or introduce formally.

> The academy director presented the new officer with her certificate.

> The lawyer presented his client to the detective.

Presents are gifts.

Prone/Supine

Someone *prone* is lying face down. Someone *supine* is lying face up. *Prone* also means having a tendency toward, while *supine* suggests willful inactivity or lethargy.

> The body was prone in the alley.

> He is prone to violence.

Prosecute/Persecute

To *prosecute* is to initiate legal proceedings.

> They were prosecuted for counterfeiting United States currency.

To *persecute* is to subject someone to hostility, often on account of their race, religion, or political beliefs.

> Pilgrims were persecuted for their religious beliefs.

Quiet/Quite

If these words are confused, it is often due to an accidental transposing of the last two letters. Something is *quiet* when it makes very little noise. *Quite* means wholly or completely. When paired with *not*, it means not wholly or not completely.

> I am quite happy with the result.

> She was not quite sure how the stolen wallet ended up in her purse.

Rain/Reign/Rein

Rain is moisture that descends from the sky. *Reign* refers to the period during which a ruling monarch is in power. A *rein* is a long strap that connects to a horse's bit and allows the rider to control its movements. To *rein* means to restrain or control.

> He found it impossible to rein in his unruly teenager.

Raise/Rise/Raze

To *raise* is to lift, elevate, grow, or promote. A *raise* is a salary increase.

> I raised my hand.

> He raised her from a young age.

> We weren't aware of the issue until she raised it.

> They voted to give everyone a 2% raise.

To *rise* is to move from a lower position to a higher one.

> I saw him rise from the couch.

> Most people rise for the National Anthem.

A *rise* is an increase in amount, extent, size, or number.

> Citizens were concerned with the rise in violent crime.

To *raze* is to destroy a building, town, or other site completely.

> They plan to raze the shopping center to make room for new townhomes.

Right/Rite/Write

Right describes that which is righteous, correct, or appropriate. *Right* also indicates direction.

> right vs. wrong

> Make the right choice.

Take your second right after the light.

A *right* is something due to a person under the law.

Americans are entitled to certain fundamental rights.

Bill of Rights

A *rite* is a ceremonial act often found in religions.

initiation rites

last rites

To *write* is to put down thoughts in words.

Set/Sit

To *set* is to place.

I know I set my laptop right here.

To *sit* is to be seated.

Sit on the curb.

Similar to *lay/lie*, *set* requires a direct object (i.e., something being set down), while *sit* does not. If you are struggling to know which word to use, try replacing it with *place*. If your sentence makes sense, the correct word is likely *set*; if not, go with *sit*.

Shone/Shown

Shone is the past participle of *shine*.

The sun shone brightly despite the cloud cover.

Shown is the past participle of *show*, which means to display or cause to be visible.

> When he was shown the photographs from the crime scene, he confessed.

Stationary/Stationery

Stationary describes a person or object that is unmoving.

> I crashed my car into a stationary vehicle.

Stationery is letterhead and other fine paper products.

> Please submit your request on official stationery.

Straight/Strait

Straight means level, upright, not bent, extending in the same direction, accurate, or honest.

> He drew a straight line.

> She was a straight shooter.

As an adverb, *straight* means directly.

> He ran straight to his mother.

A *strait* is a narrow waterway.

> Many killer whales live in the Strait of Georgia.

Tenant/Tenet

A *tenant* is a person who rents land or property from a landlord.

> The landlord collects monthly rent from his tenants.

A *tenet* is a centrally-held belief.

> Decentralization of command is a major tenet of community-based policing.

Than/Then

Than is used in comparisons.

> She is taller than me.

> He said he took more drugs than his friend.

Then indicates time.

> I didn't believe him then; I don't believe him now.

> We'll have to wait until then.

Then is not a conjunction, although it is sometimes used as one in short, parallel sentences.

> I spoke to him, then to her.

That/Which/Who

Most of the discussion around *that* and *which* comes when either word is called upon to introduce a clause. In these cases, you must first determine if the clause is essential or non-essential to the meaning of your sentence (see 13.2.3). When introducing a non-essential clause, use *which*. When introducing an essential clause, use either *that* or *which*, but remain consistent.

> The window, which was broken, has been repaired.

> The window that was broken has been repaired.

The window which was broken has been repaired.

Another issue with *that* arises when it introduces a clause about a person. In these cases, *which* is out of the question. Choose between *that* and *who*. Generally, either is acceptable.

the man that broke his arm

the man who broke his arm

Threw/Through/Thru

Threw is the past tense of *throw*, which means to cause something to move through the air.

He threw me the ball.

Through indicates movement from one side to the other.

We drove through the tunnel.

I went through the Miranda warning one more time.

Thru is an informal spelling of *through*. Although *thru* has gained more acceptance in informal writing, *through* is still preferred in formal documents such as police reports.

To/Too

To means toward or until.

I responded to the bank.

Medics transported her to the hospital.

I pursued the suspect to the county line.

Too means excessively or also.

> I ate too much food.

> I felt sick, too.

Track/Tract

A *track* is a path, course, or footprint.

> the track leading to the farm

> a racetrack

> track lighting

> a huge animal track

To *track* is to follow.

> She tracked her package online.

> The K-9 tracked the suspect.

A *tract* is an area of land, a system of body parts, or that pamphlet left on your door by religious representatives.

> urinary tract

> He purchased a tract of 162 acres.

Waive/Wave

To *waive* is to voluntarily give up a right, to refrain from enforcing, or to set aside temporarily.

> She waived her right to an attorney.

> The bank waived the overdraft fee.

He signed the liability waiver.

To *wave* is to move back and forth repeatedly.

A citizen waved me down.

A *wave* is a curled arch of water that surfers catch.

Who's/Whose

Who's is a conjunction of *who is* or *who has*.

Who's at the door?

Who's lied about their alibi?

Whose is a pronoun used to indicate possession.

Whose shoes are those?

I identified the suspect whose prints matched those at the scene.

Part V
Writing Aids and Resources

Policing can be a solitary profession. It is not un-common for police officers to handle an entire call for service without the aid of another officer. Even if the luxury of backup is available, when it comes time to write a police report or testify in court, you are individual-ly accountable for your actions.

Although no one else can write your police reports, you don't have to write them without assistance. These chapters provide assistance in the form of tools and exam-ples. Chapter 16 presents a systematic and practical writ-ing process. Chapter 17 takes the form of a workbook, walking you through the process of crafting a police re-port from start to finish. Chapter 18 provides checklists to help you remember relevant facts for numerous types of incidents. Chapter 19 gives model phrases that can be transposed into your report. Finally, chapter 20 presents three finished police reports that will help you see how the material in this book combines into a finished product.

16. The Writing Process

16.1   The Six-Step Writing Process

16.1.1   Just write

16.1.2   Revise using the COPS Method

16.1.3   Read it out loud or let a friend read it

16.1.4   Let it rest

16.1.5   Reread it

16.1.6   Submit it

16.2   The COPS Method

16.2.1   Content

16.2.2   Organization

16.2.3   Punctuation/Spelling/Grammar

16.2.4   Style

Your writing process need not be lengthy or complicated; with the demands of police work, it's better if it's not. Since you may be required to write many reports each shift, you will quickly find yourself underneath a stack of pending reports if you don't follow a standardized writing process. Remember, the goal is not to write a perfect report, only to write an effective one: your report is a product required by your employer, not a submission for the Pulitzer Prize. This book has taught you how to write effective police reports; this chapter will teach you how to do so efficiently.

16.1   The Six-Step Writing Process

In reality, the writing process begins before you ever sit down to write. As explained in Chapter 3, the effectiveness of your reports truly starts with the effectiveness of your policing. But once you begin writing, a standardized process will make it easier to get your thoughts down on paper. Such a process is summarized with six words: *Write–Revise–Read–Rest–Reread–Submit.*

The Six-Step Writing Process

1. Just **write**

2. **Revise** using the COPS Method

3. **Read** it out loud or let a friend read it

4. Let it **rest**

5. **Reread** it

6. **Submit** it

16.1.1   **Just write.** Many people struggle to write because they try to put everything down on paper perfectly the first time. No matter how experienced a writer you are, this is an impossible task. Despite all the rules and guidelines in this book, the best thing you can do when you write is to push all this information to the back of your mind and focus on getting a rough draft down on paper.

This advice isn't as easy to follow as you may think. You'll still have those voices in the back of your head questioning what you've written, and you'll still have questions you'd like to look up in this book. That's okay. Just focus on writing a basic first draft. If you get stuck at a certain point, or if you run across grammatical questions, mark the spot with three asterisks (***) and move on. You can come back to these parts later. During this step, focus solely on getting a rough draft written, no matter how terrible it may be.

16.1.2   **Revise using the COPS Method.** Most officers write their first draft, glance it over once, and then submit it. You will avoid many mistakes—and much time spent correcting them—if you immediately put your first draft through a thorough revision. Doing this will allow you to fill holes in your narrative while the details of the incident remain fresh in your mind. The COPS Method, explained in section 16.2, is a comprehensive model that helps you accomplish this. In addition to the COPS Method, consider writing your reports in a software program with a reliable grammar and spelling checker, such as Microsoft Word. This will help you catch and correct many errors. Once it's time to submit your report, copy and paste it into your agency's reporting software.

16.1.3   **Read it out loud or let a friend read it.** Once you've finished a thorough revision, it's time to get a different perspective on your writing. If you have a trusted friend who can spare the time, consider having them read through what you've written and offer their feedback. One word of caution: you are ultimately responsible for any content in your reports. Don't fall into the trap of letting your friend rewrite portions of your report for you. Instead, ask them for suggestions, and then make changes based on what you agree with. If there were places in your draft you marked with asterisks, ask them to focus specifically on those areas. Also, ensure that whoever reads your report is another sworn police officer who is allowed to view the information you have written about.

It's probably impractical to have someone else read every report you write, especially if they have their own reports to complete, so another option is to read your report out loud. Don't just mouth the words; read aloud at a normal volume. This will force you to slow down, read every word, and allow your brain to process how your writing sounds to the natural ear. If you hear something confusing or awkward, or if you stumble over your words, it's a signal that your report isn't written as clearly as it should be. Go back and revise.

16.1.4   **Let it rest.** By this point, you have read your report at least three different times: once while you were writing it, once using the COPS Method, and once as you reviewed your friend's suggestions or read your report out loud. You probably now have a solid report in front of you, but it's not yet time to submit it.

As you have read what you have written, your brain has filled gaps in your writing, whether those gaps were omitted words or missing relevant facts. What sounds complete and accurate to you now may sound different when you review your report months in the future or when your readers see your report for the first time. To account for this, let your report rest, even for just ten minutes, before doing a final read-through. Grab a bite to eat, use the restroom, chat with a coworker, or find some other distraction. This will allow your brain to rest and you to view your report with fresh eyes when you return.

16.1.5   **Reread it.** After letting your report rest, conduct a final reading. The purpose of this is not to scrutinize the smaller details—you've already done that using the COPS Method—but to ensure your report flows naturally from beginning to end. During this final reading, pretend that you have no knowledge of the incident or that you are reading this report months in the future, after you have forgotten many of the details. Ensure that your report can stand alone as a clear description of what happened during the incident. Of course, if you catch any minor errors, you should correct those too.

16.1.6   **Submit it.** After you have followed the five steps discussed above, it's time to submit your report. Remember, no report is perfect. Even after giving your best effort, your report may still contain minor grammatical errors or sections that could have been written more clearly. This is understandable. With every report comes a point of diminishing returns, where the effort you put into revising it is not worth the minimal improvements such revisions would bring.

If you have given your best effort to writing the most effective report you could, submit it with confidence. But keep in mind that some of your readers may have additional revisions. Be open to this feedback as part of your ongoing efforts to be as effective a writer as possible, and be prepared to make changes to your report based on this feedback.

16.2   The COPS Method

As part of your writing process, you should thoroughly revise every aspect of your report. You can use the COPS Method to make this daunting task more manageable. COPS is an acronym that makes it easy to remember the major areas you should focus on while revising your reports. COPS stands for *Content*, *Organization*, *Punctuation/Spelling/Grammar*, and *Style*.

16.2.1   **Content.** Content is the meat of your report. It includes all the relevant facts necessary to answer your readers' questions. You should ask yourself:

- Did I answer my readers' questions? (see Chapter 2)
- Did I include the *facts relevant to every incident*? (see 4.2.2)
- Did I include all other relevant facts? (see Chapters 1, 2, 4, and 18)
- Did I accurately quote and paraphrase statements? (see 9.4)

16.2.2   **Organization.** Organization includes the structure of your report and how well your report guides readers from beginning to end. You should ask yourself:

- Did I write in officer-chronological order? (see Chapter 5)
- Does my report guide readers along a clear fact pattern toward a reasonable conclusion? (see Chapter 5)
- Is my report organized into an effective narrative structure? (see Chapter 6)
- If necessary, does my report use section headings? (see 6.1.2)

16.2.3   **Punctuation/Spelling/Grammar.** Punctuation, spelling, and grammar include how well you used the rules of the English language to describe your incident. You should ask yourself:

- Have I used a reliable grammar/spell checker? (see 16.1.2)
- Have I looked for commonly confused words? (see Chapter 15)

- Have I constructed my sentences clearly? (see Chapters 11 and 12)
- Have I used proper grammar? (see Chapters 11 and 12)
- Have I used punctuation properly? (see Chapter 13)

16.2.4   **Style.** Style is all about how well the decisions you made as a writer increased the clarity of your report. You should ask yourself:

- Did I write in the first person, past tense, active voice? (see Chapter 7)
- Did I use action-reaction sequences? (see Chapter 8)
- Did I write from my senses? (see Chapter 8)
- Did I describe people, places, and things consistently? (see Chapter 9)
- Did I write concisely? (see Chapter 7)
- Did I adopt an appropriate, professional tone? (see Chapters 7 and 14)

The COPS Method

C — Content
- Did I answer my readers' questions?
- Did I include the *facts relevant to every incident*?
- Did I include all other relevant facts?
- Did I accurately quote and paraphrase statements?

O — Organization
- Did I write in officer-chronological order?
- Does my report guide readers along a clear fact pattern toward a reasonable conclusion?
- Is my report organized into an effective narrative structure?
- If necessary, does my report use section headings?

P — Punctuation/Spelling/Grammar
- Have I used a reliable grammar/spell checker?
- Have I looked for commonly confused words?
- Have I constructed my sentences clearly?
- Have I used proper grammar?
- Have I used punctuation properly?

S — Style
- Did I write in the first person, past tense, active voice?
- Did I use action-reaction sequences?
- Did I write from my senses?
- Did I describe people, places, and things consistently?
- Did I write concisely?
- Did I adopt an appropriate, professional tone?

17. Report Writing Walkthrough

17.1 **Description of Police Incident**

17.2 **Preparing to Write**

    17.2.1 Getting to know your readers

    17.2.2 Identifying relevant facts

17.3 **Organizing Your Information**

    17.3.1 Guiding your readers

    17.3.2 Structuring your report

17.4 **Writing Your Report**

    17.4.1 Style guidelines

    17.4.2 Describing your observations

    17.4.3 Describing your actions

    17.4.4 Describing people, places, and things

17.5 **Sample Report with Annotations**

    17.5.1 Sample report

    17.5.2 Annotations

This chapter takes a sample police incident and guides you through the report writing process using what you have learned in this book. This chapter will be most helpful if you imagine yourself as the officer who responds to the imaginary incident described in the first section. After reading the incident description, complete the exercises in the sections that follow. Refer to the indicated chapters when you need help. After completing these exercises, read the sample report provided at the end of this chapter. See if there are things you would have done differently if you had been required to write this report in real life.

17.1   Description of Police Incident

The following incident describes a shoplifting case where the suspect is identified and issued a citation. The purpose of using a basic example like this is to demonstrate how the rules, guidelines, and techniques described in this book are relevant to even the simplest of incidents. As you read the following description, consider how you would apply what you have learned in this book to document this incident effectively.

> On April 5, 2023, at 2:37 p.m., you are dispatched to a local electronics store, Best Electronics. The store manager, Ms. Delores Ruiz, has called the police non-emergency number to report a shoplifting. You learn through dispatch that Ms. Ruiz confronted the shoplifter, and he is now sitting in the manager's office waiting for police to arrive.
>
> After arriving at Best Electronics, you speak to Ms. Ruiz. She tells you that the suspect entered the store, concealed something down the front of his pants, and then walked past the cash registers without paying. Immediately upon being confronted by Ms. Ruiz, the suspect apologized and pulled two stolen Blu-ray discs from his pants.
>
> You speak to the suspect, whom you identify as Mr. Norman Terry. He confesses to stealing, stating, "I didn't have enough money to buy them, so I decided to steal them." While interviewing Mr. Terry, you notice his belt is unbuckled, and you observe what

looks like an object concealed down his right pant leg. Fearing this could be a weapon, you pat him down. When you touch the object, you can tell its shape is consistent with a DVD case. You ask Mr. Terry what it is, and he tells you it is another stolen disc. You remove the disc from his pants.

You now have a total of three stolen items: 1) *Sopranos: The Complete Series* (Blu-ray, $58.99), 2) *Identity Thief* (Blu-ray, $9.99), and 3) *Gone in 60 Seconds* (DVD, $8.99).

All the movies appear to be undamaged, so you photograph them and return them to Ms. Ruiz. You believe you have enough probable cause to charge Mr. Terry with larceny. In your jurisdiction, this offense is chargeable with a written citation, so you complete the paperwork, issue Mr. Terry the ticket, and mark yourself in service for other calls.

17.2 Preparing to Write

17.2.1 **Getting to know your readers.** Before you write, consider who will be interested in reading this report. Remember, your readers read your reports because they need the information to do their jobs. Who would be interested in an incident where a crime was committed and a suspect was charged?

A list of potential readers and their questions is started for you on the next page. Use the blank lines to fill in additional questions that these readers may ask. Additionally, see if you can identify one more reader who may be interested in this incident. Lastly, don't forget about the most important reader of your report: *you*. Try to develop three questions that will be important for you to answer when you read your report in the future. If you need help, refer to Chapter 2.

Your supervisor

- Did you make a lawful arrest?
- Did you follow proper procedures for issuing a citation?
- Do I need to notify anyone about the incident?
- _____

Prosecutor/defense attorney

- Was there probable cause for the arrest?
- Is the confession admissible in court?
- Is any restitution owed to the victim?
- _____

Crime analyst

- Are other crimes linked to this suspect?
- _____
- _____

(*Reader*) _____

- _____
- _____
- _____

You

- _____
- _____
- _____

17.2.2   **Identifying relevant facts.** Facts become relevant when they help your readers answer their questions. At a minimum, your report must contain the *facts relevant to every incident* (see 4.2.2). Additionally, your report must include whatever facts are necessary to support the general facts required by your incident. This section uses a T-Chart to outline the relevant general facts and some corresponding incident facts. Fill in the missing incident facts on the right side of the chart. Since this example incident is similar to the one presented in Chapter 4, you may find it helpful to refer to section 4.2.5 if you need additional guidance.

Incident Synopsis

I responded to a shoplifting of merchandise at Best Electronics. The suspect was detained by the store manager. I obtained a confession and charged the suspect with larceny by issuing him a citation.

General Facts	Incident Facts
Facts relevant to every incident:	
When did the incident take place?	05 April 2023 at 1437 hours
Where did the incident take place?	Best Electronics (17 Valley Circle, Fairtown, VA)
Who was involved?	*Complainant:* Best Electronics Store Manager Ms. Delores Ruiz *Suspect:* Mr. Norman Terry

What brought police to the scene?	Dispatched to a report of a shoplifting in progress.
What should happen now?	Case cleared by arrest. No follow-up action needed.

Elements of the crime of shoplifting:

willfully taking

_____

_____

_____

merchandise

_____

_____

_____

from a store

_____

_____

without paying

_____

_____

with the intent of converting the goods to one's personal use

_____

_____

_____

_____

17.3   Organizing Your Information

17.3.1   **Guiding your readers.** Now that you have identified the relevant facts of this incident, take a moment to put them into officer-chronological order. Refer to Chapter 5 for more information.

1. _____

2. _____

3. _____

4. _____

5. _____

6. _____

7. _____

8. _____

9. _____

10. _____

11. _____

12. _____

17.3.2   **Structuring your report.** If you have completed the exercise above, you now have a list of the relevant facts in the order you experienced them. Begin structuring your report by writing these facts in the blank area under each heading on the following page. If one heading contains multiple facts, you can organize them using subheadings. Refer to the section numbers next to each heading for more guidance.

Pre-Arrival (see 6.2.2)

Initial Investigation (see 6.2.3)

Follow-Up Investigation (see 6.2.4)

Administrative Actions (see 6.2.5)

Case Disposition (see 6.2.6)

Since pre-arrival information follows a standardized format, take a moment to complete the first sentence of your report by filling in the missing information below. Refer to the indicated sections for more details about how to format the information in this sentence.

On _____ at_____,
      date (see 14.6.6)   time (see 14.6.7)

I was dispatched to _____
                          location (see 9.5.1–9.5.3)

for a/an _____ _____
            incident type (see 4.2.2)   *in progress/report*

With this pre-writing information prepared, you are now ready to begin writing your report.

17.4 Writing Your Report

17.4.1 **Style guidelines.** As you begin transforming the outline you created in section 17.3.2 into a long-form narrative, keep in mind the style guidelines presented in Chapter 7. Based on the advice provided in that chapter, here are just a few things to consider as you begin to write:

- The sample incident presented in section 17.1 is written in the second-person present tense. How will you rewrite the incident in the first-person past tense?

- The sample incident states that the stolen items "appear to be undamaged." This is a conclusion. How did you come to this conclusion? Are there enough facts to support it? Did you draw this conclusion through your observations, or did the store manager tell you the items were undamaged? How will you document this important information in your final report?

- How will you remain consistent when referring to the stolen Blu-ray discs? Will you refer to them as "stolen merchandise," "stolen discs," "stolen property," or something else?

- You developed enough probable cause during your investigation to charge your suspect with shoplifting. What is the simplest way to write a sentence about this decision in your report?

17.4.2 **Describing your observations.** This incident contains a few observations that are essential to your case: Mr. Terry's unbuckled belt, the object concealed down his pant leg, and what you felt during your pat down. Reread the example police incident and determine how you will articulate these observations using sensory language instead of phrases like "I noticed" and "I could tell." Refer to section 8.1 for assistance.

While speaking with Mr. Terry, I saw _____

_____

_____

_____

During my pat down of Mr. Terry, I felt_____

_____

_____

_____

17.4.3 **Describing your actions.** You will need to use action-reaction sequences to describe your interviews with Ms. Ruiz and Mr. Terry. These are simple. Begin with a sentence introducing the interview, and then present their statement without interruption. See if you can use this formula to fill in their statements below. Refer to sections 8.2 and 9.4 if you need assistance.

I spoke with Ms. Ruiz. She told me _____

_____

_____

_____

I interviewed Mr. Terry. He said _____

_____

_____

_____

Your description of your pat down of Mr. Terry will contain a few more actions and reactions. To build this sequence, think about what action or observation led to your first reaction. Fill in the blanks with your reactions. Refer to section 8.2.3 for assistance.

I saw an object concealed down Mr. Terry's pant leg;

    therefore, I conducted a pat down.

    therefore, I felt_____

_____

    therefore, I asked Mr. Terry _____

_____

Mr. Terry told me_____

    therefore, I _____

_____

17.4.4   **Describing people, places, and things.** In this incident, two people, one place, and three things must be described. Review Chapter 9 to determine how you will refer to each of the following items on the first and subsequent mentions. Refer to the specific sections noted below for guidance and examples. The first example has been completed for you.

Store Manager: Delores Ruiz

- First mention: *the complainant, Best Electronics Store Manager Ms. Delores Ruiz*
- Subsequent mentions: *Ms. Ruiz*

Suspect: Norman Terry (see 9.1.1–9.1.5 and 9.1.8)

- First mention: _____

  _____

- Subsequent mentions: _____

Best Electronics (see 9.5.1–9.5.3)

- First mention: _____

  _____

- Subsequent mentions: _____

Stolen Blu-ray Disc #1 (see 9.6.1, 9.6.6, and 13.7.3)

- First mention: _____

  _____

- Subsequent mentions: _____

Stolen Blu-ray Disc #2

- First mention: _____

  _____

- Subsequent mentions: _____

Stolen DVD

- First mention: _____

  _____

- Subsequent mentions: _____

17.5 Sample Report with Annotations

After completing all the exercises in this chapter, try writing your own report about this incident. Once you're done, compare your report to the sample report included in this section. The annotations that follow the sample report will help you understand why certain decisions were made. As you compare your report with this sample, is there anything you would have done differently? Was your report more effective than this sample report in some areas?

This sample report is not a gold standard that your report must measure up to; every report can be improved in some way. Ultimately, you should only measure the effectiveness of your reports against one standard: how well they communicate the right information to the right people in the clearest way possible.

17.5.1   Sample report

On 05 April 2023, at 1437 hours,[1] I was dispatched to Best Electronics (17 Valley Circle, Fairtown, VA)[2] for a shoplifting in progress.[3] While en route, dispatch informed me that the suspect was being compliant and waiting in the manager's office with store employees.[4]

INITIAL INVESTIGATION[5]

Statement by Complainant, Ms. Delores Ruiz[6]

Upon my arrival,[7] I spoke with the complainant, Best Electronics Manager Ms. Delores Ruiz.[8] She told me[9] that at approximately 1400 hours today,[10] a male subject, later identified as the suspect,[11] Mr. Norman Terry (DOB: 11/21/1979),[12] entered the store and walked directly to the Blu-ray section. Ms. Ruiz[13] observed Mr. Terry take three Blu-ray discs from the shelf and conceal them down the front of his pants. Mr. Terry then walked past the point of sale.

Ms. Ruiz told me[14] she approached Mr. Terry before he exited the store. She asked him if he was planning to pay for the Blu-rays, to which Mr. Terry replied that he was sorry he stole them.[15] He then returned two stolen Blu-ray discs ("Sopranos: The Complete Series" and "Identity Thief")[16] to Ms. Ruiz.

Confession by Suspect, Mr. Norman Terry

I then spoke[17] with Mr. Terry, who was seated in the manager's office.[18] When I asked him about the discs, he said, "I didn't have enough money to buy them, so I decided to steal them."[19]

Discovery of Third Stolen Disc

While speaking with Mr. Terry, I saw[20] that his belt was

unbuckled. I also saw the impression of a square object underneath Mr. Terry's right pant leg. Thinking that this might be a weapon,[21] I conducted a pat down.[22] When I touched this object, I felt that is was hard and rectangular. I heard a sound consistent with the crinkling of plastic, leading me to believe[23] that it was a DVD case or similar item. I asked Mr. Terry what it was, and he told me it was another stolen disc. I removed the item ("Gone in 60 Seconds" DVD) from his pants.[24]

Description of Stolen Merchandise

Ms. Ruiz told me that all the merchandise was undamaged. She gave me a receipt that itemized the stolen merchandise:[25]

- Sopranos: The Complete Series (Blu-ray)—$58.99

- Identity Thief (Blu-ray)—$9.99

- Gone in 60 Seconds (DVD)—$8.99[26]

The total value of the stolen merchandise was $77.97.[27]

Ms. Ruiz agreed to cooperate with a prosecution.[28]

I issued Mr. Terry a summons for larceny (§18.2-96).[29]

ADMINISTRATIVE ACTIONS

I photographed and returned all the stolen merchandise to Ms. Ruiz.[30]

The case number was provided to Ms. Ruiz.[31]

Body camera activated.[32]

CASE DISPOSITION[33]

Case cleared by arrest. Mr. Terry's[34] court date is scheduled for June 12, 2023.[35]

17.5.2   Annotations

1. Military time is the most common time format in police reports (see 14.6.6 and 14.6.7).

2. Since this incident occurs at a business, both the street address and the proper name of the business are included (see 9.5.2, 9.5.3, and 19.3.3).

3. The first sentence of a police report grounds it in time and place (see 5.2.1). By following a structured format (see 6.2.2 and 19.1), you automatically include most of the *facts relevant to every incident* (see 4.2.2).

4. The second sentence of this report, which begins with an introductory phrase (see 13.2.1), lets readers know you learned additional information before arriving on the scene (see 6.2.2).

5. An example of a heading (see 6.1.2). This and other headings are in boldface type and set in all caps (see 14.8.2).

6. An example of a subheading (see 6.1.2). This and other subheadings are underlined (see 14.8.2).

7. This phrase transitions readers from the pre-arrival section into the actions you will take once arriving on the scene (see 5.2.2).

8. The first mention of the complainant includes her role, title, salutation, and full name (see 9.1.2).

9. This short phrase lets readers know that what follows is Ms. Ruiz's account of events (see 9.4.5).

10. Including the time and date (i.e., "today") grounds the events of this paragraph in a specific time (see 5.2.1).

11. The phrase "later identified as" allows the officer to name the suspect early in the report while simultaneously letting readers know the suspect wasn't identified until later (see 9.1.8).

12. The suspect's date of birth is included as supplemental information within parentheses (see 9.1.10 and 13.10.1).

13. Since Ms. Ruiz has already been introduced to readers, she is referred to by her salutation and last name from this point forward (see 9.1.2).

14. Starting the paragraph with "Ms. Ruiz told me" signals to readers that they are still inside Ms. Ruiz's statement of events (see 9.4.5).

15. This is a paraphrase of Mr. Terry's statement, as reported by Ms. Ruiz (see 9.4.5).

16. This parenthetical contains supplemental information about which movies were stolen (see 9.1.10). Since the titles of the movies are creative works, they are enclosed in quotation marks (see 13.7.3).

17. This phrase (see 5.2.2) shifts readers' attention to Mr. Terry's confession.

18. Mentioning the manager's office allows readers to picture where exactly this interview took place (see 5.2.1).

19. This is an example of a full inline quotation (see 9.4.1 and 9.4.11).

20. This sensory verb (see 8.1.2) begins a series of observations made by the officer. Other sensory verbs in this paragraph include *felt* and *heard*.

21. The phrase "thinking that this might be a weapon" is a conclusion (see 8.3.2) drawn from the facts presented in the previous sentence.

22. "Pat down" is police jargon that most readers will likely understand (see 14.2.1 and 14.2.2). Even if some readers don't understand the terminology, they can deduce it from the context (see 14.2.3).

23. The phrase "leading me to believe" signals to readers that what follows is a conclusion drawn by the officer (see 8.3.2).

24. This paragraph is an example of an action-reaction sequence (see 8.2) that includes sensory language (see 8.1).

25. This sentence introduces a list (see 14.5). It also lets readers know the source of the information (i.e., a receipt).

26. Each item is listed with its associated dollar amount using a block bulleted list (see 14.5.4).

27. A summary sentence gives the total value of the stolen merchandise, which is a relevant fact (see 4.2.1).

28. This sentence tells readers that Ms. Ruiz agreed to prosecute. Notice how this sentence and the next one don't elaborate on the conversation between the officer and Ms. Ruiz, which probably isn't relevant. All that matters is that she agreed to cooperate with the prosecution.

29. The plain language name of the crime and the code section are included so it's clear exactly what the suspect is being charged with (see 14.2.2).

30. The method by which the items were photographed isn't important in this particular case, nor is its sequence within the incident, so this information is grouped under the Administrative Actions section (see 6.2.5).

31. Passive voice (see 7.5 and 11.3.13) is acceptable here since readers can safely assume that the officer writing the report is the one who provided the case number.

32. Although the body camera was likely activated at the beginning of the incident and deactivated at the end, the exact sequence of these events isn't necessary to

document in officer-chronological order (see 5.1.1 and 5.1.3); therefore, it is appropriate to include this information under the Administrative Actions section.

33. This is the final heading of the report. Although information under this heading is short, and one could argue for its omission, its inclusion lets readers quickly separate the incident's conclusion from the rest of the report (see 6.2.6 and 19.4).

34. Note the correct use of the possessive case (see 13.8.1).

35. This date demonstrates an alternative format to the one used at the beginning of the report (see 14.6.6 and 14.6.7), although in an actual report, you would want to keep one consistent format throughout.

18. Relevant Facts Checklists

18.1   Basic Legal Principles

18.1.1   Consensual or non-consensual interaction

18.1.2   Investigative detention ("Terry stop")

18.1.3   Pat down for weapons ("Terry frisk")

18.1.4   Plain touch/plain feel

18.1.5   Plain view seizure

18.1.6   Protective sweep of residence (for people)

18.1.7   Protective sweep of vehicle (for weapons)

18.1.8   Probable cause search of vehicle ("Carroll search")

18.1.9   Warrantless entry into a residence

18.1.10 Probable cause to arrest

18.1.11 Miranda

18.2   Police Procedure

18.2.1   Arrests

18.2.2   Uses of force

18.2.3   Interviews

18.2.4   Crime scenes

18.2.5   Administrative actions

18.3   Incidents Involving People

18.3.1   Missing person/at-large suspect

18.3.2   Alcohol/drugs

18.3.3   Driving while intoxicated

18.3.4   Injuries

18.3.5   Death

18.4 Incidents Involving Property

18.4.1 Theft

18.4.2 Fraud

18.4.3 Weapons

18.4.4 Vehicles

18.5 Custom Lists

The checklists in this chapter provide a quick way to identify relevant facts you may need to include in your police reports (see Chapter 4); however, nothing in this chapter is all-inclusive. Your state or agency may require different information or a different level of detail than these checklists provide.

To use these checklists, first identify the topic most relevant to the incident you are writing about. Next, read the description next to each check box under that heading. Determine if the information described is relevant to your police report (not everything will be). If it is, use the techniques described throughout this book to document the relevant facts in your report. Create your own list of relevant facts using the blank checklists provided at the end of this chapter.

18.1 Basic Legal Principles

18.1.1 Consensual or non-consensual interaction[1]

☐ Conversational or confrontational nature of the interaction

☐ Public or private location of the encounter

☐ Number of officers present

---

[1] See *California v. Hodari D.*, 499 U.S. 621 (1991); *Florida v. Royer*, 460 U.S. 491 (1983); *United States v. Mendenhall*, 446 U.S. 544 (1980)

☐ Use of lights, sirens, or other emergency equipment

☐ Whether or not officers gave commands

☐ Whether or not officers restricted the subject's movements

☐ Whether or not officers displayed any weapons

☐ Whether or not officers transported the subject

☐ Whether or not the subject felt free to leave the encounter

18.1.2   **Investigative detention ("Terry stop")[2]**

☐ The criminal offense(s) the officer has reasonable suspicion to believe the person being detained has committed, is committing, or is about to commit

☐ Facts and circumstances leading to the officer's reasonable suspicion of criminal activity, such as:

  ☐ Time of day or night

  ☐ Furtive gestures or nervous behavior

  ☐ High-crime or drug-trafficking area

  ☐ Recent crimes in the area

  ☐ Suspect's headlong flight at the sight of police

  ☐ Suspect's proximity to the crime location

  ☐ Officer's knowledge of the suspect's criminal history

  ☐ Anonymous or corroborated nature of the tip

  ☐ Whether the suspect matches a lookout description or wanted flyer

☐ Length of the detention

☐ Methods used to detain the suspect

---

[2] See *Terry v. Ohio*, 392 U.S. 1 (1968); *United States v. Sharpe*, 470 U.S. 675 (1985)

18.1.3   **Pat down for weapons ("Terry frisk")**[3]

☐ Lawful reason for the detention (see 18.1.2)

☐ Facts and circumstances leading to the officer's reasonable suspicion that the subject was armed, such as:

  ☐ Furtive gestures or nervous behavior

  ☐ Clothing that could conceal a weapon

  ☐ Bulges under the subject's clothing

  ☐ Subject's demeanor

  ☐ Type of crime being investigated

  ☐ Whether a weapon was reported

  ☐ Number of officers present

  ☐ Level of suspect's compliance with officer's commands

☐ Area of the pat down

☐ Whether or not weapons were discovered

☐ Location on the body where weapons were discovered

☐ Description of weapons discovered (see 18.4.3)

18.1.4   **Plain touch/plain feel**[4]

☐ Lawful reason for the detention (see 18.1.2)

☐ Lawful reason for the pat down (see 18.1.3)

☐ Lawful reason for patting down the area where contraband was discovered

☐ Probable cause to believe the item was contraband or evidence, such as:

  ☐ Contour, shape, and mass of the suspected contraband

---

[3] See *Terry,* 392 U.S. at 1

[4] See *Minnesota v. Dickerson,* 508 U.S. 366 (1993)

☐ Technique used by the officer to determine the item was contraband (i.e., did not manipulate the item)

18.1.5 **Plain view seizure**[5]

☐ Officer's lawful reason to be present in the area where the evidence could be plainly viewed

☐ Officer's probable cause that the evidence to be seized is involved in criminal activity

18.1.6 **Protective sweep of residence (for people)**[6]

☐ Description of why officers were inside the residence (i.e., to make an arrest)

☐ Search was supported by:

☐ Reasonable suspicion that one or more people at the arrest scene posed a danger to officers making the arrest, *or*

☐ Without probable cause or reasonable suspicion, the search was "in closets and other spaces immediately adjoining the place of arrest from which an attack could be launched"[7]

☐ Areas of the residence searched (i.e., only those areas large enough to conceal a person)

18.1.7 **Protective sweep of vehicle (for weapons)**[8]

☐ Lawful reason for the detention (see 18.1.2)

☐ Reasonable suspicion a weapon was present (see 18.1.3)

[5] See *Horton v. California,* 496 U.S. 128 (1990); *Texas v. Brown,* 460 U.S. 730 (1983)

[6] See *Maryland v. Buie,* 494 U.S. 325 (1990)

[7] *Maryland,* 494 U.S. at 334

[8] See *Michigan v. Long,* 463 U.S. 1032 (1983)

☐ Areas of the vehicle searched (i.e., within the wingspan of the subject; only those areas large enough to conceal a weapon)

☐ Description of weapons discovered (see 18.4.3)

18.1.8 Probable cause search of vehicle ("Carroll search")[9]

☐ Lawful reason for the detention (see 18.1.2)

☐ Probable cause that the vehicle contained evidence or contraband of a crime

☐ Area of vehicle searched (i.e., only those areas that could reasonably contain the item(s) searched for)

☐ Description of evidence or contraband discovered, including the specific location where it was discovered

18.1.9 Warrantless entry into a residence[10]

☐ Probable cause for an arrest, plus exigent circumstances, such as:

　☐ Seriousness of the offense

　☐ Potential for destruction of evidence

　☐ Whether the suspect was present within the residence

　☐ Likelihood the suspect may escape

　☐ Amount of time required to get a warrant

　☐ Danger to officers or the public

☐ Hot pursuit of a person the officer has probable cause to believe committed a felony or other serious, jailable offense

---

[9] See *Carroll v. United States*, 267 U.S. 132 (1925); *United States v. Ross*, 456 U.S. 798 (1982)

[10] See *Payton v. New York*, 445 U.S. 573 (1980); *Warden v. Hayden*, 387 U.S. 294 (1967); *Brigham City v. Stuart*, 547 U.S. 398 (2006)

☐ Reasonable belief that a person is seriously injured or imminently threatened with serious injury[11]

18.1.10 **Probable cause to arrest**

☐ Crime the arrestee is suspected of committing

☐ Facts and circumstances leading to the officer's probable cause that the person to be arrested committed the crime, such as:

    ☐ Existing warrants

    ☐ Suspect/Victim/Witness statements

    ☐ Officer's observations

    ☐ Physical evidence

☐ Probable cause that the suspect's actions satisfy each of the elements of the crime

☐ Investigative methods used by the officer to develop probable cause

18.1.11 **Miranda[12]**

☐ Nature of detention, including whether or not it rose to the level of custody

☐ When and where the Miranda warning was issued

☐ Who issued the Miranda warning

☐ The content of the Miranda warning, including:

    ☐ the suspect's right to remain silent

    ☐ the fact that the suspect's statements can and will be used against them in a court of law

    ☐ the suspect's right to consult with an attorney and have an attorney present during questioning

---

[11] See *Caniglia v. Strom*, 593 U.S. ___ (2021)

[12] See *Miranda v. Arizona*, 384 U.S. 436 (1966)

□ the suspect's right to have an attorney provided before questioning at no cost

□ the fact that questioning will stop if the suspect asks for an attorney at any time

□ The source of the Miranda warning (e.g., department-issued Miranda warning wallet card)

18.2   Police Procedure

18.2.1   Arrests

□ Probable cause for the arrest (see 18.1.10)

□ Crimes the suspect is charged with

□ Restraint devices used

□ Force used to effect the arrest (see 18.2.2)

□ Search incident to arrest

□ Description of suspect's property, including valuables

□ Transfer of custody to jail or other location

□ Bail or bond status

□ Cruiser prisoner compartment checked for contraband

18.2.2   Uses of force[13]

□ The severity of the crime

□ Immediate threat to the safety of the officer or others

□ Whether or not the suspect was actively resisting arrest or attempting to evade arrest by flight

□ Probable cause to believe the suspect posed a threat of serious bodily injury or death

---

[13] See *Graham v. Connor*, 490 U.S. 386 (1989); *Tennessee v. Garner*, 471 U.S. 1 (1985)

- ☐ The totality of the circumstances surrounding the incident, such as:
  - ☐ Whether the officer initiated the response or was responding to a call for service
  - ☐ Whether the officer was ambushed
  - ☐ Whether the officer was readily identifiable as an officer (e.g., uniform vs. plain clothes, verbal identification as a police officer)
  - ☐ The suspect's disobedience to verbal commands
  - ☐ The size or build of the suspect compared to the officer
  - ☐ The presence or use of weapons
  - ☐ The mental state of the suspect
  - ☐ Whether the suspect was under the influence of drugs
  - ☐ Whether the suspect displayed pre-assault indicators
  - ☐ The number of assailants
  - ☐ The number of officers
  - ☐ Whether the officer called for backup
  - ☐ Injuries or exhaustion level of the officer
  - ☐ Avenues of escape for the officer or the suspect
  - ☐ The officer's prior knowledge or experience with the suspect
  - ☐ Whether the officer attempted to use de-escalation measures
- ☐ Description of suspect's or officer's injuries
- ☐ Medical aid rendered after the use of force
- ☐ De-escalation techniques used
- ☐ Supervisory notifications made

18.2.3   **Interviews**

☐ Person interviewed

☐ Role of the interviewee in the incident

☐ Consensual or custodial nature of interview (see 18.1.1, 18.1.11)

☐ Date, time, and location of the interview

☐ Method used to record the interview

☐ Inculpatory or exculpatory statements

18.2.4   **Crime scenes**

☐ Scene description

☐ Scene diagram

☐ Crime scene log

☐ Security camera locations and availability of video

☐ Evidence collected, such as:

    ☐ Fingerprints

    ☐ Blood

    ☐ Statements (see 18.2.3)

    ☐ Physical objects

    ☐ Photographs

☐ Evidence chain of custody

☐ Names of assisting officers/technicians/detectives

18.2.5   **Administrative actions**

☐ Body-worn or in-car camera activation

☐ Department paperwork filed

☐ Information entered or cleared through NCIC

☐ Notifications to supervisors or other personnel

☐ Creation and dissemination of wanted flyers/lookouts

18.3   Incidents Involving People

18.3.1   Missing person/at-large suspect

- ☐ Physical description of person
- ☐ Reason for disappearance
- ☐ Last-known whereabouts
- ☐ Direction of travel
- ☐ Method of travel
- ☐ Missing or wanted person flyers created
- ☐ Use of traditional media or social media to publish missing or wanted person's information
- ☐ Threats to the public, officers, or the missing person
- ☐ Notifications to surrounding agencies
- ☐ Resources used to search for the missing or wanted person
- ☐ Activated alert systems (AMBER alert, Silver alert, etc.)

18.3.2   Alcohol/drugs

- ☐ Signs of Intoxication
- ☐ Description of drugs, including weight
- ☐ Location where drugs were found
- ☐ Field test results
- ☐ Lab analysis results
- ☐ Description of drug paraphernalia
- ☐ Safety precautions taken when handling drugs
- ☐ Name of officer(s) who witnessed drug collection, packaging, and weighing

18.3.3   **Driving while intoxicated**[14]

☐ Driving behaviors:

   ☐ Weaving, drifting, and swerving

   ☐ Almost striking an object or vehicle

   ☐ Turning with a wide radius

   ☐ Improper stopping and signaling

   ☐ Acceleration or deceleration problems

   ☐ Varying speed

   ☐ Driving without headlights after sunset

   ☐ Following too closely

   ☐ Improper turns or lane changes

   ☐ Driving on the wrong side of the road

☐ Post-stop problems:

   ☐ Fumbling for license

   ☐ Problems exiting the vehicle

   ☐ Balance problems

   ☐ Slurred speech

   ☐ Incorrect answers

   ☐ The odor of an alcoholic beverage

☐ Interactions with the driver, including instructions given for sobriety tests

☐ Administration of sobriety tests, including the driver's ability or inability to complete them satisfactorily

☐ Breath or blood tests that were administered, and their results

☐ Arrests (see 18.2.1)

---

[14] See National Highway Traffic Safety Administration, *DWI Detection and Standardized Field Sobriety Test (SFST) Resources.* https://www.nhtsa.gov/dwi-detection-and-standardized-field-sobriety-test-sfst-resources

18.3.4   **Injuries**

☐ Description of injuries

☐ Cause of injuries

☐ Medical assistance provided or offered

☐ Statements from injured person (see 18.2.3)

☐ Notifications to family, supervisors, etc.

☐ Weapons involved (see 18.4.3)

☐ Photographs of injuries

18.3.5   **Death**

☐ Time of death

☐ Person pronouncing death

☐ Cause or manner of death

☐ Medical history

☐ Attending physician

☐ Names of next-of-kin

☐ Notifications to family, supervisors, etc.

☐ Crime scene information (see 18.2.4)

18.4   Incidents Involving Property

18.4.1   **Theft**

☐ Property description

☐ Property owner information

☐ Serial numbers

☐ Method of theft (larceny, robbery, etc.)

☐ Total monetary loss

☐ Insurance information

☐ Recovery of stolen item(s)

☐ NCIC entries

18.4.2   **Fraud**

- ☐ Method of fraud (computer, embezzlement, etc.)
- ☐ Description of damages
- ☐ Total monetary loss
- ☐ Reimbursement of losses by bank, credit card company, insurance, etc.
- ☐ Bank or insurance information, including account numbers
- ☐ Dates and times of fraudulent transactions/activities

18.4.3   **Weapons**

- ☐ Type of weapon (gun, knife, etc.)
- ☐ Make, model, and color of the weapon
- ☐ Serial number, caliber, etc.
- ☐ Owner of the weapon
- ☐ Name or description of the suspect who used the weapon
- ☐ How the weapon was used
- ☐ Injuries sustained (see 18.3.4)
- ☐ NCIC checks

18.4.4   **Vehicles**

- ☐ Vehicle description, including make, model, color, year, and distinguishing features
- ☐ Vehicle license plate state, number, and VIN
- ☐ Registered owner information
- ☐ Insurance information
- ☐ Damage description and cost
- ☐ Description and number of vehicle occupants
- ☐ Registration or stolen status of vehicle
- ☐ NCIC entries or checks

18.5   Custom Lists

(*List Heading*) _____

- ☐ _____
- ☐ _____
- ☐ _____
- ☐ _____
- ☐ _____
- ☐ _____

(*List Heading*) _____

- ☐ _____
- ☐ _____
- ☐ _____
- ☐ _____
- ☐ _____
- ☐ _____

(*List Heading*) _____

- ☐ _____
- ☐ _____
- ☐ _____
- ☐ _____
- ☐ _____
- ☐ _____

19. Model Phrases

19.1   Initial Response

19.1.1   Dispatched call

19.1.2   Dispatched call with contextual information

19.1.3   Self-initiated activity

19.1.4   Arrival on scene

19.2   Describing Actions

19.2.1   Generally

19.2.2   Interviews

19.2.3   Uses of force

19.3   Describing Observations

19.3.1   Generally

19.3.2   People

19.3.3   Places

19.3.4   Things

19.3.5   Knowledge, training, and experience

19.3.6   Compliance with law and policy

19.4   Case Disposition

19.4.1   Arrest & case closed

19.4.2   Open investigation

The model phrases in this chapter will give you a place to start if you get stuck while writing your reports. To use these model phrases, first find the section corresponding to what you are trying to articulate. (For example, if you are trying to articulate a use of force, refer to section 19.2.3.) Next, find the model phrase most closely resembling what you are trying to say. Replace the words shaded in gray with your own wording. Shaded words in SMALL CAPS describe the category of information you may wish to insert into your sentence. Shaded words set in italics give example words you may want to use.

For example, if you are trying to articulate where you found a knife at your incident scene, and you refer to section 19.3.4, you'll find this model phrase:

I saw OBJECT *on/under/above/near* LOCATION.

Based on this model phrase, your resulting sentence may read like this:

I saw the steak knife on the kitchen counter.

Using this model phrase as a starting point, you may decide you need to add additional information, like this:

I saw the steak knife on the kitchen counter, directly to the right of the kitchen sink.

Think of these model phrases as ways to generate ideas rather than as set formulas. So long as these model phrases help you express your ideas clearly, they will have achieved their purpose.

19.1 Initial Response

19.1.1 Dispatched call

On DATE at TIME, I was dispatched to LOCATION for *a/an* INCIDENT TYPE *in progress/report*.

19.1.2 **Dispatched call with contextual information**

On DATE at TIME, I was dispatched to LOCATION for *a/an* INCIDENT TYPE *in progress/report*. Prior to my arrival, dispatch told me RELEVANT INFORMATION.

19.1.3 **Self-initiated activity**

On DATE at TIME, I was in the area of LOCATION when I ACTION/OBSERVATION.

19.1.4 **Arrival on scene**

I arrived on the scene and ACTION/OBSERVATION.

Upon my arrival, I ACTION/OBSERVATION.

19.2 Describing Actions

19.2.1 **Generally**

I *approached/asked/directed/grabbed/inspected/*ETC....

19.2.2 **Interviews**

I spoke with the ROLE, SALUTATION/TITLE FIRST NAME LAST NAME, who told me PARAPHRASED STATEMENT.

TITLE/SALUTATION LAST NAME *explained/told me* PARAPHRASED STATEMENT.

TITLE/SALUTATION LAST NAME said, "QUOTED STATEMENT."

19.2.3 **Uses of force**

I saw TITLE/SALUTATION LAST NAME ACTION, so I intervened by ACTION.

I felt TITLE/SALUTATION LAST NAME resisting my ACTION by ACTION, so I responded by ACTION.

I gained control of TITLE/SALUTATION LAST NAME using the NAME OF TACTIC as it was taught to me at the NAME OF TRAINING ACADEMY OR CLASS.

I attempted to de-escalate the situation by ACTION.

19.3   Describing Observations

19.3.1   Generally
I *saw/heard/smelled/felt/tasted*...

19.3.2   People
TITLE/SALUTATION LAST NAME is a RACE ETHNICITY SEX AGE, approximately HEIGHT tall, WEIGHT pounds, with HAIR DESCRIPTION and COLOR eyes.

TITLE/SALUTATION LAST NAME last saw the *suspect/subject* wearing CLOTHING DESCRIPTION and traveling DIRECTION *on foot/ in a vehicle/on a bicycle*/ETC.

19.3.3   Places
This incident occurred at BUSINESS NAME (ADDRESS).

I located the PERSON/OBJECT/LOCATION DISTANCE DIRECTION of LANDMARK.

19.3.4   Things
I saw OBJECT *on/under/above/near* LOCATION.

I saw *a/an* OBJECT DESCRIPTION in LOCATION, which appeared to be OBJECT NAME.

The OBJECT was a COLOR MAKE MODEL SERIAL NUMBER.

While searching TITLE/SALUTATION LAST NAME, I felt OBJECT DESCRIPTION in LOCATION.

I entered the OBJECT into evidence as ITEM NUMBER.

I smelled the strong odor of *an alcoholic beverage/ marijuana/etc.*

19.3.5   Knowledge, training, and experience

Based on my *training/experience* in SPECIFIC AREA, I knew that DESCRIPTION OF KNOWLEDGE.

Based on my prior interactions with the subject, I knew that DESCRIPTION OF KNOWLEDGE.

19.3.6   Compliance with law and policy

Based on these facts, I developed *reasonable suspicion/probable cause* to...

Based on the elements of the crime of CRIME NAME described in STATE code CODE SECTION, I *found/did not find* probable cause to ACTION.

In accordance with POLICY NAME, I ACTION.

Pursuant to code section CODE NUMBER AND NAME, I ACTION.

19.4   Case Disposition

19.4.1   Arrest & case closed

TITLE/SALUTATION LAST NAME is being held at the JAIL NAME on BOND STATUS. TITLE/SALUTATION LAST NAME has a court date on DATE in COURT NAME. This case is cleared by arrest.

19.4.2   **Open investigation**

This case remains active.

This case is open and turned over to *criminal investigations/crash reconstruction/patrol/*ETC.

20. Sample Reports

20.1   **Basic Report**

20.2   **Basic Report with Headings and Subheadings**

20.3   **Detailed Follow-Up Report**

This chapter includes three sample police reports that demonstrate how the rules, guidelines, and techniques explained throughout this book work together to produce an effective written account of a police incident. Since these reports document fictional police incidents, don't worry if the investigations described here differ from your agency's policies and procedures. What's important is to focus on how well each report tells the *right people* the *right information* in the *clearest way possible.*

As you read these reports, pay attention to things that worked well and things you would have done differently if you were the author. Whenever you identify such examples, take a moment to add the ideas to your swipe file (see 3.3.5) and, more importantly, to incorporate what you have learned into future reports you write about real-life incidents.

20.1   Basic Report

On November 7, 2022, at approximately 0330 hours, I was on routine patrol in the 500 block of Piper Avenue when I observed a light on inside Tony's Carpet Repair (597 Piper Avenue). Based on my prior patrols of this area, I know this business normally closes at 2100 hours.

I walked the perimeter of the business, checking doors and windows for signs of entry. The front door of the business was closed and locked. The plate glass window was intact. The rear exit of the business was closed but unlocked. I held my position at the rear of the business while I waited for an additional unit to arrive on scene.

Officer Y. Ebert (#88523) arrived on scene. We knocked and announced our presence, and we both cleared the building without incident. Based on my observations inside the business, nothing appeared to be out of place. The cash register and safe were both present and undamaged. There were no signs of forced entry on the rear door.

I left my business card on the desk in the back office. I secured the rear door by turning the interior lock and closing the door tightly.

This incident is being documented for suspicious activity reporting purposes.

Body camera activated.

Case closed as a public service.

20.2   Basic Report with Headings and Subheadings

On October 8, 2023, at 1109 hours, I was dispatched to Corner Mart (71 Hilldale Drive) for a larceny in progress.

INITIAL INVESTIGATION

Witness' Description of Suspect & BOLO

Upon my arrival, I met with the complainant, Corner Mart Manager Mr. Leo VEGA (DOB: 05/16/1949), who told me that an unknown male subject entered the store at approximately 1045 hours today and stole a twenty-ounce bottle of Diet Dr. Pepper and a Twinkie.

Mr. Vega described the suspect as a white male, approximately 20–25 years old, wearing black shorts and a green tee shirt with yellow writing on the front. He said the suspect fled south on Hilldale Drive on a motorized scooter.

Mr. Vega showed me surveillance video, where I witnessed events consistent with his statement. I broadcast a lookout for the suspect and sent a screenshot from the surveillance footage to other officers who were on duty.

Description of Stolen Property

Mr. Vega provided me with a receipt for the stolen merchandise (total loss: $3.48):

- One (1) 20 oz. bottle of Diet Dr. Pepper, valued at $2.49
- One (1) Twinkie, valued at $0.99

FOLLOW-UP INVESTIGATION

Identification of Suspect, Mr. Bo Lavoie

Approximately ten minutes after I broadcast the lookout description, Officer D. Alvarado (#25411) located a subject matching the suspect's description standing in front of 251 Sierra Avenue. I responded to the scene and identified the subject as Mr. Bo LAVOIE (DOB: 02/27/1995) using his state-issued identification card. During my initial encounter with Mr. Lavoie, I made the following observations:

- Mr. Lavoie matched the suspect description provided by Mr. Vega.

- Mr. Lavoie matched the images of the suspect in the surveillance footage, including the clothing he was wearing.

- Mr. Lavoie was holding a 20 oz. bottle of Diet Dr. Pepper.

- There was a Twinkie, still in its wrapper, sitting on the stone ledge next to Mr. Lavoie.

- A motorized scooter was parked on the sidewalk less than 20 feet from our location.

Interview with Suspect & Confession

Mr. Lavoie initially denied being inside the Corner Mart or taking any merchandise. When I confronted him with the evidence against him, he admitted to stealing the items and stated, "alright, alright, you caught me."

Issuance of Summons and Trespassing Notification

I issued Mr. Lavoie a summons for misdemeanor larceny. I also issued him a Notice of Trespass (Form #584) for Corner Mart.

ADMINISTRATIVE ACTIONS

I returned the Twinkie and soda to Mr. Vega and issued him a witness subpoena.

I provided Mr. Vega with my business card and case information.

Body-worn camera active.

Signed copy of Form #584 forwarded to the Records Division.

CASE DISPOSITION

Mr. Lavoie has a court date scheduled for November 10, 2023 in the district court.

Case cleared by arrest.

20.3   Detailed Follow-Up Report

Case Number:	202300238
Incident Date:	January 14, 2023
Incident Time:	2354 hours
Incident Type:	Robbery — Home Invasion
Incident Location:	4111 Laurel Rd. #136-A
Victim:	Luis Nagy (DOB: 08/14/2001)
Suspect #1:	Alisha Beltran (DOB: Unknown)
Suspect #2:	Unknown B/M
Investigator:	Detective T. Luther (#1346)
Disposition:	ACTIVE

Synopsis

The victim, Mr. Luis Nagy, alleged that on 14 January 2023, he invited Ms. Alisha Beltran over to his apartment. Shortly after her arrival, an unidentified male entered the apartment, pointed a gun at Mr. Nagy, and robbed him of $750 in cash. This report documents crime scene processing and an interview with the victim.

INITIAL SCENE SURVEY

I responded to the scene of this incident on 14 January 2023 at approximately 2245 hours.

Incident Location Description

This incident occurred at a residential condominium located at 4111 Laurel Road, #136-A (hereafter "the Apartment"), which belonged to the victim, Mr. Luis Nagy. The Apartment was located on the second level of the apartment building in the northeast corner. I accessed the Apartment by ascending fifteen concrete steps to the building entrance and then two flights of stairs to the second level of the building.

The interior of the Apartment consisted of a living room, a galley kitchen, one bedroom, and one bathroom. The robbery took place in the bedroom, which is located at the rear of the Apartment, directly adjacent to the bathroom (see Scene Diagram #1).

APARTMENT EXTERIOR

Point of Entry/Exit

The front door of the Apartment was the suspect's point of entry/exit. There were no signs of forced entry.

The door was unlocked at the time the suspect entered.

There were no latent prints or items of evidence at this location.

APARTMENT INTERIOR

Point of Entry/Exit

There were no signs of forced entry on the interior side of the front door. There were no latent prints or items of evidence on the door itself. There was a drop of apparent blood on the floor immediately inside the front doorway.

Living Room

The living room is the first room accessed upon entering the apartment.

There were no latent prints or items of evidence in this location.

Kitchen

There were no latent prints or items of evidence in this location.

Bathroom

There were no latent prints or items of evidence in this location.

Bedroom

The bedroom measured approximately 14'6" x 11'0". The bedroom contained the following furniture (see Scene Diagram #2):

- A wooden dresser that had been tipped over

- A mattress with a comforter, blanket, and pillows

- A large beanbag chair

- A nightstand

- Two (2) plastic storage totes filled with miscellaneous clothing

I observed the following items of note in the bedroom:

- A broken lamp on the ground next to the nightstand

- Clear fluid on the floor next to the mattress

- One (1) piece of toilet paper with apparent blood on the floor next to the mattress

- One (1) apparent blood smear on the molding of the bedroom door

- Three (3) apparent drops of blood on the carpet within the threshold of the bedroom door

- Possible latent prints on the inside molding of the bedroom door

EVIDENCE COLLECTION

Photography

I photographed the incident location. The photographs are categorized in the following file name groups:

- DSCN2412–DSCN2432 — Apartment building exterior
- DSCN2433–DSCN2444 — Apartment front door
- DSCN2445–DSCN2451 — Apparent blood near front door
- DSCN2452–DSCN2498 — Living room, kitchen, and bathroom
- DSCN2499–DSCN2536 — Bedroom
- DSCN2537–DSCN2598 — Closeups of items of note in bedroom
- DSCN2599–DSCN2615 — Final walkthrough of apartment

Physical Evidence Collection

I collected the following items from the scene:

- One (1) sample of clear fluid from the floor next to the mattress (item #57556-01)
- Five (5) samples of apparent blood from the molding of the bedroom door (item #57556-02)
- Six (6) samples of apparent blood from the carpet within the threshold of the bedroom door (item #57556-03)

- One (1) piece of toilet paper with apparent blood from the floor next to the mattress (item #57556-04)

- Two (2) samples of apparent blood from the floor immediately inside the front door of the Apartment (item #57556-05)

Fingerprint Collection

I processed the following locations in the bedroom for fingerprints:

- Dresser—No results

- Nightstand—No results

- Door molding—Three (3) prints collected (items #57556-06 through #57556-08)

CASE INVESTIGATION

Interview: Luis Nagy

On 15 January 2023, at approximately 0215 hours, I interviewed Mr. Nagy at police headquarters (92 Annabelle Drive) in Interview Room #6. The interview was audio and video recorded.

Mr. Nagy told me that on 14 January 2023, he received a "match" on an online dating app for a female who identified herself as "Alisha Beltran." Mr. Nagy invited Ms. Beltran over to his apartment and she arrived in the apartment building lobby at approximately 2130 hours.

Mr. Nagy said he escorted Ms. Beltran up to his apartment. Upon entering the apartment, Mr. Nagy and Ms. Beltran walked directly to the bedroom and sat down on the mattress. Mr. Nagy did not remember whether or not he locked the front door of his apartment. Ms. Beltran then pulled out her phone, appeared to type in a few words, and put the phone back in her pocket.

Mr. Nagy said that approximately five minutes after entering the apartment, he heard what sounded like loud footsteps running through the living room. Just as he was standing up to investigate the noise, he observed a masked suspect enter his room and point a gun at him. Mr. Nagy immediately ran at the suspect, and a short scuffle ensued. During the scuffle, the dresser was knocked over, and the suspect struck Mr. Nagy in the face with the side of the pistol. Mr. Nagy said he remembered touching his face, seeing blood on his hands, and becoming "mad with adrenaline." He began screaming at the suspect, and the suspect fled on foot.

Mr. Nagy said he turned around to ensure that Ms. Beltran was okay, but he didn't see her. He searched for her throughout his apartment, but she was not there. Mr. Nagy said he became worried for her safety until he went back to his bedroom and discovered that his wallet, which contained $750 in cash, was missing from the top of his nightstand. Mr. Nagy searched his bedroom but could not find the wallet. He concluded that Ms. Beltran must have been involved with the plot to rob him and steal his wallet.

<u>Mr. Nagy's Description of the Suspects</u>

Mr. Nagy described Ms. Beltran as a white hispanic female, approximately 5'4" tall, 110 lb., with shoulder-length brown hair and brown eyes. He provided me a picture of Ms. Beltran from her dating profile, which he confirmed was consistent with her appearance at the time of the incident.

Mr. Nagy described the masked suspect as a black male, 5'8"–6'2", 170–200 lb., with brown eyes, wearing red shoes, dark jogging pants, and a black zip-up jacket. Mr. Nagy said that despite the suspect being masked, the eye holes in the mask were large enough that he could determine the suspect's race and eye color.

<u>Mr. Nagy's Injuries</u>

Mr. Nagy sustained the following injuries:

- 1.5" laceration above his right eyebrow

- contusion on his right cheekbone

- numerous small abrasions on the knuckles of his right hand

EVIDENCE CHAIN OF CUSTODY

On 15 January 2023, I entered the following items into evidence under #57556.

- #1 — one (1) clear fluid sample

- #2 — five (5) apparent blood samples

- #3 — six (6) apparent blood samples

- #4 — one (1) toilet paper with apparent blood

- #5 — two (2) apparent blood samples

- #6 — one (1) lifted fingerprint

- #7 — one (1) lifted fingerprint

- #8 — one (1) lifted fingerprint

- #9 — one (1) Scene Diagram #1

- #10 — one (1) Scene Diagram #2

- #11 — one (1) printed screenshot of Ms. Beltran's dating profile picture

- #12 — one (1) USB drive containing crime scene photographs

CASE DISPOSITION

This case remains open for further investigation.

Attachments: Scene Diagram #1, Scene Diagram #2, Picture of Ms. Alisha Beltran's dating profile

cc: Evidence Section

Appendix

Appendix A
Tables

References are to page numbers.

Example Primary and Secondary Readers	19
Sample Questions Your Readers May Ask	27–29
Five Parts of a Police Report Narrative	75
Personal Pronouns	209
State Abbreviations	258
Types of Lists	260
Currency Symbols and Formatting	265
Conjugations of "to Lay"	299
Conjugations of "to Lie"	300
The Six-Step Writing Process	318
The COPS Method	324

Appendix B
Figures

References are to page numbers.

Two Groups of Readers   21

The Investigation-Report Cycle   35

T-Chart   57

Officer-Chronological Order   63

Sample Report with Sections, Headings, and Subheadings   81

Appendix C
Example Police Incidents

References are to page numbers.
Asterisks (*) indicate complete report examples.

Two males detained outside convenience store   6–7, 34–36
    Constitutionality of investigative detention

Subject smashing out car windows in a parking lot   7–9
    Compliance with agency policy and procedure

Subject driving under the influence   10
    Reasonableness of officer's actions

Gas station robbery with a deadly weapon   22–26
    Primary and secondary readers and their questions

Machete attack during a drug deal   39–40
    Correct way to document mistakes

Shoplifting of beer at a convenience store   47–49, 53–60, 66
    Relationship of incident facts and general facts, T-Chart

Subject with a replica firearm   64–65
    Presenting facts in officer-chronological order

Two witnesses interrupting each other   67
    When to avoid officer-chronological order

Foot pursuit where suspect drops a gun in the alley   86–88
    First-person point of view

Disorderly subject walking in the roadway   101–105, 109–114
     Writing from your senses

Surveillance of two subjects on a car lot   114–116
     Action-reaction groups

Drunk subject at a bar   177–181*
     Documenting uses of force

Theft at electronics store   326–344*
     Walkthrough of report writing process

Open door during business check   368*
     Basic report without headings

Theft from convenience store   369–371*
     Basic report with headings and subheadings

Home invasion robbery   372–379*
     Detailed follow-up report

Appendix D
Referenced U.S. Supreme Court Cases

References are to page numbers.

Brigham City v. Stuart, 547 U.S. 398 (2006) — 350

California v. Hodari D., 499 U.S. 621 (1991) — 346

Caniglia v. Strom, 593 U.S. ___ (2021) — 351

Carroll v. United States, 267 U.S. 132 (1925) — 52, 350

Elkins v. United States, 364 U. S. 206 (1960) — 162

Florida v. Royer, 460 U.S. 491 (1983) — 346

Graham v. Connor, 490 U.S. 386 (1989) — 9, 63, 162, 164–165, 168, 352

Horton v. California, 496 U.S. 128 (1990) — 349

Maryland v. Buie, 494 U.S. 325 (1990) — 349

Michigan v. Long, 463 U.S. 1032 (1983) — 349

Minnesota v. Dickerson, 508 U.S. 366 (1993) — 348

Miranda v. Arizona, 384 U.S. 436 (1966) — 351

Payton v. New York, 445 U.S. 573 (1980) — 350

Tennessee v. Garner, 471 U.S. 1 (1985) — 162, 166, 168, 352

Terry v. Ohio, 392 U.S. 1 (1968) — 162–164, 347–348

Texas v. Brown, 460 U.S. 730 (1983) — 349

United States v. Mendenhall, 446 U.S. 544 (1980)   346

United States v. Place, 462 U.S. 696 (1983)   166

United States v. Ross, 456 U.S. 798 (1982)   350

United States v. Sharpe, 470 U.S. 675 (1985)   347

Warden v. Hayden, 387 U.S. 294 (1967)   350

Appendix E
Suggested Readings

The following is a list of books that any student of police report writing or the English language would do well to find on their shelves.

Associated Press. 2004. *The Associated Press Stylebook and Briefing on Media Law: With Internet Guide and Glossary*. Cambridge, Mass.: Perseus Books.

Chicago Press. 2017. *The Chicago Manual of Style*. Chicago: The University of Chicago Press.

Dreyer, Benjamin. 2019. *Dreyer's English: An Utterly Correct Guide to Clarity and Style*. New York: Random House.

Fowler, H W, and Jeremy Butterfield. 2015. *Fowler's Dictionary of Modern English Usage*. Oxford, United Kingdom: Oxford University Press.

Garner, Bryan A. 2016. *The Chicago Guide to Grammar, Usage, and Punctuation*. University of Chicago Press.

Garner, Bryan A, and Henry Campbell Black. 2021. *Black's Law Dictionary*. St. Paul, Mn: Thomson Reuters.

Merriam-Webster. 1989. *The Merriam-Webster Dictionary of English Usage*. Springfield, Mass.: Merriam-Webster.

Miller, Larry S, and John T Whitehead. 2014. *Report Writing for Criminal Justice Professionals*. Routledge.

O'Conner, Patricia T. 2019. *Woe Is I: The Grammarphobe's Guide to Better English in Plain English*. New York: Riverhead Books.

Random House. 2008. *Random House Webster's Grammar, Usage, and Punctuation.* New York: Random House Reference.

Scalise, Frank, and Douglas Strosahl. 2012. *Street Officers Guide to Report Writing (Book Only).* Cengage Learning.

Skillin, Marjorie E. 1974. *Words into Type.* Prentice-Hall, Inc.

Index

References are to section number unless otherwise indicated.

A

a/an, 11.8.2–3

a lot/allot, p. 273

abbreviations, 14.3.1–4,
    acronyms, 13.1.4, 14.3.2
    capitalizing, 14.7.1
    clipped words, 14.3.1, 14.3.4
    dates, 14.6.6
    initialisms, 13.1.4, 14.3.1, 14.3.3
    jargon, 14.2.1
    money, 14.6.5
    punctuation:
        parentheses, 13.10.2, 14.3.2
        periods, 13.1.3
        slashes, 13.12.6
    specific:
        aka, 9.1.11
        cc, 6.3.4
        ft./in., 9.2.6
        lb., 9.2.7
        sic, 9.4.9
    state, 14.3.5
    times, 14.6.7
    weights and measures, 14.6.10
    see also acronyms; initialisms

abstract language, 7.6, 8.1.1, 8.1.3

accents, spoken, 9.4.6

accept/except, p. 274

acronyms, 13.1.4, 14.3.2
    see also abbreviations

action-reaction groups, 8.2.5

action-reaction sequences, 8.2.1–5,
    16.2.4
    avoiding gaps, 8.2.3
    evaluating effectiveness, 8.2.3
    paragraph form, 8.2.4
    uses of force, 10.2.3
    variations, 8.2.5
    see also actions

actions, p. 100, 8.2.1–5, 19.2.1
    benefits of effectively describing,
        3.2.2
    evaluating without hindsight, 5.1.1
    extended, 8.2.5
    as facts, 4.1.2
    grouped, 5.1.3, 8.2.5
    linking reactions, 8.2.3
    as observations, 8.2.2n
    relevant vs. irrelevant, 8.2.4
    uses of force, 10.2.3
    see also action-reaction sequences;
        Administrative Actions;
        reasonableness

active voice, 7.5, 11.3.13

actus reus, 1.1.4

adapt/adopt, p. 274

addresses, 9.5.1–3
    business names, 9.5.3
    commas, 13.2.7
    numbers, 14.6.1
    virtual locations, 9.5.9
    see also URLs

adjectives, 11.1.5, 11.4.1–3
    ages, 9.2.5
    comparisons, 11.4.2
    compound, 13.9.2, 11.4.3
Administrative Actions, 5.1.3, 6.2.5,
    18.2.5
    see also *Five Parts of a Police Report
    Narrative*
adults, 9.1.5, 9.1.9, 9.2.5
adverbs, 11.1.5, 11.5.1–2
    connecting, 13.2.4, 13.3.2
advice/advise, p. 274
affect/effect, p. 275
age, 9.2.5
agreement
    pronoun-antecedent, 11.6.3, 12.4
    subject-verb, 12.3
aid/aide, p. 276
aka (also known as), 9.1.11
alcohol, 18.3.2
all right/alright, p. 276
allusion/illusion/allude/elude, p. 276
alternate/alternative, p. 277
a.m./p.m., 13.1.4, 14.6.7n
among/between, p. 277
antecedents, 11.6.2
    interrogative pronouns, 11.6.9
    pronoun agreement, 11.6.3, 12.4
    pronoun confusion, 12.5
    pronoun gender, 11.6.6, 14.1.5
apostrophes, 13.8.1–5
    contractions, 13.8.3, 14.4.1
    measurements, 9.2.6, 13.8.5
    plurals, 13.8.4
    vs. prime marks, 13.7.5n
appearance, describing physical, 9.2.2
appraise/apprise, p. 278
approximately/about, 9.2.6–7
arrests, 18.2.1, 19.4.1
arrival on scene, 19.1.4

articles, 11.1.5, 11.8.1–3
    a/an, 11.8.2–3
    definite vs. indefinite, 11.8.2
    the, 11.8.2
articulation
    decision making, p. 3–4, 3.2.1
    evaluating effectiveness, 8.2.3
    poor, 3.4.3
    reports as tools for, 3.1, 3.2.1–2,
    3.3.1–5
    seizures, 10.1.3
assure/ensure/insure, p. 279
at-large suspect, 18.3.1
attachments, 6.3.3

B
background information, 8.3.1
badge numbers, 9.1.7
baklava/balaclava, p. 279
bare/bear, p. 279
baseless conclusions, 7.8
bias, 14.1.1–5
    gendered language, 14.1.5
    implicit vs. explicit, 14.1.1
    offensive terms, 14.1.3–4
    person-first language, 9.2.2, 14.1.4
    race, 9.2.3
    religion, 14.1.1–2
    stereotypes, 14.1.2
block quotations, 9.4.11
blonde/blond, p. 280
boarder/border, p. 280
body cameras
    documenting use of, 5.1.3, 6.2.5,
    10.1.7
    field of view vs. human eye, 8.1.5
    observations, 8.1.5
    recorded statements, 9.4.3
boldface text, 6.1.2, 14.8.2
brackets, 9.4.9, 13.11.1
brake/break, p. 281

brand names, 9.6.7
breath/breathe, p. 281
bullet points, 14.5.4
   see also lists
business names, 9.5.3
buy/by, p. 282

C

canned phrases, 10.3.1
canvas/canvass, p. 282
capital/capitol, p. 282
capitalization, 14.7.1–7
   abbreviations, 14.7.1
   acronyms, 13.1.4
   cardinal directions, 14.7.6
   colon, first word after, 14.7.2
   country names, 14.7.5
   direct quotations, 14.7.2
   job titles and ranks, 14.7.4
   languages, 14.7.5
   nationalities, 14.7.5
   proper nouns, 11.2.2, 14.7.3
   seasons, 14.7.7
   semicolon, first word after, 14.7.2
   sentences, 11.1, 14.7.1–2
carat/karat/caret/carrot, p. 283
cardinal directions, 9.5.4–5, 9.5.7,
   14.7.6
cardinal numbers, 14.6.2
Carroll doctrine, 4.2.3, 18.1.8
case, pronoun, 11.6.7
Case Disposition, 4.2.2, 6.2.6, 6.3.1,
   18.2.5, 19.4.1–2
   see also *Five Parts of a Police Report
     Narrative*
casual/causal, p. 283
cc (carbon copy), 6.3.4
chord/cord, p. 283
chronological order, 5.1.1–3
   see also officer-chronological order
cite/sight/site, p. 284

clarifying information, 13.11.1
clarity, p. xx–xxi, 5.1.3, 7.1–2, p. 187,
   p. 223, 16.1.3, 16.2.3–4
   vs. brevity, 7.9
clipped words, 14.3.1, 14.3.4
clothing, 9.2.2, 9.2.11
coarse/course, p. 285
collective nouns, 11.2.4
colons, 13.4.1–4
   capitalization after, 14.7.2
   headings, 13.4.4
   joining sentences, 13.4.2
   lists, 13.4.1
   quotation marks, 13.7.6
   vs. semicolons, 13.4.2
   spaces, 13.13.3
   times, 13.4.3, 14.6.7
comma splice, 12.1, 13.2.2
commas, 13.2.1–8, 13.2.9
   addresses, 13.2.7
   conjunctions, 13.2.2
   connecting adverbs, 13.2.4, 13.3.2
   dates, 13.2.8
   direct quotations, 13.2.6
   essential and non-essential
     information, 13.2.3
   introductory phrases, 13.2.1
   joining sentences, 13.2.2
   lists, 13.2.5
   names, 13.2.9
   numbers, 14.6.4
   offsetting phrases, 9.1.8
   omitting, 13.2.2
   Oxford, 13.2.5
   quotation marks, 13.7.6
   quotations, 13.2.6
   spaces, 13.13.4
   see also comma splice
common nouns, 11.2.2
commonly confused words, avoiding,
   16.2.3

compass points, *see* cardinal directions

complement/compliment, p. 285

complex sentences, 11.1.3

compound adjectives, 13.9.2, 11.4.3

compound sentences, 11.1.3

compound words, 11.4.3, 13.9.2

conciseness, *see* clarity

conclusions

    guiding readers toward logical,
        p. 61, 8.2.1, 16.2.2

    stereotypes, 14.1.2

    supporting information, 8.3.2

    supporting with facts, 7.8, 8.1.3,

concrete language, 7.6, 7.8–9, 8.1.3–4,
    10.3.1, p. 273,

conjugation, 11.3.3–8, 11.3.14–15

    lay/lie, p. 298

conjunctions, 11.1.5, 11.9.1–4

    commas, 13.2.2

    coordinating, 11.9.2

    correlative, 11.9.3

    joining sentences without, 12.1,
        13.3.1

    subordinating, 11.9.4

    then, p. 311

    who's, p. 314

    see also run-on sentences

connecting adverbs, 13.2.4, 13.3.2

conscience/conscious, p. 285

consensual or non-consensual
    interaction, 18.1.1

consequently/subsequently, p. 286,
    13.2.4, 13.3.2

consistency, p. xx, p. 72, p. 123, 7.10,
    16.2.4

Constitution, United States, 1.1.1–2

    Fourth Amendment, 10.1.2–5

constitutional, compliant, and reasonable,
    1.1, 1.1.3, 1.1.6, p. 61, 5.1.2

constitutional policing, 1.1.1

context, p. 4, 4.1.2–3, 9.4.4, p. 273,
    14.2.3

continual/continuous, p. 286

contractions, 13.8.3, 14.4.1

coordinating conjunctions, 11.9.2

COPS Method, 16.1.2, 16.2.1-4

corps/corpse, p. 287

correlative conjunctions, 11.9.3

counsel/council, p. 287

count nouns, 11.2.3

country names, 14.6.5, 14.7.5

court, 1.1.3, 3.4.2, 10.1.3–6

creative works, 13.7.3

crime scenes, 18.2.4

crimes, documenting, 1.1.4, 10.1.3,
    10.2.2

cross-examination tool, 3.3.2

cue/queue, p. 287

currency, 14.6.5

custom labels, 9.1.1, 9.1.6, 9.1.12,
    9.5.10

    parentheses, 13.10.2

D

dashes, 13.9.1, 13.9.6–9

    em, 13.9.1, 13.9.7–9, 13.13.5

    en, 13.9.1, 13.9.6, 13.13.5

    vs. hyphens, 13.9.1

    spaces, 13.13.5

dates, 7.10, 13.2.8, 13.12.3, 14.6.6

deadly force, 10.1.5

deaths, 18.3.5

decimals, 9.5.8, 13.1.6, 14.6.8, 14.6.10

declarative sentences, 11.1.4

definite articles, 11.8.2

dependent clause, 11.1.2–3

descent/dissent/decent, p. 288

dessert/desert, p. 288

device/devise, p. 289

die/dye, p. 289

digital evidence, 9.6.5

direct objects, 11.3.13
lay, p. 298
set, p. 309
direct questions, 13.5.1
direct quotations
  capitalization, 14.7.2
  interjections, 11.10.1
  necessity, 9.4.2
  profanities, 13.9.9
  punctuation:
    commas, 13.2.6
    ellipses, 13.1.7
    em dashes, 13.9.9
    exclamation points, 13.6.1
    periods, 13.1.1
    question marks, 13.7.1
direction of travel, 9.5.4, 9.5.5
disabilities, 9.2.2, 9.2.12, 14.1.3–4
disassociate/dissociate, p. 290
discreet/discrete, p. 290
disinterested/uninterested, p. 290
dispatched call, 19.1.1, 19.1.2
dissemination, 6.3.4
documents, 9.6.4
drafting reports, 16.1.1–3
driving while intoxicated, 18.3.3
drugs, 18.3.2
dual/duel, p. 291
duplicate names, 9.1.9

E
effective police reports, p. xx,
  effect on others' jobs, p. 1, 2.1.1,
    2.2
  inseparable from effective policing,
    p. xvi, 3.1, 3.2, 3.2.2, 16.1,
ellipses, 13.1.7
em dashes, 13.9.1
  changes in thought, 13.9.8
  vs. parentheses, 13.9.7
  profanities, 13.9.9

spaces, 13.13.5
supplemental information, 13.9.7
eminent/imminent, p. 291
en dashes, 13.9.1
  number ranges, 13.9.6
  spaces, 13.13.5
envelop/envelope, p. 291
errors, in quotations, 9.4.9
essential information, 13.2.3
ethnicity, 9.2.3
evaluation tools, reports as, 3.2.1
eventually, 10.3.2
evidence numbers, 9.6.9
evoke/invoke, p. 291
exclamation points
  direct quotations, 13.6.1
  directive/imperative sentences,
    11.1.4
  exclamations/exclamatory
    sentences, 11.1.4
  with quotation marks, 13.7.6
  with spaces, 13.13.2
exclamatory sentences, 11.1.4
exercise/exorcise, p. 292
explicit/implicit, p. 292
explicit bias, 14.1.1
extended actions or reactions, 8.2.5
eyes, 9.2.2, 9.2.9

F
facts and circumstances, 1.1.4,
  10.1.4–6,
facts relevant to every incident, 4.2.2,
  6.2.2, 16.2.1
facts, 4.1.1–3
  general vs. incident, 4.1.2–3
  grouping, 4.2.3
  instead of assumptions, 14.1.2
  supporting conclusions with, 7.8,
    8.3.2
see also relevant facts

fair/fare, p. 293

farther/further, p. 293

faze/phase, p. 294

feedback, receiving, 16.1.3, 16.1.6

feet/ft., 9.2.6, 9.2.8

figures, 14.8.6

filler words and phrases, 8.1.4, 9.4.10,

first-person point of view, 7.1

first-person pronouns, 11.6.5, 11.6.8

Five Parts of a Police Report Narrative,
    6.2.1–5, 6.2.6, 16.2.2
    additional parts, 6.3.1–4
    uses of force, 10.2.1

fix promptly, document honestly, 3.4.2

flair/flare, p. 294

fleeing felon rule, 10.1.5

flier/flyer, p. 295

Follow-Up Investigation, 6.2.4
    see also *Five Parts of a Police Report
        Narrative*

following/as follows, 13.4.1, 13.5.4

fonts, 14.8.4–5

forego/forgo, p. 295

formally/formerly, p. 295

forth/fourth, p. 296

Fourth Amendment, *see* Constitution,
    United States

fractions, 13.12.4, 14.6.5, 14.6.8,
    14.6.10

fraud, 18.4.2

full quotations, 9.4.1

G

gender, pronoun, 11.6.3, 11.6.6, 14.1.5

gendered language, 14.1.5

general facts, *see* facts

GPS coordinates, 9.5.1, 9.5.8

Graham factors, 10.1.4

grammar, p. xxi, p. 83, p. 183, p. 273,
    16.1.2, 16.2.3

graphs, 14.8.6

H

hair, 9.2.8

hangar/hanger, p. 296

hanged/hung, p. 296

headers, 6.3.1

headings, 6.1.2, 16.2.2
    colons, 13.4.4
    to label *Five Parts of a Police Report
        Narrative*, 6.2.1-5
    line breaks, 13.13.1, 13.13.6
    text formatting, 14.8.2–3, 14.8.5
    three-part use of force model,
        10.2.1

height, 9.2.6

hindsight, 5.1.1–2

Hispanic/non-Hispanic, 9.2.3

home in/hone, p. 296

homeless, bias-free terms for, 14.1.1n

however, 13.2.4, 13.3.2

hyphens/hyphenation, 13.9.1–5
    ages, 9.2.5
    compound adjectives, 11.4.3
    vs. dashes, 13.9.1
    fractions, 13.12.4, 14.6.8
    list items, 14.5.4
    numbers, 13.9.4
    prefixes, 13.9.3
    spaces, 13.13.4
    weights and measures, 14.6.10

I

identity, of people,
    avoiding bias, 9.2.1–2, 14.1.1–2
    confidential, 9.1.12
    custom, 9.1.12
    discovered later in investigation,
        9.1.8
    juveniles, 9.1.6
    unknown, 9.1.12
    see also people

imperative mood, 11.3.11

imperative sentences, 11.1.4

implicit bias, 14.1.1

imply/infer, p. 297

inches/in., 9.2.6, 9.2.8, 9.2.10, 13.7.5

incident facts, *see* facts

incident type, 4.2.2, 6.2.2, 6.3.1

including, 13.4.1

indefinite articles, 11.8.2

independent clause, 11.1.2–3

indicative mood, 11.3.11–12

indirect questions, 13.1.2

indirect quotations, *see* paraphrases

infinitive verb, 11.3.2

Initial Investigation, 6.2.3, 10.2.1

    see also *Five Parts of a Police Report Narrative*

initialisms, 13.1.4, 14.3.1, 14.3.3

    see also abbreviations

injuries, 9.3.1–4, 10.1.6–7, 18.3.4

inline quotations, 9.4.11

interjections, 11.1.5, 11.10.1

internment/interment, p. 297

interrogative pronouns, 11.6.9

interrogative sentences, 11.1.4

interviews, 8.2.5, 18.2.3, 19.2.2

    transcripts, as attachments 6.3.3

intransitive verbs, 11.3.13

introductory phrases, 13.2.1

investigation-report cycle, 3.2.1–2

investigative detentions, 1.1.1, 3.2.2, 4.1.2–3, 18.1.2

irregular verbs, 11.3.4, 11.3.8, 11.3.15

italicized text, 14.8.2

J

jargon, 14.2.1–3

    abbreviations, 14.2.1

    agency-specific, 9.5.10, 14.2.3

    slang, 9.4.7, 14.2.1

    technical terms, 14.2.1

job titles, 14.7.4

juveniles, 9.1.6, 9.1.9

K

knowledge, training, and experience, 8.3.1, 19.3.5

L

landmarks, 9.5.1, 9.5.7

languages, capitalization, 14.7.5

later/latter, p. 298

later identified as, 9.1.8

law, compliance with state, 10.1.7, 19.3.6

lay/lie, p. 298

lb., 9.2.7, 14.6.10

lead/led, p. 300

lessons learned tool, 3.3.3

liability, 1.1.2, p. 160

lightening/lightning, p. 301

line breaks, 13.13.1, 13.13.6–7, 14.5.1, 14.5.4

lists, 14.5.1–5

    block, 14.5.1, 14.5.4–5

    bulleted, 14.5.1, 14.5.4

    indentation, 13.13.1

    inline, 14.5.1–3

    numbered, 14.5.1, 14.5.3, 14.5.5

    punctuation:

        colons, 13.4.1

        commas, 13.2.5

        parentheses, 13.10.4

        periods, 13.1.5

        semicolons, 13.3.3

    sentences within, 13.1.5

    unstyled, 14.5.1–2

loose/lose, p. 301

M

M.O. (modus operandi), 2.2.1, 9.4.8,

marks, *see* scars and marks

maybe/may be, p. 301
measurements
    apostrophes, *feet*, 13.8.5
    combined with landmarks, 9.5.7
    formatting, 14.6.10
    hair, 9.2.8
    height, 9.2.6
    quotation marks, *inches*, 13.7.5
    weight, 9.2.7
medical conditions, 9.2.2, 9.2.12, 9.3.1,
    9.3.4
memory aids, reports as, 3.1
mens rea, 1.1.4
military time, 14.6.7
miner/minor, p. 302
mini-debrief tool, 3.3.1
Miranda warning, 18.1.11
mispronunciations, 9.4.8
misquoting, 9.4.2
missing person, 18.3.1
mistakes, proper documentation of,
    3.4.1-3, 9.4.9
modifiers, misplaced and dangling, 12.6
money, 14.6.5
mood, of verbs, 11.3.11
Mr./Ms., 9.1.2, 9.1.4, *see also* salutations
mucous/mucus, p. 302

N
namely, 13.4.1
names, 9.1.1–12
    adults, 9.1.5, 9.1.9, 9.2.5
    brands or products, 9.6.7
    businesses, 9.5.3
    commas, 13.2.9
    country, 14.7.5
    creative works, 13.7.3
    discovered later in investigation,
        9.1.8
    duplicate, 9.1.9
    hairstyles, 9.2.8

incident facts, 4.1.2
    italicized, 14.8.2
    juveniles, 9.1.6, 9.1.9
    nicknames, 9.1.11
    police officers, 9.1.7
    salutations, 9.1.2–5, 9.1.9
    tactics, 10.2.3
    vessels, 13.7.4
    virtual locations, 9.5.9
narrative vs. incident details, p. xxi
nationalities, capitalization, 14.7.5
negative constructions, 7.4
nicknames, 9.1.11
non-count nouns, 11.2.3
non-essential information, 13.2.3
nouns, 11.1.5, 11.2.1–4
    acronyms functioning as, 14.3.2
    capitalization, 14.7.3
    collective, 11.2.4
    common, 11.2.2
    concrete language, 7.6, 8.1.3
    count, 11.2.3
    hyphenated prefixes, 13.9.3
    non-count, 11.2.3
    plural, 11.2.3–4
    possessive, 13.8.1
    prepositions, 11.7.1
    proper, 11.2.2, 14.7.3
    sentence subject, 11.1.1
    see also affect/effect
numbers, 14.6.1–10
    cardinal, 14.6.2
    commas, 14.6.4
    dates, 7.10, 13.2.8, 13.12.3, 14.6.6
    decimals, 13.1.6
    documents, 9.6.4
    en dashes with, 13.9.6
    evidence, 9.6.9
    fractions, 13.12.4, 14.6.5, 14.6.8,
        14.6.10
    hyphens with, 13.9.4

lists, 14.5.3, 14.5.5
money, 14.6.5
ordinal, 14.6.2
parentheses, 13.10.3–4, 14.6.3
percentages, 14.6.9
separating thousands, 14.6.4
Social Security, 13.9.4, 14.6.1,
    14.6.4
spelling, 14.6.3
telephone numbers, 13.9.4, 14.6.4
times, 14.6.7
weights and measures, 14.6.10

O
object, of preposition, 11.7.2
objective case, of pronouns 11.6.7
objective reasonableness, 10.1.2n,
    10.1.4–5, *see also* reasonableness
objectivity in writing, 3.4.2, 7.8, 9.4.4,
    14.1.1
observations, 8.1.1–5, 19.3.1–6
    actions as, 8.2.2n
    incident facts, 4.1.2
    within *Five Parts of a Police Report
        Narrative*, 6.2.3
    supporting information, 8.3
    uses of force, p. 160, 10.1.2
offensive terms, 14.1.3–4
officer-chronological order, 5.1.1–3,
    16.2.2
    avoiding, 5.1.3, 6.2.5, 8.2.5
    transitional phrases, 5.2.2
omissions, documenting, 7.4
open investigations, 19.4.2
or, 13.12.1
ordinal numbers, 14.6.2
ordinance/ordnance, p. 302
organization, 16.2.2
    see also structure, report
over-quoting, 9.4.3
Oxford comma, 13.2.5

P
paragraphs, 6.1.1–2, p. 83, 8.2.5, 9.4.5
    line breaks and indentation
        13.13.1, 13.13.7, 14.5.1
paraphrases, 9.4.1–4, 9.4.5, 16.2.1
    ellipses, 13.1.7
    quotation marks, 9.4.5, 13.7.1
    vs. quotations, 9.4.2
parentheses
    abbreviations, 13.10.2, 14.3.2
    business names, 9.5.3
    custom labels, 9.1.12, 13.10.2
    vs. em dashes, 13.9.7
    lists, 13.10.4
    nicknames, 9.1.11
    numbers, 13.10.3–4, 14.6.3
    plain language descriptions, 9.2.12
    spaces, 13.13.2
    supplemental information, 9.1.10,
        13.10.1
partial quotations, 9.4.1
participles, 11.3.2, 11.3.9, 11.3.11,
    11.3.13, p. 299, p. 309–310
parts of speech, 11.1.5
passed/past, p. 303
passive voice, 7.5, 11.3.13
pat down for weapons, 18.1.3
patience/patients, p. 303
pauses, 9.4.10
peace/piece, p. 303
peak/peek/pique, p. 303
pedal/peddle, p. 304
people, 18.3.1–5, 19.3.2
    adults, 9.1.5, 9.1.9, 9.2.5
    age, 9.2.5
    clothing, 9.2.2, 9.2.11
    disabilities, 9.2.2, 9.2.12, 14.1.3–4
    ethnicity, 9.2.3
    eyes, 9.2.2, 9.2.9
    hair, 9.2.8
    height, 9.2.6

injuries, 9.3.1–4, 10.1.6–7, 18.3.4
juveniles, 9.1.6, 9.1.9
names, *see* names
nicknames, 9.1.11
police officers, 9.1.7
race, 9.2.3
roles, 4.2.2, 9.1.2, 9.1.3, 9.6.2
salutations, 9.1.2–5, 9.1.9
scars and marks, 9.2.2, 9.2.10
sex, 9.2.4
supplemental information, 9.1.10
titles, *see* titles
weight, 9.2.2, 9.2.7
see also identity, of people; names
per, 13.12.2
percentages, 14.6.9
periods, 13.1.1–6
   abbreviations, 13.1.3
   direct quotations, 13.1.1
   ellipses, 13.1.7
   ending sentences, 11.1.4, 13.1.1
   initialisms, 14.3.3
   lists, 13.1.5
   quotation marks, 13.7.6
   spaces, 13.13.2
   weights and measures, 14.6.10
   see also decimals
permanent records, 1.1.6
person-first language, 9.2.2, 14.1.4
person, grammatical, 11.3.10, 11.6.5
personal/personnel, p. 304
photographs, 6.3.3, 9.6.4, 10.1.7
phrases
   abbreviations, 14.3.1
   bias, 14.1.1, 14.1.4
   canned, 10.3.1
   conjunctions, 11.9.1
   essential vs. non-essential, 13.2.3
   establishing time and place, 5.2.1
   filler, 8.1.4
   introductory, 8.2.5, 9.4.5, 13.2.1

may be, p. 301
   text formatting, 14.8.2
   transitional, 5.2.2
   verb, 11.3.13, 11.5.1
physical characteristics, *see* people
places, 19.3.3
   addresses, 9.5.1–2
   business names, 9.5.3
   cardinal directions, 9.5.4–5, 9.5.7,
      14.7.6
   custom labels, 9.5.10
   direction of travel, 9.5.4, 9.5.5
   GPS coordinates, 9.5.1, 9.5.8
   landmarks, 9.5.1, 9.5.7
   positioning events within, 5.2.1
   reference points, 9.2.8, 9.2.10,
      9.5.4, 9.5.6–7
   relative positions, 9.5.5–7
   virtual locations, 9.5.9
plain/plane, p. 304
plain language, 9.2.9, 9.2.12, 9.3.3–4,
   9.5.10, 14.2.2–3
plain touch/feel, 18.1.4
plain view seizure, 18.1.5
plural
   apostrophes, 13.8.4
   nouns, 11.2.3–4
   pronouns, 11.6.4, 11.6.8, 14.1.5
   verbs, 11.3.8, 11.3.12, 11.3.14–15,
      12.3–4
point of view, 7.1, 16.2.4
police officers, 9.1.7
policies, compliance with agency, 1.1.2,
   4.1.2, 5.1.3, p. 83, 10.1.7, 19.3.6
pore/pour/poor, p. 305
possessive case, of pronouns, 11.6.7,
   13.8.2
possessive nouns, 13.8.1
pounds, 9.2.7
Pre-Arrival information, 6.2.2, 8.3.1,
   19.1

see also *Five Parts of a Police Report Narrative*

precede/proceed, p. 305

predicates, 11.1.1

predicting the future, 7.3

prefixes, hyphenated, 13.9.3

prepositions, 11.1.5, 11.7.1–2

prescribe/proscribe, p. 306

presence/present/presents, p. 306

prime marks, 13.7.5n

probable cause, 1.1.4, 4.1.3, 4.2.3, 10.1.2, 10.1.5, 18.1.8, 18.1.10

product names, 9.6.7

profanities, 13.9.9

prone/supine, p. 306

pronouns, 11.1.5

    with adjectives, 11.4.1

    antecedents, 11.6.2–3, 11.6.6, 11.6.9, 12.4–5, 14.1.5

    case, 11.6.7

    demonstrative, 11.6.11

    gender, 11.6.3, 11.6.6, 14.1.5

    interrogative, 11.6.9

    number, 11.6.4

    objective, 11.6.7

    person, 11.6.5

    plural, 11.6.4, 11.6.8, 14.1.5

    possessive, 11.6.7, 13.8.2

    prepositions, 11.7.1

    reflexive, 11.6.7

    relative, 11.6.10

    subjective, 11.6.7

    see also *who's/whose*

proper nouns, 11.2.2, 14.7.3

property, lost, damaged, or stolen, 9.6.6

prosecute/persecute, p. 307

protective sweep of residence, 18.1.6

protective sweep of vehicle, 18.1.7

punctuation, p. xxi, p. 83, p. 183, p. 223, 16.2.3

    joining sentences, 12.1

    with other punctuation, 13.7.6, 13.13.2–3

    terminating, 13.1.1, 13.5.1, 13.6.1

purpose of police reports 1.1.1–6

    communication tools, p. xx

    documentation tools, p. xx, 3.2.1

    evaluation tools, 3.2.1

    input for others' jobs, p. 1

    memory aids, 3.1

    products for employers, p. xxiv

Q

question marks

    direct questions, 13.5.1

    direct quotations, 13.7.1

    to end sentences, 11.1.4, 13.1.1

    with quotation marks, 13.7.6

questions

    answering readers', p. xx, p. 1–2, 2.2.1–4, 4.2.1–2, 8.1.1–2, 16.2.1

    direct questions, 13.5.1

    indirect questions, 13.1.2, 13.5.1

    interrogative pronouns, 11.6.9

    periods, 13.1.2

    question marks, 13.5.1

    unanswered, 1.1.3, 3.3.2, 3.3.4, p. 45, 8.1.1

quiet/quite, p. 307

quotation marks, 13.7.1–6

    colons, 13.7.6

    commas, 13.7.6

    to indicate feet, 9.2.6

    italicizing text, alternative to, 14.8.2

    nicknames, 9.1.11

    with other punctuation, 13.7.6, 13.13.2

    paraphrased statements, 9.4.5, 13.7.1

    prime marks, alternative to, 13.7.5n

    quotations, 9.4.11, 13.7.1

semicolons, 13.7.6
slang, 9.4.7
spaces, 13.13.2
quotations
    block, 9.4.11
    capitalization, 14.7.2
    direct, 13.7.1
    full vs. partial, 9.4.1
    indirect, *see* paraphrases
    inline, 9.4.11
    interjections, 11.10.1
    necessity, 9.4.2
    vs. paraphrases, 9.4.2
    profanities, 13.9.9
    punctuation:
        commas, 13.2.6
        ellipses, 13.1.7
        em dashes, 13.9.9
        exclamation points, 13.6.1
        periods, 13.1.1
        question marks, 13.7.1
        quotation marks, 9.4.11, 13.7.1
    recorded, 9.4.3

R
race, 9.2.3
rain/reign/rein, p. 307
raise/rise/raze, p. 308
rank, 9.1.7, 14.7.4
reactions, *see* actions
read out loud tool, 16.1.3
reader-centric approach, p. xxi
readers
    examples, 1.1.5, p. 17, 2.1.1, 2.1.2,
        2.2.1, 2.2.4
    guiding, p. 61, 5.2.1–2, 8.2.1,
        16.2.2
    identifying, p. xx–xxi, p. 1, 2.2.1–2
    most important, p. 31
    primary, 2.1.1, 2.2.2

secondary, 2.1.2, 2.2.3
    see also questions: answering readers'
reasonable suspicion, 4.1.2, 10.1.3
reasonableness, 1.1.3, 5.1.1, 8.3.1,
    see also objective reasonableness
recorded statements, 9.4.3–4
recording devices, p. 3, 5.1.3,
    see also body cameras
records management systems, 1.1.6,
    3.1, 6.3.3, 13.12.4, 14.8.1
reference points, 9.2.8, 9.2.10, 9.5.4,
    9.5.6–7
reflexive case, of pronouns, 11.6.7
regular verbs, 11.3.4–7, 11.3.14
relative positions, 9.5.5–7
relevant facts, 4.2.1–5
    action-reaction sequences, 8.2.4
    grouping, 4.2.3
    missing, 16.1.4, 16.2.1
    officer-chronological order, 5.1.2
    structuring, p. 71, 6.2.1, 10.2.1
    uses of force, 10.1.1–8
    see also facts; *facts relevant to every*
        incident; T-Chart
religion, 14.1.1–2
restrictive vs. non-restrictive, 13.2.3n
right vs. wrong or *good vs. better*, p. 183
right/rite/write, p. 308
roles, 4.2.2, 9.1.2, 9.1.3, 9.6.2
run-on sentences, 12.1

S
said/stated/told me, 9.4.5, 13.2.6
salutations, 9.1.2–5, 9.1.9
scars and marks, 9.2.2, 9.2.10
seasons, 14.7.6
seizures, 10.1.2–6, 18.1.5
self-initiated activity, 19.1.3
semicolons, 13.3.1–3
    capitalization, 14.7.2
    vs. colons, 13.4.2

connecting adverbs, 13.3.2
joining sentences, 13.3.1–2
lists, 13.3.3
quotation marks, 13.7.6
spaces, 13.13.3
senses, writing from, 7.6, p. 100, 8.1.1,
   8.1.3–4, 16.2.4
sentence complement, 11.1.1
sentences, 11.1.1–5
   beginning with sensory verbs, 8.1.2
   capitalization, 11.1, 14.7.1–2
   common errors, 12.1–6
   complex, 11.1.3
   compound, 11.1.3
   declarative, 11.1.4
   exclamatory, 11.1.4
   imperative, 11.1.4
   interrogative, 11.1.4
   joining:
      with colons, 13.4.2
      with commas, 13.2.2
      with semicolons, 13.3.1–2
   joining without conjunctions, 12.1,
      13.3.1
   as list items, 13.1.5
   as parts of paragraphs, 6.1.1
   periods, 13.1.1
   predicates, 11.1.1
   preposition placement, 11.7.2
   run-on, 12.1
   simple, 7.7, 11.1.3
   spaces after, 13.13.3
   structures, 11.1.3
   subject, *see* subjects, of sentences
   terminating punctuation, 13.1.1,
      13.5.1, 13.6.1
set/sit, p. 309
sex, 9.2.4
sexual identity, 14.1.1–2, 14.1.5
sharing information, 1.1.5
shone/shown, p. 309

sic, 9.4.9
similar descriptions, items with, 9.6.8–9
slang, 9.4.7, 14.2.1
slashes, 13.12.1–6
   abbreviations, 13.12.6
   alternatives, 13.12.1
   dates, 13.12.3, 14.6.6
   fractions, 13.12.4
   or, 13.12.1
   per, 13.12.2
   URLs, 13.12.5
Social Security numbers, 13.9.4, 14.6.1,
   14.6.4
spaces, 13.13.1–7
   after punctuation, 13.13.2–5
   character, 13.13.1
   headings, 13.13.6
   indentations, 13.13.1, 13.13.7
   line breaks, 13.13.1, 13.13.6–7,
      14.5.1, 14.5.4
   paragraphs, 13.13.7
   times, 14.6.7
   types of, 13.13.1
   weights and measures, 14.6.10
spelling, 13.9.5, 14.6.3, 16.2.3
standard time, 14.6.7
statements, 9.4.1–11, 9.6.4
stationary/stationery, p. 310
stereotypes, 14.1.2
straight/strait, p. 310
structure, report, p. 71, 6.1.1–2, 7.10,
   p. 160, 16.2.2
   see also *Five Parts of a Police Report
      Narrative*
structure, sentence, 11.1.3
style, p. xxi, 3.3.5, p. 83, p. 85, 7.10,
   14.5.1, 16.2.4
subheadings, *see* headings
subject, to refer to person, 9.1.3n
subjective case, of pronouns, 11.6.7

subjects, of sentences, 7.5, 11.1.1, 12.3, 13.2.2
    pronouns, 11.6.7–8, 12.4–5
    verbs, 11.3.1, 11.3.13, 12.3
subjunctive mood, 11.3.11
subordinating conjunctions, 11.9.4
subsequently, 13.2.4, 13.3.2
such as, 13.4.1
supervisor standards, 2.1.1, p. 183
supplemental information, 8.1.5, 9.1.2, 9.1.10, 13.9.7, 13.10.1, 14.8.6
supplemental reports, 6.2.4, 7.3
supporting information, p. 99, 8.3.2, 9.1.11
swipe file tool, 3.3.5
synopsis, 4.2.5, 6.3.2

T
T-Chart, 4.2.5
tables, 14.8.6
tactics, describing, 10.2.3
tattoos, 9.2.2, 9.2.10
technical terms, 14.2.1
telephone numbers, 13.9.4, 14.6.4
tenant/tenet, p. 310
tense shifts, 7.2, 12.2
tenses, 7.2–3, 11.3.4–9, 16.2.4, *see also* verbs
terminating punctuation marks, 13.1.1, 13.5.1, 13.6.1
Terry frisk, *see* pat down for weapons
Terry stop, *see* investigative detention
testimony, based on police reports, 1.1.4, 3.1, p. 315
text alignment, 14.8.3
text formatting, 14.8.1–6
than/then, p. 311
that/which/who, p. 311
the, 11.8.2
the following, 13.4.1
theft, 18.4.1

then, p. 311
therefore, 13.2.4, 13.3.2
things, describing, 9.6.1–9, 19.3.4
three-part use of force model, 10.2.1–3
threw/through/thru, p. 312
time
    abbreviations, 14.6.7
    avoiding *eventually* and *until*, 10.3.2
    colons, 13.4.3, 14.6.7
    military vs. standard, 14.6.7
    positioning events in, 5.2.1
    respecting readers', 4.2.4
    spaces, 14.6.7
    see also verbs: tense
titles
    capitalization, 14.7.4
    citizens, 9.1.2, 9.1.4, 9.1.5
    creative works, 13.7.3
    job, 14.7.4
    police officers, 9.1.7
    vessels, 13.7.4
to/too, p. 312
to be, conjugation of, 11.3.8
tone, 7.10, 13.1.1, 16.2.4
totality of the circumstances, 1.1.3, 10.1.6
track/tract, p. 313
transitional phrases, 5.2.2
transitive verbs, 11.3.13

U
unanswered questions tool, 3.3.4
underlined text, 6.1.2
unknown, ethnicity, 9.2.3
until, 10.3.2
URLs, 13.1.6, 13.12.5
usage, p. 183, p. 248
uses of force, 10.1.1, 18.2.2, 19.2.3
    guidelines for documenting, 10.3.1–3

identifying relevant facts, 10.1.1–8
three-part model, 10.2.1–3

V

value, of property, 9.6.6
vehicles, 9.5.5, 9.6.2, 18.1.6–7, 18.4.4
verbal commands, 8.2.3, 10.1.6,
    10.2.2–3, 10.3.3
verbiage, eliminating, 8.1.4,
verbs, 11.1.5, 11.3.1–15
    conjugation, 11.3.3–8, 11.3.14–15,
    infinitive, 11.3.2
    intransitive, 11.3.13
    irregular, 11.3.4, 11.3.8, 11.3.15
    mood:
        imperative mood, 11.3.11
        indicative, 11.3.11–12
        subjunctive, 11.3.11
    number, 11.3.12
    participles, 11.3.2, 11.3.9, 11.3.11,
        11.3.13, p. 299, p. 309–310
    person, 11.3.10
    phrases, 11.3.13, 11.5.1
    plural, 11.3.8, 11.3.12,
        11.3.14–15, 12.3–4
    regular, 11.3.4–7, 11.3.14
    sensory, 8.1.2
    sentence predicate, 11.1.1
    stem form, 11.3.2
    tense:
        future, 7.2–3, 11.3.4, 11.3.7
        past, 7.2–3, 11.3.4–5, 11.3.8
        perfect, 11.3.9, 11.3.11
        perfect-progressive, 11.3.9,
            11.3.11
        present, 7.2, 11.3.4, 11.3.6,
            11.3.8, 11.3.12
        progressive, 7.2, 11.3.9,
            11.3.11
        simple, 11.3.9

tense shifts, 7.2, 12.2
transitive, 11.3.13
voice, 7.5, 11.3.13
vessels, names of, 13.7.4
virtual locations, 9.5.9

W

waive/wave, p. 313
warrantless entry into residence, 18.1.9
weapons, 9.6.3, 18.4.3
weight, of people, 9.2.2, 9.2.7
weights and measures, 14.6.10
which included, 13.4.1
who-what-where-when-why pattern,
    4.2.2
who's/whose, p. 314
words, referring to, 13.7.2, 13.9.5
writing process, p. 317, 16.1.1–6
    see also COPS Method
wrong words, quoting, 9.4.9

About the Author

Benjamin J. Smith is an active-duty law enforcement officer in Virginia. He has taught hundreds of officers the art of police report writing. Smith holds a bachelor's degree in English and a master's degree in organizational leadership. He is a certified general instructor, defensive tactics instructor, and Force Science analyst. Smith has served as a patrol officer, detective, crisis negotiator, training coordinator, adjunct academy instructor, and patrol supervisor. He currently serves as a lieutenant.